RACE,
SCHOOLS,
&
HOPE

African Americans and
School Choice After *Brown*

RACE, SCHOOLS, & HOPE

African Americans and School Choice After *Brown*

Lisa M. Stulberg

Teachers College, Columbia University
New York and London

Published by Teachers College Press, 1234 Amsterdam Avenue, New York, NY 10027

Library of Congress Cataloging-in-Publication Data

Stulberg, Lisa M.
  Race, schools, and hope : African Americans and school choice after Brown / Lisa M. Stulberg
    p. cm.
  Includes bibliographical references and index.
  ISBN 978-0-8077-4853-4 (hardcover) — ISBN: 978-0-8077-4852-7 (pbk.)
    1. School choice—Political aspects—United States. 2. African Americans—Education. 3. West Oakland Community School. I. Title.
  LB1027.9.S88 2008
  371.829'96073—dc22   2007041739

ISBN: 978-0-8077-4852-7 (paper)
ISBN: 978-0-8077-4853-4 (hardcover)

Printed on acid-free paper
Manufactured in the United States of America

15 14 13 12 11 10 09 08   8 7 6 5 4 3 2 1

For Akiyu Hatano and Eric Rofes:
school visionaries, trusted mentors, and beloved friends.
I miss you both very much
and I love the world that you dreamed.

Hope enacts the stance of the participant who actively struggles against the evidence in order to change the deadly tides of wealth inequality, group xenophobia, and personal despair. . . . To live is to wrestle with despair yet never to allow despair to have the last word.
—Cornel West, *Restoring Hope: Conversations on the Future of Black America*

Contents

Acknowledgments

I am incredibly fortunate to have so many people who have filled my life and work with meaning and purpose. My apologies to those I have not properly acknowledged here.

I have been supported in this project by the National Science Foundation Graduate Fellowship; the University of California at Berkeley; and New York University's Steinhardt School of Culture, Education, and Human Development; with additional support of a grant-in-aid from the Berkeley chapter of Sigma Xi.

For their research assistance, I thank Jonathan Green and Alan Divack of the Ford Foundation archives, Lucinda Manning of the United Federation of Teachers archives, David Mintz and Betty Weneck of the New York Board of Education archives, and Marylène Altieri at the Harvard Graduate School of Education Gutman Library Special Collections. A special thanks to Nina Pessin-Whedbee, who provided thorough, smart, and invaluable research help at NYU.

Thank you to the staff at Teachers College Press, particularly Lori Tate for all of her time and careful work and Marie Ellen Larcada for her ongoing support and encouragement.

I am grateful for the time, information, and intellectual and political exchange that many have been generous enough to provide in the research and writing of this book. These people include Michael Ames, Andy Barlow, Crystal Byndloss, Marilyn Gittell, Henry Izumizaki, Jerry Karabel, David L. Kirp, Don Levine, Amanda Lewis, Jabari Mahiri, Ron Miller, Beryl Nelson, Pedro Noguera, Gary Orfield, Orlando Patterson, Dan Perlstein, Bob Peterson, Eric Premack, Diane Ravitch, Raka Ray, Kay Schlozman, Jonathan Schorr, Mwalimu Shujaa, Barrie Thorne, Preston Wilcox, Margaret Weir, and Jack Wuest. In particular, I thank my dissertation chair, Nancy Chodorow, for her patient generosity. Her mark on this book is pervasive, particularly as she has encouraged me to find my voice in and through my writing.

For wise input on my writing at various stages, thanks to Robert Bulman, Howard Fuller, Wendy Schwartz, Debbie Stulberg, Leslie Stulberg, and Mark Stulberg. I also appreciate the astute feedback on my work-in-progress from David Kirp's fall 1998 "Education Reform for the Next Generation" seminar at Berkeley, Orlando Patterson's spring 2000 "Race and Public Policy" workshop at Harvard, and the ongoing Education Workshop group at NYU.

For providing an always-lively and ever-supportive environment in which I do my work, thanks to my colleagues in the Department of Humanities and Social Sciences in the Professions at NYU Steinhardt. Thanks, especially, to Rene Arcilla, Richard Arum, Floyd Hammack, Pedro Noguera, Mitchell Stevens, and Jon Zimmerman, who provided mentorship and guidance throughout this project; to Cynthia Miller-Idriss, who has been a great source of support in the department; and to Tamika Bota and Lucy Frazier, without whom I could not do my work.

This project would not exist without the openness, trust, partnership, and vision of the West Oakland Community School founding group. For their time, support, and feedback on chapters of the book, I particularly thank Japheth Aquino, Greg Hodge, Shawn Ginwright, Macheo Payne, Derek Peake, Anthony Reese, Celsa Snead, Dirk Tillotson, and Ted Uno. Also for their love and friendship, as well as limitless support, I thank two amazing women: Marjorie Wilkes and my dear missed friend, Akiyu Hatano.

I owe so much to the friends and family who have provided guidance, encouragement, research help, input on my writing along the way, or simply much-needed diversions from my work. Thanks in particular to Beth Berkelhamer, Tony Chen, Cori Flam, Brad Meltzer, Christy Getz, Kate Grossman, Lauri Hornik, Elise Huggins, John and Melissa King, Jill Kneerim, Jason Mark, the late Eric Rofes, David and Jann Stulberg, Debbie Stulberg, Leslie Stulberg and Jerry Levy, Mark Stulberg, and Madhavi Sunder.

I am so grateful to Evan Rudall for love and true partnership. I have infinite respect for the way that he lives the vision of those activists who fill these pages. Finally, my two beautiful children, Avery and Eli: Thank you for bringing joy to absolutely everything. Thank you for reminding me every day why I exist in the world.

CHAPTER I

Introduction

"America never was America to me," Langston Hughes proclaimed in a 1936 poem, describing the way in which American notions of freedom, liberty, and opportunity exclude so many Americans. This lament describes much of the way that American public schools have failed to serve African American students, and the way in which a racially stratified system of public education is often taken for granted, even as it presents an affront to this country's ideals. But Hughes's poem, though it condemns the injustices of American inequality, is actually quite hopeful. In his poem, entitled "Let America be America Again," Hughes urges:

O, yes,
I say it plain,
America never was America to me,
And yet I swear this oath—
America will be!

Hughes's simultaneous rejection of American perils and embrace of American possibilities encapsulates the complexity of African American participation in school choice reforms of the last half century.

I was part of a predominantly African American group that founded an African American–centered charter school in West Oakland, California, in the late 1990s. At this time, news reports abounded about school voucher and charter school supporters who ostensibly had given up on public schooling and turned their backs on public school students. In particular, reporting about African American voucher and charter proponents often painted them as cynical or desperate people willing to leave public schools behind and, sometimes, as unreflective dupes who joined against their interests in partnership with White, Republican, conservative choice supporters and funders to embrace choice reforms. These characterizations did not match my experience. When our charter school group began meeting to plan our school, our initial conversations were filled with hope. Many in the group were angry with the woefully inadequate public schooling in Oakland, the turn away from affirmative action and the general state of race politics in California, and the seeming indifference of local and national leaders to the continued underachievement of African American children. But many in the group were also very hopeful about what one small, alternative public school could do to create social change. Group members placed an incredibly heavy—and quite optimistic—charge on the school they dreamed.

In my experience lies the puzzle at the heart of this book, the puzzle Hughes provides through his poetry: How can school choice be a form of both giving up on American public schools *and* a form of hope and faith in American schooling? How can many who oppose school choice paint its proponents as hopeless and desperate parents and educators who have given up on American education, yet school choice advocates over the past 50 years, particularly African American advocates, talk about schools as if they hold so much promise?

My answer is that debates surrounding school choice, especially when they include discussions of race, tap into an emotional and political dialogue about American participation, about who can share in American institutions, who can expect these institutions to accommodate them and serve them equally. In this highly charged discussion of American inclusion, there is a real *grappling* with the promises and shortcomings of American education, not simply a *giving up* on schooling.

This book examines school choice as a strategy for African Americans to retain hope in American schooling. I argue that the existing literature on race and school choice is inadequate to help us make sense of why and how African Americans participate in and lead school choice reforms. This literature often quickly dismisses choice strategies as being anti–public schooling or anti–racial integration. It misses the complexity of the politics of these reforms. It also misses the extent to which these have been hopeful ventures for their participants. For the most part, these choice reforms have not been simply about the rejection of schooling, public schooling, integration, or American institutions. They have represented a complicated mixture of despair and hope, integrationism and nationalism, faith in and rejection of public schooling. They have been a mechanism to, in Hughes's words, let America be America again.

School choice debates provide a terrain for a national conversation about the politics of race, nation, and schooling, particularly at key moments of shift in these politics. Sometimes, the discussion about

African American participation and leadership in choice reforms is explicitly about race politics. For example, African Americans have used school choice debates to grapple with and work out a definition of racial equality and a strategy of racial justice. Sometimes, these race politics combine with a politics of nation, as African Americans, through school choice, work out a relationship to the nation: the American welfare state and its institutions. Sometimes, African American participation in choice reforms and debates is less about race and nation, *per se*, than about working out a vision of schooling and a definition of what it means to educate African American young people at a particular moment in history.

SCHOOL CHOICE TODAY

School choice means many things. Historically, school choice reforms have included magnet schools, which draw students and families with competitive educational programs or specialties such as performing arts or technology; small alternative public and private schools that are either community-controlled or district-run; and district-wide "controlled choice," in which every student must affirmatively choose his or her school (Henig, 1994; Wells, 1993). Students and families also exercise school choice when they choose to live in a community for the quality of its public schools, when they vie for particular teachers or classes within schools, and when they prepare to take exams to enter selective district and magnet or specialty schools (Rofes & Stulberg, 2004).

In current parlance, *school choice* often means publicly funded voucher programs, which provide government money for students to attend private and parochial schools, and charter schools, which are public schools that have significant autonomy with respect to governance, budget, personnel, and curriculum and programming. The following chapters include much more about these two reforms and their roots in school choice efforts of the past 4 decades.

Current voucher and charter reforms began in the early 1990s, with an unusual collection of supporters. Republican lawmakers interested in removing government from schooling and injecting marketlike competition into the public school system joined with communities of color fed up with dismal district school options for their children, teachers' unions (in the case of charter schools) hoping to gain increased participation and control for teachers, business leaders betting that schools could turn profits for them, and other legislators trying to balance the needs of their constituents for decent schools with the limitations they felt in providing these schools through state and local governance (Bulman & Kirp, 1999; Carl, 1996).

The first publicly funded voucher program, the 1990 Milwaukee Parental Choice Program, did not spark a broad, national voucher movement, however. Currently, Cleveland, the District of Columbia, and the state of Ohio have the only other publicly funded voucher programs in the country, though many other states have considered voucher plans through their legislatures or through ballot initiatives. Charter schooling, which began in 1991 in Minnesota, has grown significantly over the past 15 years. Currently, 40 states and the District of Columbia have charter laws on their books, and more than one million students are served in more than 4,000 charter schools, according to the pro-charter Center for Education Reform (Center for Education Reform, 2007). Charter schools enroll approximately 2% of the nation's K–12 students (Vanourek, 2005).

In this book, I use the term *school choice*, or *school choice reform*, to refer to any reform effort that seeks to give parents more control over the *school assignment* of their children and/or more control over the *kind* of school that their children attend (in terms of staffing, curriculum, and programming, for example). I use the term *African American school choice* to mean African American–led choice efforts or school choice efforts designed explicitly to serve African American young people and communities.

MY EXAMINATION OF AFRICAN AMERICAN SCHOOL CHOICE

My own introduction to school choice began when I was a graduate student at the University of California at Berkeley. During graduate school, I taught in an after-school program in a West Oakland middle school, and, through this work, I became involved in education policy work in Oakland. This led to my joining the founding team of the West Oakland Community School (WOCS), a small community-based charter middle school by and for African Americans in Oakland.

The charter school's founding group of educators, parents, community and youth activists, and nonprofit leaders first met to plan this school in the spring of 1996, amid an active race politics in the state. Our group watched the University of California (UC) regents annul affirmative action by race and gender in hiring and admissions in the UC system in the summer of 1995. We then witnessed California voters support and put into law Proposition 209, which effectively ended affirmative action in the state. The charter school was largely a response to these politics of affirmative action and to recent data in Oakland that suggested the district schools were severely under-serving African American students.

I initially was interested in examining the ways in which the race and school politics of California in the mid-1990s came together in this one small charter school. I envisioned an ethnographic examination of the founding and first year of the middle school and the race and school politics it embodied. But, as I began this research in earnest, I turned to history to understand our work more fully and to help me raise some of the sociological and political questions that might structure my study of the charter school. I started my historical investigation with the references that those involved in the charter school provided, those that they drew on in dreaming their school: the community control movement in Ocean Hill–Brownsville, New York; the African American independent school movement; Ella Baker and the youth activism of the civil rights movement; and the Black Panthers and their community programs in Oakland and elsewhere.

In truth, until I started this project, I had heard and read very little about some of these historical referents, particularly the public school community control movement and the African American independent school movement. This seemed odd to me. I had been a longtime student of race and school politics and history, yet these nondesegregation-focused movements were overshadowed by the story of desegregation and civil rights that dominated the historical and sociological literature. The more I read about African American choice initiatives of the past, the more I was able to learn about the charter school I was studying and helping to build. At a time in my research when I was having trouble gaining enough distance from WOCS to be able to ask good sociological questions, history helped to raise these questions for me. I decided to make this historical narrative central to my investigation.

I learned that I could only fully understand the charter school and the politics that surrounded it if I understood it as part of a historical trajectory of African American school choice initiatives (see Forman, 2005). I also learned that we must understand the past 50 years of school choice reforms in the context of the broader politics of race and schooling in America. We cannot understand community control initiatives, independent school efforts, vouchers, or charters without understanding the complexity of the move from civil rights to Black

Power in the mid-1960s, the debates around Black nationalism in the late 1960s and early 1970s, and the current race politics of desegregation and affirmative action.

I also learned that history can bring hope. Howard Zinn (1994) teaches us this. History is many things: tragic, joyous, shameful, a source of pride, the maker of heroes and villains, celebrated, and forgotten. But radical historian and consummate optimist Zinn implores us that if we train our historian's eye in the right place, history can bring hope. He looks to the people who are not featured in textbooks, not answers to questions on standardized history tests, not the namesake of a national or even regional holiday. In countless brave, everyday people, Zinn finds a hopeful story to tell. From them he learns that "To be hopeful in bad times is not just foolishly romantic. It is based on the fact that human history is a history not only of cruelty, but also of compassion, sacrifice, courage, kindness" (p. 208).

Contemporary American schools could really use some hope—especially the schools that the majority of African American students attend. Amid the good news of marginally rising national test scores in some cities, sparks of innovation and humanity in teachers who give themselves almost completely to their jobs, beacons of academic excellence and community engagement in some alternative schools, is the bad news that many now take for granted as an eternal part of the story of American public schooling. This news is of crumbling and overcrowded urban schools, listless teaching, indifferent administrators, parents who feel shut out of their children's school experience, deadlocks between unions and districts, perennial reforms of questionable academic merit, and a persistent and unwavering racial academic achievement gap.

With this bad news, much of the debate and scholarship on race and schooling is curiously ahistorical. Many students of American schooling, when they weigh in on the current school issues of the day, do not take care to locate their positions historically. Many of those who are experts or who make policy on the key educational issues of our time do not take care to learn from history. In overlooking history, we lose valuable analytical tools, we ignore questions and answers that our forbears have raised nicely for us. We also lose an opportunity for hope.

In my examination, I primarily am interested in expanding the way that scholars understand African American school choice efforts and the participation of African Americans in school choice debates since the Supreme Court's landmark desegregation decision of 1954,

Brown v. Board of Education. The scholarship on current and past choice initiatives, when it deals with race at all, tends to focus almost exclusively on a *desegregation* framework and the narrow question of whether and how choice initiatives exacerbate segregation and reject or ignore integration as a goal (Stulberg, 2004). The history of African American school choice and an examination of some current forms of choice in the context of this history help us build a more complicated picture. Through this investigation, we see that the reason why school choice has been so politically heated is *not* because it is a simple rejection of American values or American ideals of diversity and integration, but because it is a space to *contest* these values and ideals.

This book is an attempt to broaden our current understanding of school choice politics by focusing on the complex participation of African Americans in choice reforms. I present here a primarily political examination of these reforms, not an educational assessment (though I address the educational potential of these reforms in the concluding chapter). I argue that regardless of the success or failure of these reforms—highly debatable concepts given their politicized nature—they represent an important political phenomenon in American schooling and in African American history and politics.

In the following chapters, I investigate four examples of African American school choice reforms, four forms of school choice that some African American educators, parents, policymakers, scholars, and other leaders have embraced to serve African American young people and communities. The first section of the book focuses on African American school choice in the post-*Brown* period. Here I examine the ways in which these choice reforms became a response to desegregation politics and policies and a space for African American leaders to debate the strategy of school integration and the limits and possibilities of the American welfare state and its institutions. The second half of the book focuses on a current example of African American school choice. Here I examine the ways in which charter schooling has provided a site in the post–civil rights era to grapple with a retreat from civil rights–era gains and policies and to fashion a politically feasible strategy of equal schooling and racial equality.

In Chapter 3, I begin my historical investigation with the fight for public school community control in New York City in the mid- to late 1960s. This effort represents the first significant school choice reform by and for communities of color in the post-*Brown* era. It also represents an important moment in African American race and school politics, as it was one of the earliest and most substantial rejections of desegregation as a solution to racial inequality in schooling by African American activists, educators, and parents after the *Brown* decision. It also provided the organizational and ideological roots for a number of subsequent African American school choice initiatives.

Chapter 4 continues my historical look at choice with an examination of African American independent schools of the 1970s and 1980s. I focus particularly on the Council of Independent Black Institutions (CIBI) and its member schools. CIBI is a national organization that grew out of pan-Africanism and Black cultural nationalist theory and activism. The schools of this organization represented the next phase of African American school choice movement, after public school community control, and were a significant alternative to desegregation and public schooling in their time. CIBI, too, was a direct outgrowth and extension into schooling of African American social movement activism of the time. Yet these independent schools are significantly underexamined in the literature on post-*Brown* African American schooling.

In Chapter 5, I examine school vouchers since conservative economist Milton Friedman proposed his voucher plan in the 1950s and early 1960s, and since sociologist Christopher Jencks proposed his own voucher plan from the political left in the late 1960s and early 1970s. In particular, I turn to published media reports to examine the range of ways in which African Americans were featured in, participated in, and led voucher debates and efforts over the past half century. African American responses to early voucher plans are virtually entirely unexamined in the literature. I focus, again, on the ways in which African American voucher politics reveal a broader debate about the capacity and limitations of the American welfare state and its proper role in serving American children and communities. I also focus on the way in which voucher politics have been a part of a new, post–civil rights era Black politics.

Charter schooling, with vouchers, has largely been the focus of school choice debates since 1990. In Chapters 6, 7, and 8, I examine the charter school movement through an ethnographic examination of the charter middle school that I helped to found. Like the public school community control and independent school initiatives before it, and the concurrent voucher movement, the West Oakland Community School has been a site for an African American community in Oakland to rearticulate a broad vision of educational quality, debate its view of integrated schooling, and rethink its stance on the role of public schooling in struggles for racial justice and identity.

WHY STUDY THESE EXAMPLES

With these four school choice examples, we see African Americans with a wide range of politics placing their faith in schools of choice and choice reforms. A variety of school choice mechanisms allowed for this space in schooling. Often, embracing school choice was a strategic calculation on the part of African American educators and leaders: These school choice reforms provided new opportunities for involvement in and control of schooling, new forms of political activism, and new sites for broader social movements of their time.

I chose these four examples for a number of reasons. First, I was particularly interested in examining non-desegregation-focused school reform efforts. Here I aim to fill a significant hole in the literature on African American schooling since *Brown*, which focuses primarily on desegregation efforts and progress, including desegregation-focused forms of choice (like magnet schools or districtwide controlled choice). The history and politics of African American schooling reveals a *relationship* between integrationism and nationalism rather than a simple embrace or rejection of integration as a goal. I believe that the school choice reforms that I chose to study here allow a particularly fruitful examination of these interconnected race politics.

Second, I chose these four examples because they represent four significant, but underexamined, forms of African American school choice since *Brown*. They are not *representative* of African American schooling in their times, as each of these reforms drew relatively few students. These four school reforms are not even representative of the forms of school choice employed by African American parents, educators, and activists. School choice takes many forms, the most mundane of which rarely make headlines. I do not examine these forms of choice here, though they are important to acknowledge. Rather, the four examples of choice that I study are the most politically contested choice reforms since *Brown*. They receive extensive criticism for being ostensibly anti-integration and/or anti–public schooling. They often are considered the most controversial and the most substantial rejections of American public schools and institutions—the least hopeful of school reform efforts. Precisely *because* they are so contentious, it is important to examine the nuances of these reforms and the ways in which they represent active sites for the negotiation of the politics of race and nation.

Third, I chose these cases because I was interested in building a kind of historical trajectory of African American school choice. This should not be read as an argument about *progress*. As I see it, this trajectory is not particularly linear. For instance, we cannot say that community control activists in the late 1960s embraced a form of nationalism that became linearly more or less pronounced by the time that WOCS founders built their charter school in the 1990s. We cannot say that African American independent school builders in the early 1970s offered a rejection of American institutions in a way that had been linearly strengthened or weakened by the time that African American activists in Milwaukee pushed for a voucher program in the early 1990s. But we can say that public school community control organizationally, discursively, and politically prompted the development of African American independent schools, and that these independent school builders impacted voucher and charter movements in their time. There are strong connections among all of these choice reforms, both for their similarities and for the way in which they are shaped by historical contingencies, the differences that come with being part of different political and educational eras.

MY METHOD

To investigate these four examples of school choice, I blend the methods of educational historians, historical sociologists, and ethnographers. Ethnographic work and historical archival research are not often done together, yet they have much to teach each other. The richness of human interaction that is available to ethnographers underscores some of the limitations of historical research and teaches us to be vigilant for subtleties of meaning in our archival studies. In my work at the West Oakland Community School, I constantly was struck by how much symbolic shorthand the group used, how one-word references to touchstone events stood in for some of the most significant moments in the group. Words become even more nuanced among people who know each other well and have years of shared history. These subtleties are generally more difficult to glean from written records or accounts (Hughes, 1984). Yet historical archival work also teaches us about the nuance of meaning, as we see the same words and concepts taking on very different connotations through time. Through historical investigation, we learn to question the origin of the often taken-for-granted language and concepts that we come across in the field. We learn to take these as historical constructs and choices that have stories that extend beyond the research site. As Margaret Placier (1998) argues, in her exploration of the ways in which historical investigation can enhance and deepen ethnographic research in education, we also learn an attention to historical and political context; with some historical distance we can more clearly see how organizations and people are always embedded in these contexts.

For my studies of New York City community control, African American independent schools, and the voucher movement, I depend primarily on archival material and an assessment of public documents and published accounts. This historical work is guided by historical sociologists who advocate empirically rigorous, comparative studies of the interactions among ideas, politics, and policy and the ways in which these relationships change through time (Evans, Rueschemeyer, & Skocpol, 1985; Skocpol, 1984; 1985). My work is also motivated by the conception of schooling that is central to the method of educational historians such as David Tyack and Elisabeth Hansot (1982). They promote a study of the history of education that pays particular attention to the interaction between meaning-making and institution-building, discursive and material change. This approach extends an ethnographic eye on history—one that catches conflict, nuance, negotiation, and how these processes drive the building and organization of institutions.

My investigation of the West Oakland Community School is based primarily on extensive fieldwork. Ethnography allows for a rich, extended, and inductive approach to schooling. It is a particularly useful method for the research questions I ask, on vision-building and meanings given to schooling and the institutionalization of these meanings through the creation of a school of choice (Hughes, 1984). As I was part of the founding group—then the board—of this charter school, I was able to act as a participant observer from the very first meeting of the school's planning group. Beginning with the second meeting of the founding group, I became the group's note-taker and produced meeting summaries after each meeting. Many of the quotations I include in this book come from these meeting summaries and represent, as accurately as possible, comments of individual group members. In addition, I took extensive fieldnotes, interviewed founders multiple times, and attended nearly every meeting related to the school's planning from May 1996 to the summer of 1999, when I left California. After the school opened, I returned a number of times to do follow-up classroom observations and interviews with school founders, teachers, other staff, and a few parents and students.

In my fieldwork, I drew on a number of models that encourage self-reflexivity and advocate ethnography as a way to investigate the connection among individuals, institutions, and systemic sociopolitical relationships. The work of ethnographers such as Paul Willis (1977),

Carole Joffe (1986), Dorothy E. Smith (1987), and Michael Burawoy (1991a; 1991b) helped me to construct a method that places the institution of the school and the people who build that institution at its center, but that understands that a school is a fulcrum for a number of discursive, political, and material relationships and conflicts. In conjunction with a focus on the macro and the external, an attention to the micro and the internal life of the school is also an important part of my field research. To inform this work, I turned to the example of school ethnographers, such as Barrie Thorne (1993), who have a keen eye and ear for the rich details of life in schools, and who bring the story of schools alive by documenting everyday negotiations in classrooms, hallways, and playgrounds.

REFLECTIONS ON MY ROLE

There are a number of political, ethical, and methodological issues raised by my research, particularly the ethnographic study. Many of these relate to my position as both an insider and an outsider in this work.

In some ways, I was the ultimate insider in the charter school research: I studied a school that I was—during the school's 3 planning years—a daily part of building. I studied documents that I helped to write, meetings in which I actively participated, and colleagues who became close friends. As I worked to make sense of my dual role as participant and researcher, I turned to the long tradition of insider research in education and sociology. Many ethnographers have written about the theoretical and methodological benefits and challenges that accompany the difficult yet productive position of being both an insider and an outsider to a research site. As Everett C. Hughes (1984) wrote: "The unending dialectic between the role of member (participant) and stranger (observer and reporter) is essential to the very concept of fieldwork. It is hard to be both at the same time" (p. 502; see also Collins, 1991a; 1991b; Ladner, 1973; Simmel, 1950; Smith, 1987; Thorne, 1983; Willis, 1980).

There are certainly ways in which my "insiderness" has impacted what I saw and what I have written about WOCS. From the beginning, I had a difficult time gaining critical distance from the school. My initial notes were more like meeting minutes than fieldnotes, and I struggled to stop feeling guilty about recording anything that I would not say publicly to the WOCS group. As I worked to turn my notes into a manuscript, I received feedback from advisors and colleagues that the chapters on WOCS read more as an advocacy piece than as a sociological investigation. I have worked to strike a balance here: to be honest about the challenges and the shortcomings of this school, its vision, and its planning process, while honoring my belief in the school's mission and conveying the deep sense of respect and admiration I have for its founders and staff. As an insider, too, I know that I have had access and trust that an outsider might not have had. I have worked to be cognizant of this and to respect it in the story I tell.

For all of the ways in which I am an insider at WOCS, in some ways, too, I am an outsider at the school. In particular, I was the only White member of the WOCS founding group for most of the planning phase and one of very few White people involved in the school over the years. During my years as an active participant in the building of WOCS, I thought and talked a lot about my position as a White founder and researcher, and I often have been asked to reflect on what it has meant to participate in the building of this African American–centered school.

In some ways, race has mattered immensely in the building and the chronicling of this school. I do not take for granted that the school's African American founders were making an active choice to participate in a *multiracial*, even if predominantly African American, effort to build an explicitly African American school. I also do not take for granted that the founders of the school allowed me and trusted me to do research on the school and to make this work public. I do not deny that I often felt that I had to build trust anew when I was the only White person at new gatherings for the school: parent orientations, Kwanzaa celebrations, my returning visits to observe classes and interview new staff members.

In the beginning, I was very aware of being White—and sometimes of being Jewish—at WOCS meetings. I grew to be less awkward about my Whiteness at WOCS meetings as I developed friendships and real working relationships with my cofounders. As a 25-year-old, at the first WOCS meeting, I did not know that in the process of building our small school, the WOCS group would share many celebrations and tragedies. The intimacies of the friendships I developed through WOCS certainly do not make race unimportant. They just mean that race is not all that matters, and the ways and extent to which it matters vary significantly with context.

My involvement in WOCS, as both participant and researcher, has been deeply personal. The years I spent as part of the WOCS founding team were among my first years as a young adult, living on my own 2,000 miles away from my family. I grew up with my WOCS friends and colleagues. We earned degrees, bought and sold houses, celebrated weddings and births, endured divorces, gained and lost jobs and friendships and loves together. Now, as a parent, I make the daily and often heart-wrenching choice to place my two children in day care so that I can write about the school and its politics (a choice that I also know I am very privileged to be able to make). Why would I make this choice if this work is not deeply meaningful to me? I do not see personal connection to my work as something to hide or to overcome. I deny that social scientists can be truly removed from the work they pour their lives into, and I cannot see why they would strive for such detachment. Furthermore, I do not believe that personal or emotional connection to one's work must come at the expense of rigor and intellectual honesty. A contentious topic like school choice, in particular, demands a nuanced, accurate, and politically and methodologically responsible investigation. I believe that this is possible to achieve.

It is difficult, though, especially now, to talk with any degree of detachment about this work and my own role in it when premature funerals draw me back to Oakland and to WOCS. I write this in the weeks after I have had to say goodbye to my friend Akiyu Hatano, a cofounder and founding principal of WOCS. She was a teacher in San Francisco when the WOCS group convened in the spring of 1996. Nine years after we met, I attended her wedding. One year after that, in July 2006, I attended her funeral. She was 38 years old when she died. In this context, as I mourn my friend alongside the entire WOCS community, I know that I will never achieve detachment from this work.

There is one other consideration as an insider and as researcher-outsider that is important to mention here. As an insider, I was never denied my request to use the real name of the school or of any individuals I interviewed. I know that the use of pseudonyms can provide necessary protection and is sometimes the only ethical choice in sociological research. But I chose to name the school and many of its participants for a number of reasons. I felt that it was important that the school's founders receive the recognition they deserve as tireless builders of an amazing school and advocates for African American and West Oakland youth. I also felt that the Oakland political and educational context was important to highlight. The story I tell about the charter school is also a story about urban politics and urban schooling, and obscuring the city's name would have made this story impossible to tell. Once I chose to name the city, naming the school, which would have been recognizable with even the briefest description, was inevitable.

The loss of Akiyu makes more complicated the ethics of writing of WOCS without pseudonyms. I sent a near-final version of the manuscript to many from the founding group. Akiyu died, however, before she could provide feedback. I wonder if I am chronicling her school and her vocation in a way that she would like or even recognize. I cannot ask her now. I can only guess and endeavor to write in a way that is both honest and reflective of the profound admiration and awe that I have for those I know who wake up each morning to do this work. I have to guess at Akiyu's blessing by working as hard as I can to earn it. I hope this work reveals my love and my deepest respect for her and her vision.

CHOICE AND AMERICAN HOPE

Schools always have been contested political spaces. School choice mechanisms have been among the most contested school reforms of the last half century. This makes nuanced discussion and scholarship difficult. Often, the current history and sociology of school choice tend narrowly to read African American participation in school choice efforts as a *rejection* of American public schools and the ideal of racial integration. My examination of African American participation in school choice reveals, rather, a *wrestling* with the limits and possibilities of American public schools and *debates* about the efficacy and desirability of integration as a strategy of schooling. These debates are a terrain for a struggle over American participation and the limits and possibilities of the state to serve all of its people. Many forms of school choice, too, are both an opting out of a key American institution *and* a reliance on key American symbols and principles—of choice, market, individualism, and competition.

Conversations about the meaning of African American racial justice and equality and the best means to achieve these goals through schooling are still quite active, despite the current absence of a mass social movement for racial justice. School choice has been, and continues to be, a key site for these conversations. My aim is to expand the discussion about African American participation in choice reforms to more than simply the ecstatic reporting of it from school choice proponents on the political left and right and the lament/head-scratching from opponents, particularly on the left, who often believe that these choice reforms work against racial equality.

Also, my look at school choice efforts of the past half century uncovers a long-standing strategy of African American schooling that did not begin when policymakers and politicians turned their attention to charter schools and the latest form of vouchers in the late 1980s and early 1990s. This historical point is important to understanding the current school choice moment and the current politics of race and schooling, yet it is often glaringly absent from the current school choice discourse.

Roberto Mangabeira Unger and Cornel West concluded their 1998 book on progressivism with a hopeful call to change. They wrote that those who take the time to understand the past horrors and dream of the future redemption of America are true patriots. They love their country enough to pour energy into changing it:

> To understand your country you must love it. To love it you must, in a sense, accept it. To accept it as it is, however, is to betray it. To accept your country without betraying it, you must love it for that in it which shows what it might become. America—this monument to the genius of ordinary men and women, this place where hope becomes capacity, this long, halting turn of the no into the yes—needs citizens who love it enough to reimagine and remake it. (p. 93)

Throughout this book, we see groups of African American educators and their supporters who loved their schools enough to "reimagine and remake" them through choice reforms. As we settle in to the next century of American schooling, the choice strategies I discuss in the following chapters instruct and inspire, both as categories of historical and sociological understanding and as means of social change.

CHAPTER 2

Schooling and Hope: The Integration Debate

Schooling in the United States always has been about something else, other than just academics, and it always has served a number of political, social, and economic purposes. As major institutions at the center of the country's economic and state-building efforts and at the heart of many communities, public schools have, historically, been central sites of political struggle. As politically and personally charged spaces, public schools have been institutions through which Americans have envisioned their future and dreamt their legacy (Tyack & Cuban, 1995). In this way, schools also always have been about hope—or at least the promise of hope (Lewis, 2003; Noguera, 2003).

PURPOSES OF AMERICAN SCHOOLING

When Progressive reformers in the late 1800s built a centralized, professionalized system called American public schooling, they did so simultaneously to sort, assimilate, and homogenize American immigrants and citizens, to nation-build, to stir democratic ideals, and to facilitate modernization and urbanization. Ira Katznelson and Margaret Weir (1985) show that, even before this time, in the early part of the 19th century, the United States adopted widespread public education, and it became a state-building mechanism. Early public schooling before the Civil War developed an American citizenry by teaching "civic responsibility" and "republican virtues" (p. 30). These schools fostered the development of a democratic, industrialized nation-state with a common set of values and helped create a secular state by taking education largely out the hands of the church. As Lawrence A. Cremin (1980; 1988) argues, public education was also a nation-building force after the Civil War, when schools became a primary vehicle of the "redemption through education" (1988, p. 212) of the former Confederacy. The establishment of both the federal Freedmen's Bureau schools for African Americans after the Civil War and the systematization of public schooling in the South in the late 1800s played a significant role in bringing the Confederate states under national rein (see also Perkinson, 1995).

The development of mass public education was about state-building and the creation of a common national culture. By the end of the 19th century, it also was about managing and acculturating newcomers. Immigration expansion in the years from 1880 to 1920 coincided with the development of the Progressive movement. For the large number of immigrants who came from Eastern and Southern Europe during these years, Progressive educators saw assimilation and acculturation as the means to economic success in the United States. But Progressive educators and reformers also saw education as a tool of class and status differentiation in the burgeoning capitalist nation. These reformers envisioned that school would be accessible to everyone, but that not every student would have the same needs and talents. Therefore, reformers believed that students should receive different kinds of education and training, preparing them for different positions within the national economy (Tyack & Cuban, 1995; Tyack & Hansot, 1982).

Because the American public schooling system was built on sorting, containing, and managing difference, it historically has provided a ready terrain for struggles around ethnicity, religion, and class. So, too, it has been a primary site of race politics. For African Americans, schooling has been a focal point for the conversation about the meaning of racial equality and the most effective and desirable means to this goal. Integrationists and nationalists alike have turned to schools to build and institutionalize their political and philosophical visions.

INTEGRATIONISM AND NATIONALISM
IN AFRICAN AMERICAN SCHOOLING

The long-standing conversation among African Americans about whether and how American public schools can be used to achieve racial justice often has taken shape as a debate about the efficacy of racial integration. This debate has been a central feature of school choice politics of the past half century, as well, so the debate is important to introduce here.

Defining Terms

First, some discussion of terminology is important. Unless otherwise noted, I use the terms *desegregation* and *integration* interchangeably. Some have argued that desegregation is only a tactical and legal accomplishment, whereas integration is an interpersonal and emotional one (Kirp, 1982b). In 1962, Martin Luther King, Jr., made this distinction:

> *Desegregation* is eliminative and negative, for it simply removes these legal and social prohibitions. Integration is creative, and is therefore more profound and far-reaching than desegregation. Integration is the positive acceptance of desegregation and the welcomed participation of Negroes into the total range of human activities. Integration is genuine intergroup, interpersonal doing. . . . Integration is the ultimate goal of our national community. (1986, p. 118. Emphasis in original.)

These differences in connotation are important to acknowledge and understand. But most scholars and educators do not carefully distinguish between *desegregation* and *integration* in their scholarship or their advocacy. Unless I believe that this distinction is important to the actors in the stories I tell, I do not use these terms in qualitatively different ways.

Integrationism often is opposed, in the literature, to a second general strain of African American politics and thought called either *nationalism* or *separatism*. Nationalism tends to be a broader category than separatism, as not all nationalists are separatists. The literature has characterized African American integrationists and nationalists in many different ways. Historian William L. Van Deburg's (1992) typology is particularly helpful (see also Van Deburg, 1997). He writes that there are three ideological approaches to African American racial justice: *assimilationism, pluralism*, and *nationalism*. Assimilationists, he argues, "view the collective expression of grievances as a short-term strategy for ultimate integration into the mainstream." Pluralists, by contrast, "view society as being composed of various ethnic and interest groups. . . . An amicable coexistence of diverse groups would, unlike assimilation, allow each subculture to remain relatively intact." Nationalists, finally, "are skeptics. They are suspicious of claims that radically divergent groups long can live in peace and on a basis of equality while inhabiting the same territory or participating in the same societal institutions" (p. 25).

According to Van Deburg, there are three primary forms of Black nationalist ideology: *territorial nationalism, revolutionary nationalism,* and *cultural nationalism.* Territorial nationalists focus on community control of African American institutions within the United States, an independent African American–governed territory within or outside of the United States, or "repatriation" of African Americans to Africa. The Nation of Islam is an example of a territorial nationalist organization, according to Van Deburg. By contrast, revolutionary nationalists—like the Black Panther Party—hold a sweeping critique of America and see African American freedom fights as part of broader (multiracial) world struggles against colonialism and the imperial effects of capitalism. Cultural nationalists, such as Maulana Ron Karenga (the founder of the holiday Kwanzaa) and Amiri Baraka (former beat poet LeRoi Jones), believe that culture, style, and aesthetics hold the key to African American liberation (Van Deburg, 1992).

The concepts of integrationism and nationalism help me to organize the 50-year-old story I tell in this book. But this focus is not meant to imply that any strategy that is not expressly desegregation-focused or multiracial in aim is necessarily nationalist, a suggestion that would imply that these are the only two options available to racial and ethnic minorities as they structure their lives and their politics. It is also not meant to suggest that the integrationism/nationalism distinction infuses all intraracial school choice politics. Finally, it is not meant to imply that these concepts are mutually exclusive or fixed. Racial identity is fluid and complicated, and people of any racial or ethnic background may be integrationist in some aspects of their lives while reserving some spaces for racial/ethnic homogeneity or for more explicitly nationalist politics. This is important to the story I tell. In fact, my critique of the existing literature suggests that this recognition of the complexity of racial identity is *absent* in much of the writing on racially separate school strategies, which tends to be overly and almost automatically dismissive of these strategies.

Pre-*Brown* Schooling Debates

Integrationist and nationalist thinking and strategies have been part of school debates and policies throughout American history. As James Anderson (1988), Thomas Sowell (1974; 1976), Vanessa Siddle Walker (1996b), and other scholars of segregated African American schools before the civil rights movement argue, there has been a long tradition of separate, quality schooling by and for African Americans. Some African Americans, like other American racial, ethnic, and religious minorities, have sought to control their political, moral, and social development through their own, separate schools. Although the philosophies of these schools vary widely, some of these schools have represented a nationalist approach to African American schooling.

On the integrationist side, as early as 1849, an African American parent in the North, Benjamin Roberts, challenged Boston's school segregation policy. The Supreme Judicial Court of Massachusetts ruled against him, in *Roberts v. City of Boston*, allowing the schools to remain segregated by law in Massachusetts (until the legislature banned such school segregation in 1855) and providing precedent for legal segregation in a number of other states (Kluger, 1975). John H. Bracey, Jr., August Meier, and Elliott Rudwick (1970) also write that abolitionist Frederick Douglass successfully fought school segregation in Rochester, New York, in the 1850s, a century before legal school segregation was outlawed by the Supreme Court in the *Brown v. Board of Education* decision.

In the early 20th century, a number of prominent African American intellectuals weighed in on the role of schooling in racial justice struggles. W.E.B. Du Bois and Booker T. Washington very publicly debated the appropriate form and purpose of African American education. Du Bois also participated directly in the debate over integrated schooling. In his 1903 classic, *The Souls of Black Folk*, Du Bois wrote that African Americans *are* rightful Americans:

> Actively we have woven ourselves with the very warp and woof of this nation,—we fought their battles, shared their sorrow, mingled our blood with theirs, and generation after generation have pleaded with a headstrong, careless people to despise not Justice, Mercy, and Truth, lest the nation be smitten with a curse. Our song, our toil, our cheer, and warning have been given to this nation in blood-brotherhood. Are not these gifts worth the giving? Is not this work and striving? Would America have been America without her Negro people? (p. 215)

Like other integrationists before and after him, Du Bois (1903) seemed to believe that America could be a land of equality and democracy, writing: "If somewhere in this whirl and chaos of things there dwells Eternal Good, pitiful yet masterful, then anon in His good time America shall rend the Veil and the prisoned shall go free" (p. 215). As a cofounder, as well, of the National Association for the Advancement of Colored People (NAACP), Du Bois worked within the American legal system to effect social change.

But, by 1935, Du Bois asked the question: "Does the Negro Need Separate Schools?" and answered this question in the affirmative. This undercited piece was a soaring critique of White racism, African

American self-loathing, and narrow integrationism. The early integrationist sounded quite nationalist in this essay. Here, Du Bois presented a pessimistic view of American mainstream institutions, including schools, writing that he had little hope that these schools could provide a humane and quality education for African American students:

> I am no fool; and I know that race prejudice in the United States today is such that most Negroes cannot receive proper education in white institutions. If the public schools of Atlanta, Nashville, New Orleans and Jacksonville were thrown open to all races tomorrow, the education that colored children would get in them would be worse than pitiable. It would not be education. And in the same way, there are many public school systems in the North where Negroes are admitted and tolerated, but they are not educated; they are crucified. (1935, pp. 328–329)

The only alternative, given intractable White racism, was separate schools for Black students. Du Bois called for separate schools that built African American "self-knowledge and self-respect" (p. 331) and that taught African American history and culture:

> Thus, instead of our schools being simply separate schools, forced on us by grim necessity, they can become centers of a new and beautiful effort at human education, which may easily lead and guide the world in many important and valuable aspects. It is for this reason that when our schools are separate, the control of the teaching force, the expenditure of money, the choice of textbooks, the discipline and other administrative matters of this sort ought, also, to come into our hands, and be incessantly demanded and guarded. (pp. 334–335)

Like nationalists before and after him, Du Bois called for Black-controlled institutions for Black children that could combat internalized racism through a focus on Black culture, history, and accomplishment.

Another prominent African American intellectual of the early twentieth century, historian Carter G. Woodson, also was intensely critical of the American education system and its impact on African Americans. Like Du Bois in his 1935 essay, Woodson took a nationalist approach to African American education. In his 1933 classic, *The Mis-education of the Negro*, Woodson focused on the internalization of racism through the American school system and other American institutions as a significant barrier to racial equality. Also like Du Bois, Woodson recognized schooling as a life or death issue, calling education "the most important thing in the uplift of the Negroes" (p. 22). The solution to cultural death was a form of educational self-determination: "The Negro must now do for himself or die out as the world undergoes readjustment" (p. 107).

Brown and Beyond

Du Bois and Woodson, writing in the 1930s, argued for educational self-determination at a time when the civil rights establishment, led by the NAACP, was strengthening its focus on school integration as a means to educational equality. The 1954 Supreme Court ruling in *Brown* was the end result of two decades of efforts by the NAACP to lay the groundwork to challenge the unconstitutionality of educational segregation (Kluger, 1975). The *Brown* ruling outlawed *de jure* segregation on the grounds that "[s]eparate educational facilities are inherently unequal" and, thus, in violation of the Equal Protection Clause of the Fourteenth Amendment (quoted in Kluger, 1975, p. 782).

Brown established desegregation as the national strategy to combat racial inequality in schooling. It also more broadly established public schooling as a central terrain of race politics, creating a new focus on public schooling as a site to address racial inequalities and tying quality schooling to racial equality (Katznelson & Weir, 1985; Newby & Tyack, 1971). Through its unprecedented wedding of race and school politics, and the importance with which it imbued schooling in determining the life chances of young Americans, even this symbol of integrationism left a legacy beyond desegregation (see Kirp, 1982b).

After *Brown*, at the height of the civil rights movement, from 1954 to the mid-1960s, integrationism was the primary focus of the broader racial justice movement and of those concerned with schooling as a site of race politics. But, as early as 1963, there were challenges to this focus. By 1966, there was a notable division among African American activists on the desirability and efficacy of school integration as a strategy of racial justice or educational equality. Here again in American history, we see schools as the site for the politics of integrationism and nationalism, as African American leaders and their supporters turned to new forms of alternative, community-controlled schools that institutionalized various forms of nationalist thought.

Through the mid- to late 1960s and early 1970s, community-controlled public schools, African American independent schools, Black Panther schools, and other educational institutions that grew out of the social movements of the day challenged the integrationist assumptions and goals of the civil rights movement. Stokely Carmichael, for instance, coauthor of *Black Power* in 1967 and a leader of the Black Panther Party and the radicalized Student Nonviolent Coordinating Committee (SNCC) of the latter half of the 1960s, called for community-controlled institutions, including schools. Carmichael was considered by some scholars to be a pluralist, in that he modeled the African American strategy he proposed after White ethnic groups that gained both strength in ethnically homogeneous communities *and* in integration and in that he did not fully give up on American institutions or the possibility of African American participation and leadership in these (McCartney, 1992; Van Deburg, 1992). However, Carmichael and Charles V. Hamilton wrote, in 1967, that school integration had not worked. They envisioned, instead, autonomous, community-controlled Black schools: "The point is obvious: black people must lead and run their own organizations. Only black people can convey the revolutionary idea—and it is a revolutionary idea—that black people are able to do things themselves" (p. 46).

Others during the late 1960s and early 1970s who were identified with a form of Black nationalism that did not hold out the possibility for eventual integration had an even more pessimistic view of America and its institutions. But they, too, saw schools as critical to the building of strong, self-governed Black communities. For instance, Haki R. Madhubuti (1973), an African American intellectual who cofounded an African American independent school in Chicago during the period that I discuss in Chapter 4, echoed territorial and cultural nationalists before him in his critique of America and his view that African Americans should identify first as Africans (or "Afrikans"[1]), not Americans. He viewed schooling as a central institution to the survival of African American people and to African American self-determination, but he held a nationalist view of the shape this schooling should take:

> [O]nly Black educators can fulfill the educational needs of Black people; to expect our needs to be met by our natural enemies is circus talk at best. The Black educator must realize that *it is unrealistic to talk about change if you are not moving to control the instruments of change in your community.* Genocide comes in many forms, but the most subtle and damaging is the genocide of the mind and at this point in time we can't plead ignorance. (1973, p. 41. Emphasis in original.)

In his view, schooling held significant power to both harm and liberate African American communities.

Through the 1970s and 1980s, as well, debates about integrationism and nationalism continued, and schools were a central focus. Magnet schooling became a new, politically palatable strategy of school integrationists (Henig, 1994; Wells, 1993). Magnet schools, as public schools of choice, were and are oriented toward a curricular theme, such as college preparation or the arts. By design, they also must maintain a certain racial balance. Although students choose these schools, rather than being assigned to them, they are governed like any public school in their district and do not, therefore, represent a form of community control. Many northern cities developed magnet schooling in the 1970s and early 1980s as a "vehicle for managing integration" (Henig, 1994, p. 106). During this period, as well, Afrocentrism, a new form of pan-Africanism and cultural nationalism, was introduced in both K–12 schooling and higher education (Asante, 1994; Ginwright, 2004). Also, the 1990s and the first few years of the new millennium have seen the integrationist/nationalist debate play out in schooling as courts, legislatures, educators, and communities of color rethink desegregated schooling as a strategy of equal schooling and as new forms of alternative school-building have been possible, at least in part, through the new school choice reforms of the past 15 years.

INTEGRATIONISM, NATIONALISM, AND HOPE

So, where does *hope* enter into these politics and debates? Hope is often a key theme of African American politics and philosophy. Even now, the most high-profile African American politicians often draw on the theme—from the Reverend Jesse Jackson and his decades-long urging to "keep hope alive," to presidential hopeful and Illinois senator Barack Obama's recent book, *The Audacity of Hope: Thoughts on Reclaiming the American Dream.* It is not surprising that one of the key distinctions between integrationists and nationalists is about hope: hope and faith in America and American institutions (Cone, 1991; McCartney, 1992; West, 1996). According to scholars, integrationists always have held out hope that American institutions—like schools, the law, and the welfare state—could be salvaged and put to work for racial justice and African American communities (Cone, 1991; McCartney, 1992). They, therefore, have looked to mainstream American institutions as sites of social change: They integrate schools in the belief that, with integration, schools would change to accommodate and equally serve as tools of social mobility for Black students; and they rely on legal action, legislation, voting, and party politics in the belief that the U.S. Constitution and the institutions it upholds could be mobilized to ensure and protect African American rights.

Nationalists, on the other hand, have had no such hope for America (Cone, 1991). They believe that America was founded on White supremacy and that White power is endemic and intractable in the United States. They believe that the very founding documents of the country, from the Declaration of Independence to the U.S. Constitution, were built on White privilege and African American oppression, and that American mainstream institutions could not be fixed, especially using tools (such as the Constitution) that codified this inequality. They therefore look to alternative forms for African American racial justice: autonomous, racially defined community-controlled schools, businesses, and political parties (Cone, 1991; Marable, 1990; Pinkney, 1976).

James H. Cone (1991), a scholar of African American religion and theology, writes of the "two great resistance traditions in African-American history—integrationism and nationalism" (p. 3): "Integrationist thinkers. . . believe it is possible to achieve justice in the United States and to create wholesome relations with the White community" (p. 3), while "nationalist thinkers have rejected the American side of their identity and affirmed the African side" (p. 4). This distinction between integrationists and nationalists is an important one to understanding school politics of the past 50 years.

COMPLICATING THE
INTEGRATIONISM–NATIONALISM DISTINCTION

There is, clearly, variation in the degree of hope with which integrationists and nationalists approach America as an idea, a state, and a set of institutions. However, the distinction between integrationists and nationalists is often too starkly understood. Although it is true that nationalists generally reject American institutions and integrationists hold out hope that these institutions can change, there is more nuance in the integrationist–nationalist binary than we often see in the literature, particularly the education literature. We actually miss the extent to which African American educators and other school leaders have grappled, quite hopefully, with schools if we focus too sharply on a strong distinction between integrationism and nationalism.

Integrationism and nationalism are best understood in relationship to each other rather than as clear opposites. Some of the leading scholars of African American history and politics embrace this approach, but it is not the popular wisdom in most education research or analysis. Those who evaluate African American educational reforms often take simplistic views of school reform's grounding in and impact on integrationist or nationalist goals. Much of the education literature completely ignores the historical and philosophical scholarship on the complicated relationship between African American integrationism and nationalism and on the nuances of each of these philosophies throughout American history. The mainstream American narrative—whether taught through high school and college history courses or through American popular culture—supports this blunt distinction. It paints integrationists like the Reverend Martin Luther King, Jr., as the rational, moral "good guys" (Cone, 1991, p. 245) who turn the other cheek in the face of violence and who steadfastly and hopefully believe in America. On the other hand, this narrative portrays nationalists, like the Black Panthers—if it portrays them at all—as cynical, violent, young, macho hotheads who have given up on the American Dream.

This tendency is problematic for a number of reasons. For one, the use of this binary distinction generally allows mainstream scholars and educators—who often are grounded in the integrationist paradigm of the early civil rights movement—to ignore or dismiss out of hand any school reform effort that appears to be separatist, race-based, or community-controlled. As a result, education scholars often do not accurately assess the politics or political and educational impact of a wide range of African American educational initiatives.

There are a number of ways in which it makes more sense to understand integrationism and nationalism as interconnected, coexistent, reinforcing strategies that often are quite referential to each other. First, often individual people and organizations have adopted elements of both integrationism and nationalism (Bracey, Meier, & Rudwick, 1970; Cone, 1991). Sociologist and civil rights activist Du Bois is an important example of this phenomenon. The quote cited above from *The Souls of Black Folk* demonstrates the extent to which Du Bois believed in the promise of America. As an early integrationist, Du Bois helped to found one of the preeminent integrationist organizations of the 20th century, the NAACP. But he later became critical of the middle-class, integrationist bent of the organization (Bracey, Meier, & Rudwick, 1970), and he opted instead for a philosophy of racial justice that incorporated elements of nationalism. Du Bois broke with the NAACP and increasingly "became disillusioned about the possibilities for solving the race and class question in America" (McCartney, 1992, p. 72). He eventually left the United States, moving to and dying in Ghana. Some scholars identify Du Bois as one of the few African American leaders in American history to combine integrationist and nationalist approaches to African American liberation struggles (Cruse,

1967; Marable, 1990). Du Bois demonstrates that one can hold both integrationist and nationalist beliefs: a seemingly simple point, but one that often is lost on scholars who employ these concepts to assess school reforms and reformers.

A second way in which integrationism and nationalism are more related than many acknowledge is that many activists and theorists have seen the benefit of the philosophies and tactics to which they did not subscribe. Cone's (1991) work on the relationship between Dr. King and Malcolm X is illustrative of this point. Cone argues that historians and the popular narrative tend to view "Martin and Malcolm" as opposing ideological and political forces in African American liberation thought and activism. King is viewed as the consummate integrationist and Malcolm X as the ultimate nationalist. But, Cone argues, the two leaders should not be understood as so starkly opposed. They both were influenced by both strands of African American thought and, in fact, they moved ideologically closer to each other over the course of their short lives. Malcolm and Martin exemplify the "interrelationship of integrationism and nationalism in African-American history" (p. 3). Cone argues that the two philosophies are "two different but interdependent streams of black thought" (p. 4) and that "no sharp distinction can be drawn between the traditions, because representatives of both were fighting the same problems—the power of 'white over black' and its psychological impact upon the self-esteem of its victims" (p. 15). While Cone is speaking of Martin and Malcolm here, he also is speaking more broadly of the philosophies of Black liberation ideology that each embodies:

> Martin's and Malcolm's movement toward each other is a clue that neither one can be fully understood or appreciated without serious attention to the other. They *complemented* and *corrected* each other; each spoke a truth about America that cannot be fully comprehended without the insights of the other. (p. 246. Emphasis in original.)

Cone argues that scholars must understand the interconnection between the two philosophies if they are fully to understand African American history and freedom struggles.

Third, there has been so much variation among adherents of integrationism and nationalism within and between historical periods that it does not make sense to talk of them in binary or fixed terms. For instance, the terms and their connotations do not remain static with the passing of time. Being a racial integrationist in 1930 was, for instance, much more radical than it was in 1968 or 1998.

Fourth, the integrationism–nationalism dichotomy does not take into account all of the other intersecting identities with which African American activists approach and define their race politics. Surely, if history teaches us anything about identity politics, it teaches us that we cannot assume that everyone who shares a racial designation understands their racial identity in the same way (e.g., Giddings, 1984). African American racial identities and approaches to racial justice often are informed by—among other things—gender, sexual orientation, class, religion, and immigration status. Black women who have embraced nationalism have reminded us that gender, for instance, has been quite a relevant organizing category among some Black nationalist groups and that gender can significantly impact the way in which nationalists define and organize themselves (Brown, 1992).

Given these complexities, then, the question when one examines the race politics of school reforms is not whether nationalism can, should, or does effectively replace integration as a strategy for racial justice. Rather, the more accurate question is: What is the relationship between integrationist and nationalist goals, and how is this relationship negotiated and realized in specific strategies for racial justice? Addressing this question necessitates an attention to the nuances and complexities of the meanings of integrationism and of nationalism. It also requires a broad understanding of racial equality that does not presume a stark a priori opposition between integrationism and nationalism. This understanding, when applied to school debates, must allow for African American educational autonomy and community-centered approaches to schooling without seeing these as necessarily threatening to American integration. This approach, I believe, allows room for us to see hope in places where scholars often deny that it exists: in the struggling over a view of racial equality, one that may accept some tenets of integrationism and reject others.

SCHOOL CHOICE AND THE POLITICS OF INTEGRATION

Scholars often approach African American educational history with the assumption that, at various historical moments and with various reforms, nationalism has replaced integration as a strategy of African American racial justice. Some lament the loss of an ostensible consensus on integration and offer schools of choice that do not have a core goal of integration as examples of this loss (Jacoby, 1998). Others understand that America never enjoyed this consensus, and they view African American schools of choice as a response to failed desegregation efforts. But they are driven by the belief that integrated schooling is a key component of equal educational opportunity (Orfield, 1996b; 1996c; 1996e; Ravitch, 1981). Some assume an understanding of integration that discounts any appreciable affirmative attention to race or "community" in public policy (Ravitch, 1981; Sleeper, 1997). These beliefs drive some scholars to portray the kinds of school choice reforms presented in this book as threatening to interracial relationships, to civil rights coalitions, and to American inclusion.

The question of whether and how strategies like those employed by the Council of Independent Black Institutions or the West Oakland Community School impact racial integration and the integration politics of their time is an empirical one that should be studied as such. In order to approach this empirical study with an open mind, education scholars who tend to view the world through an integration lens would do well to study the history of the interrelationship between integrationism and nationalism in school choice reforms and elsewhere, and to learn from historians who question the rigidity with which these categories have been used and understood. We can best understand school choice in this country if we acknowledge the centrality of race politics to the school choice debate, if we understand that these race politics are part of a broader conversation about American participation and inclusion, and if we believe that these politics and debates often involve a complex combination of philosophies and approaches to racial justice and school quality.

Since the mid-1980s, schools have become increasingly racially segregated (Frankenberg & Lee, 2002; Orfield & Yun, 1999). Despite this fact, persistent school segregation is now almost a taken-for-granted feature of American public schooling. Few policymakers, politicians, and academics focus on racial segregation in schooling as a problem to solve. There is some indication that, in recent years, White parents and parents of color have not viewed school integration as a relatively important route to educational excellence and equality (Farkas, Johnson, Immerwehr, & McHugh, 1998). Also, in the past decade or so, courts and legislatures have been increasingly willing to terminate long-standing desegregation orders in urban districts from Buffalo, New York, to Charlotte-Mecklenburg, North Carolina, to San Francisco, California (Frankenberg & Lee, 2002; Guthrie, 1999; Hendrie, 1998a; 1998d; 1998e; Reid, 2001b). In June 2007, two voluntary school desegregation plans, which explicitly took race into account in student assignment, in Louisville and Seattle, were struck down by a 5–4 Supreme Court ruling. This Court decision could substantially impact the use of race in public school choice and assignment in districts across the country—even when the use of race is for integration purposes (Greenhouse, 2006; 2007).

Now, the racial achievement gap—often operationalized as the standardized test-score gap between White and African American students—is the primary target of those whose scholarship focuses on racial inequality in schooling. As part of a broader attention to school standards, testing, and accountability, the race-based achievement gap often supplants school segregation as the school civil rights issue of the day (Jencks & Phillips, 1998), and segregation rarely gains significant attention as a problem to be overcome.

The current politics of vouchers and charters, however, is one place where the conversation about school segregation is still quite active. Since the emergence of charter schools and publicly funded school vouchers in the early 1990s, those who address the race politics of these initiatives often focus on the extent to which these reforms contribute to school segregation. Critics worry that charter schools and vouchers will exacerbate school segregation, or at least that they will do nothing to mitigate existing segregation. For charter and voucher critics who care about social equality, their understanding of the impact of charters and vouchers on school segregation significantly informs their negative view of the reforms. So, too, as I illustrate in the following chapters, African American communities continue to debate the efficacy and desirability of school choice reforms, and the question of the effect of school choice on racial segregation is an important facet of these debates.

School choice reforms of the past 50 years also provide a site for a long-standing debate among African Americans about the promise and possibility of American institutions. While African American school choice politics uncovers a debate about integrationist and nationalist strategies, it more broadly reveals a concern about American participation and the potential of American democracy: a concern about how hopeful to be about America as an ideal and a set of institutions. One of the primary reasons why school choice politics garner so much public attention, despite the relatively small number of students and schools that it impacts, is that it provides a new site for the integrationism–nationalism debate and for the centuries-old conversation about who is an American and who can lay claim to American institutions. It is these debates that form the core of the case studies that follow.

CHAPTER 3

Community Control and Post-*Brown* Politics of Race and Nation

In this chapter and the following one, I turn to two historical examples of African American school choice: the public school community control movement in New York City and the African American independent school movement. Some of the history of these two reforms is well known, and some of it is barely known by those who study race and schooling (Stulberg, 2004). Yet these school initiatives are direct forbears of the current voucher and charter school movements.

The community control and the African American independent school movements are school choice initiatives in slightly different ways. Public school community control was not primarily about parents' choice of school *enrollment*, but it was about parents' and communities' choice to shape the schools to which their young people were assigned: through control over personnel and school leadership, budget, curriculum, and programming. The Independent Black Institutions (IBIs) I study here were school choice initiatives in the way we typically understand private schools to be today. They were schools that parents chose, as parents opted out of public schooling. They were also schools that African American communities controlled. Together, while these two forms of African American schooling generally are not included as part of the school choice debate, they have a lot to teach us that can be applied to our current thinking about school choice.

The New York community control movement and the African American independent school movement provided sites to negotiate the shift to Black Power from a civil rights focus on access and desegregation that had dominated African American politics since *Brown*. At a particularly charged moment in history, these school choice initiatives became places through which to examine the broader political question of the extent to which assimilation into American mainstream reforms and institutions was a viable and desirable strategy for African American racial equality and identity.

The questions of the continued relevance of school integration and the particular characteristics of an alternative program of self-determination are explicitly political questions. In this way, these two school initiatives were explicitly political movements, tied more heavily to urban and Black social movements and power politics than they were to any movement for educational reform. Yet these political issues were mapped onto educational reforms. Community control and African American independent schooling were also educational movements that furnished a way to reconcile the importance of schooling as a key community commodity and means of social mobility with a critique of American educational institutions and the race and class hierarchies they supported.

In this chapter, I examine the politics of desegregation, nationalism, and American inclusion of those who worked to implement public school community control in New York in the late 1960s. The community control movement came after a number of years of a largely unrealized movement for desegregated schooling in New York and other Northern cities. It also came at a time when the civil rights movement was contending with new Black Power ideology and activism. The struggle for community control of schools in New York City provided an opportunity to assess the relevance and viability of school desegregation as a strategy of racial equality. Ultimately, community control became part of a larger strategy of both critique of and inclusion into American institutions and structures. Through their public reconciliation of desegregation and community control goals, supporters grappled with the legitimacy of American institutions and the role they envisioned African Americans should play in these institutions.

COMMUNITY CONTROL CONTEXT

New York City's Board of Education acted soon after the 1954 *Brown* ruling to declare its support for school desegregation. Yet 12 years later—despite an active local movement for school desegregation—the city's schools were still, and increasingly, racially segregated (Ravitch, 1974; Rogers, 1968). In the North, in general, progress toward desegregated schooling was barely under way by 1966. Southern urban and rural school desegregation began in earnest after the passage of the Civil Rights Act of 1964, which prohibited discrimination in any institution that received federal funds, and the passage of the 1965 Elementary and Secondary Education Act, which significantly increased federal funding to urban schools, thus raising the stakes for Southern schools deemed to be out of compliance with the 1964 civil rights law (Orfield, 1996d; Ravitch, 1981). But Northern school segregation—which was primarily achieved by residential segregation, housing discrimination, and school zoning patterns rather than by law—was more difficult to mitigate (Coleman, 1981; Orfield, 1996c). Whereas Southern schools desegregated through court action and the work of the Department of Health, Education and Welfare (HEW) in the latter part of the 1960s, neither the Supreme Court nor the federal government generally intervened on behalf of Northern school integration until a short-lived period in the early 1970s (Orfield, 1981; 1996b).

In New York City and in the country in general, there also was increasing attention to race and class inequalities in schools and to the deleterious effects of race and class segregation on student achievement. The *Brown* decision and the subsequent New York Board of Education's declaration of support were grounded in the assumption that segregated schooling had negative academic effects on students of color. This required the documentation of educational inequities in segregated schools. Yet this data did not exist in New York City until 1966, when activists and pro-integration educators pushed the Board to disaggregate its data by school (Perlstein, 1994). For the first time, the Board published reading scores for individual schools. These scores revealed that schools serving middle-class White students had average reading levels 3 to 5 years above schools serving majority Black and Puerto Rican students (Fantini, Gittell, & Magat, 1970). Nationally, the high-profile Coleman Report of 1966, *Equality of Educational Opportunity*, documented further race and class disparities in schooling. Among its findings, the report demonstrated that not only did African American students in northeastern cities begin school behind their White counterparts (as measured by achievement on standardized tests), but that this gap widened as students progressed through school.

The summer of 1966 marked a turning point in both race and education politics. With an emerging Black Power movement, there was now a public Black voice that urged that true freedom would only come when African Americans had power and control over key American institutions (Van Deburg, 1992). Community control of schools was part of a larger, growing effort to control the significant institutions of Black communities. The tension between civil rights and Black Power activists and the new literature of Black Power informed and lent urgency to the public school community control movement. The schools of Harlem and Ocean Hill–Brownsville, Brooklyn, became a significant site of this transition within the movement (Eisenberg, 1971).

When Stokely Carmichael first shouted "Black Power" in a Mississippi speech in June 1966, he crystallized long-brewing ideological divisions within the civil rights movement, economic frustration in U.S. cities, and anger with the unrealized promises of racial equality through desegregation and equal access fights. Carmichael's call was a culmination of a politics that had been percolating in the civil rights movement since at least the August 1963 March on Washington (Anderson, 1997). Civil rights activist and commentator Bayard Rustin (1976) argued that with the passage of the Civil Rights Act of 1964 and the Voting Rights Act of 1965, many African American leaders and activists recognized that truly combating racial inequality would demand more than a legislative agenda focused on legal race discrimination in the South. Rather, it would require attention to economic structures and the condition of city ghettos, especially in the North. Mass urban uprisings in Northern cities, beginning in Watts in August 1965, underscored the limits of legislation like the 1964 Civil Rights Act in mitigating the daily effects of poverty, racial discrimination, and segregation (Matusow, 1972).

During these years, a number of the movement's core organizations, including the Student Nonviolent Coordinating Committee (SNCC) and the Congress of Racial Equality (CORE), adopted comprehensive programs for Black self-determination that revolved around the development of Black-owned and Black-controlled community institutions, banks, businesses, and social services (Matusow, 1972; Powledge, 1991; Van Deburg, 1992). Other organizations emerged at the time and came to define Black Power ideology and thinking. The Black Panther Party was founded in Oakland in October 1966 by Huey P. Newton and Bobby Seale and quickly gained national and international support. The root of the Panther program was community organization and control, through police patrols, breakfast programs, and Panther schools such as the Oakland Community School (Newton, 1991; Van Deburg, 1992).

THE SHORT-LIVED "EXPERIMENT"

The New York City Board of Education's footdragging on desegregation and its increasingly public failure to educate poor students of color furnished an important context and catalyst for community control demands (Fantini et al., 1970; Ravitch, 1974). The community control movement in New York began, in 1966, with a broken promise by the New York City Board of Education to integrate a new intermediate school in Harlem. Once parents of the new Arthur Schomburg Intermediate School 201 (I.S. 201) learned that the school would not—as promised—be racially integrated, they boycotted and made new demands: If the Board would not desegregate the new middle school, then it should give them "total community control" over the school (Minter, 1967; Ports, 1970; Wasserman, 1970). Local activists urged the Board to cede some control, so that they could hire staff, install a Black principal, have a say in the courses their children would take, and decide for themselves how their money would be spent. This demand for a semi-independent school, in the summer and fall of 1966, began the community control movement in New York City.[1]

When parents and activists of I.S. 201 called for significant local control, the New York City Board of Education eventually conferred this autonomy on a trial basis to a small district of the Harlem middle school and its four feeder elementary schools. It granted similar autonomy, in 1967, to a few other clusters of schools, including two middle schools and their six feeder elementary schools in the predominantly African American Ocean Hill–Brownsville neighborhood in Brooklyn. Ocean Hill-Brownsville parents and activists also had begun to demand more participation in and control of local school governance. Like the I.S. 201 group in Harlem, this Brooklyn group had asked that it have a significant decision-making role in a new intermediate school, I.S. 55, which was slated to be integrated but was built on a site that would ensure that it was not (Brownsville, Ocean Hill Independent Local School Board petition, 1966). When the East Harlem and Brooklyn neighborhoods (along with a neighborhood on Manhattan's East Side called Two Bridges) became "demonstration districts," they were to experiment with circumscribed local control over personnel, budget, and curriculum (Ford Foundation, 1969; Ward, 1967). The head of the Ford Foundation, McGeorge Bundy, agreed to commit start-up funds for a number of these projects.

Community control advocates envisioned a fundamental redistribution of power in a number of key aspects of school governance, including budget, facilities, curriculum and programming, and personnel. A flier for a march at J.H.S. 271 in Ocean Hill asserted: "Our Children are Not Learning in our Public Schools!: WE DEMAND TOTAL CONTROL OF OUR SCHOOLS." These demands were:

(1) Right to hire and fire all principals, assistant principals and teachers. Those who work hard to teach our children, are welcome to stay; those who won't cooperate—must and will go!

(2) Right to control all our own money, in our own bank signed by our own people.

(3) That every child in our district gets the same amount of money that [*sic*] children in white neighborhoods.

(4) Right to buy our own books and supplies by direct purchase.

(5) Right to build and rehabilitate our schools using black and Puerto Rican companies and workers from our community. (Ocean Hill–Brownsville School District flier, n.d.)

Some authority shifted from the central office to an elected representation of the community (defined by both race and geography). With the aid of Ford Foundation funding, the demonstration districts in Harlem and Brooklyn elected local governing boards of parents and community representatives by the end of 1967. These governing boards began to develop new curriculum and programming and hired a number of new school administrators and teachers who were supportive of community control. The goal for many, as political scientist Charles V. Hamilton (1968) wrote, was to devise "an educational system which is functional, not dysfunctional, to the needs of black people" (p. 322).

The initial educational proposals by the communities for the Harlem and Brooklyn demonstration districts focused on self-concept-building. Curricula that enhanced students' sense of "beauty and worth" (Ocean Hill–Brownsville Teaching Staff, 1968, p. 1) often tied self-esteem-building to racial identity ("Proposal for Academic Excellence," 1967). This connection between student self-concept and racial identity fueled the call for "relevant" curriculum and programming. One of the primary architects of the New York community control movement was Preston R. Wilcox, an African American community activist and an assistant professor at the Columbia University School of Social Work. He called for a "'Blackenization' of all areas" of school curriculum (1968, p. x). Designing relevant curricula and holding students accountable for knowledge of the history and culture of their ancestors was one important way in which community control advocates sought to redefine educational excellence (Podair, 2002; Vann, 1970; Wilson, 1969).

The first school year of community control, 1967–1968, did not go without clashes between the teachers' union and the community districts. But it is the following school year, 1968–1969, on which many of the accounts of the community control movement focus. The event that touched off the 1968 school year confrontation was the Ocean Hill–Brownsville governing board's "termination of employment" of 19 union teachers and administrators in the community district in May 1968. These teachers were all, with the exception of one, White (Podair, 1994). The personnel committee of the governing board claimed that this "small, militant group of teachers who continue to oppose" the new governance of the district was endangering the district's students and undermining the project (Marshall, 1968, p. 4). The teachers' union, the United Federation of Teachers (UFT), claimed that the dismissal of these teachers violated their due process rights (Fantini et al., 1970).

When the Ocean Hill governing board refused to follow the ruling of a trial examiner and reinstate the educators in the fall of 1968, the union responded by calling a citywide teachers' strike for the beginning of the school year. This strike was followed by two more, shutting down more than 900 schools across the city for much of the fall (for an extensive telling of the story, see Berube & Gittell, 1969). During the 1968–1969 school year, national and local media featured vigorous debates among New York City politicos, teachers, and intellectuals on the due process question and on the issue of the breakdown of the traditional civil rights coalition of African Americans, Jews, and labor.

The end of the community-controlled districts came before the completion of their second year, in April 1969, when the state legislature passed a school decentralization bill that divided the city into between 30 and 33 local districts. These districts were to be comprised of a minimum of 20,000 students each, thus eliminating the smaller demonstration districts (Fantini et al., 1970; Gittell, 1969; Ravitch, 1974).

THE DOMINANT VIEW OF COMMUNITY CONTROL

The New York community control movement came at a time of enormous change in American history, especially with regard to race politics. Yet, because it came to be framed as a labor struggle or a conflict between African Americans and Jews, the nuanced ways in which community control impacted and was impacted by these race politics are often obscured or ignored. The existing scholarship generally dismisses community control as simply a marginal and militant aberration from school desegregation.

The primary scholarship on community control laments the decline of desegregation as a strategy for equal educational opportunity. It also dismisses community control advocates as militant and out of touch with what most parents wanted. Historian of education Diane Ravitch represents this dominant understanding of community control. Ravitch's (1974) contribution to the study of the New York movement is significant, particularly in that she recognizes the extent to which the confrontation between labor and the Ocean Hill community was a major political event in the city's school history. But she dismisses the aims of community control supporters as overly sectarian and pedagogically misguided. In doing so, Ravitch does not take community control seriously enough as a strategy of quality schooling or racial equality, nor does she adequately acknowledge the complexity of community control politics.

Particularly relevant to my discussion here is Ravitch's understanding of the race politics of New York City's community control movement. Ravitch rejects the movement as a turn away from desegregation toward a kind of "black militancy" and misguided separatism (1983, p. 173). In so doing, she does not sufficiently recognize the nuances of these politics or the intraracial politics of desegregation. She readily dismisses the judgment of community control leaders, painting them as irrational and blaming them for failing to recognize the ultimate benefits of racial integration. She writes:

> The leaders of Ocean Hill-Brownsville [must] be faulted for failing to understand that the interests of their people would be best advanced by breaking down the barriers of race and class and by overcoming the self-limitations of separatism. (1974, p. 378)

She ultimately dismisses the community control movement as a "distract[ion]" for the "liberal imagination" orchestrated by rampant and capricious militant "ethnic separatists" (1983, pp. 168, 270).

Following Ravitch are Jim Sleeper (1990), a writer and columnist in New York City, and Tamar Jacoby (1998), a journalist and senior fellow at the conservative Manhattan Institute for Policy Research. These two writers also lament the community control movement for its turn away from integration and the long-lasting stress they believe it placed on liberal coalitions. As Jacoby (1998) writes in her introductory chapter, entitled "What Ever Happened to Integration":

> A tiny minority, black or white, have repudiated integration outright, but increasingly on both sides there is a new contradictory mood. . . . Together, wittingly or not, we as a nation are dropping the flag, turning our backs on the great achievement of the civil rights era—the hopeful consensus that formed in the 1960s around King's vision of a single, shared community. (p. 3)

Jacoby overestimates the level of consensus in the early 1960s so that she can paint the supposed diversions in sharp relief. She, like Ravitch (but with much more hyperbole and much less rigor than Ravitch), depicts community control supporters and practitioners as simple and self-serving "race-obsessed" separatists who "killed all hope of racial harmony" and duped White liberal do-gooders into supporting them (pp. 216–217).

Ravitch and her intellectual descendants represent the dominant reading of community control. Even as they applaud *integrationist* politics, they believe that, on balance, schooling and the politics of race should be separate endeavors. They therefore dismiss New York's movement for community control as a political project with little pedagogical worth. As Ravitch (1974/2000) writes: "I no longer believe that the public schools should be a 'battlefield of social change'; instead, the schools should be centers of learning" (p. xvii). Driven by this understanding of schooling, Ravitch and others do not recognize the community control movement as a legitimate and important site for working out a nondesegregation-based strategy of African American racial and educational justice.

In response to this literature, my analysis of the New York City movement builds on the work of participants and, later, scholars who acknowledge the centrality and the complexity of race politics in the New York movement. The participant writers in this vein tended to be White professionals sympathetic to decentralization and community control, many of whom had their own relationships with the community districts and their own professional interests in the projects (e.g., Berube & Gittell, 1969; Fantini et al., 1970; Gittell, 1971). Other scholars, who recently have added to a sympathetic scholarship on the New York movement, recognize the ways and extent to which community control represented a struggle for "local black institution-building and empowerment" (Podair, 2002, p. 32) and became a site of the renegotiation of African American school and race politics (e.g., Byndloss, 2001; Gordon, 2001; Perlstein, 2004; Podair, 2002). In particular, building on this scholarship, I believe that we should reexamine the community control movement's politics of desegregation and politics of American participation.

DEBATING THE GOAL OF DESEGREGATION

New York City's community control movement was not simply a critique of the failure of school integration. Rather, community control was a means to negotiate the changing politics of integration at a time of tremendous ideological flux in African American race politics (Perlstein, 2004; Podair, 2002). For some, the community control alternative allowed a way out of the goal of integration. For others, it provided an opportunity to redefine school integration. Of particular debate among community control supporters and others concerned with African American educational equality was the question of whether community control *replaced* or simply *delayed* racial desegregation in schooling and other aspects of American sociopolitical life. Although the debate quickly became polarized, due in large part to the confrontation between the teachers' union and the community districts, there was actually significant nuance in the positions of community control supporters. Despite the racial polarization portrayed by most media coverage of the confrontation, the lines drawn in the fight for community control were not carved neatly along racial lines.

On balance, those who were frustrated with the pace of change in New York City schooling, and who ultimately weighed in on community control, had deep ambivalence about how or whether to turn away altogether from desegregation as a strategy (Perlstein, 2004). Contrary to much of the literature's narrative, the movement for community control was not hijacked by "militants." Although there were some peripheral yet vocal supporters, such as Brooklyn CORE leader Sonny Carson (Abubadika, 1972; Perlstein, 2004), who more closely resembled Ravitch's or Jacoby's characterization of the entire movement, they were not the main actors in the community districts. Many community control advocates were former desegregation activists, like the long-standing desegregation activist Reverend Milton A. Galamison, whose primary goal was to find a viable way to provide quality education for African American children in the city (Perlstein, 2004). Others were parents and educational practitioners with similar objectives. They wanted better schools, not so radically defined, for their children.

Reconciling Two Goals

Most school leaders and the families they served did not envision the community-controlled schools as a means to secede from the American mainstream. Rather, they saw the schools as a strategy for preparing students to excel in college and in future careers, given the failure of the city to deliver desegregated schooling (Eisenberg, 1971). An education activist in East Harlem wrote that, in their demand for community control, parents were saying to the Board of Education:

We recognize, that though your policy is quality integrated education, you cannot deliver. Therefore, we know we will have segregated school. In that case we want a segregated school that will deliver quality education, the kind that will assure our children the opportunity to advance in the world. (Jones, 1966, p. 20)

Toward this end, political scientist and community control supporter and aide Marilyn Gittell (1971) concluded, in her study of the demonstration districts, that most parents "expressed traditional expectations, looking to improve students' basic skills." In fact, teachers who advocated more fundamental educational change often faced resistance from administrators and parents (p. 129). For most parents and advocates, community control, like desegregation before it, was a vehicle primarily for the attainment of quality education for students denied it by virtue of their race and class (Eisenberg, 1971; Fantini, 1972; Perlstein, 2004).

Yet quality education under community control meant, often explicitly, "quality segregated education" (Goldberg, 1966–1967, p. 2). There was a range of support for this segregated education among community control activists. Some who supported community control were not willing to explicitly denounce desegregated schooling. They worked to reconcile desegregation goals with community control by expanding the definition of school desegregation (Perlstein, 2004). They recast segregation as not simply a measure of the division of students by racial designation, but as the extent to which institutions were *controlled* by White or Black outsiders who did not have the interests of Black communities at heart.

This was not a huge ideological leap from the thinking of the "militantly integrationist" Galamison, who always had embedded an adamant critique of American power relations in his call for school integration (Perlstein, 1994, p. 267). New York–Harlem CORE wrote, in its proposal for an independent Harlem school board in March 1967, that the "chief characteristic of a segregated system is that it is *imposed* on a group of people and they have no control over it" (New York–Harlem CORE, 1967, p. 4. Emphasis in original). Later that year, one of the organizations central to the community control movement, the African-American Teachers Association, similarly recast segregation in a resolution:

WHEREAS—we understand that we must demand control of all schools that service our community, we demand an end to a segregated educational system—a system in which control of our education rests in the hand of outsiders. . . . A school is not segregated because it is all black. A school is segregated when it is controlled by outsiders whose only interest is exploitation. (African-American Teachers Association, 1967, p. 1)

This strategy of redefining segregation as lack of control over schools followed the thinking of many Black Power theorists of the time, in the shift of emphasis from access to control. But, by putting the struggle for control of institutions in these terms, these community control proponents avoided having to reject school desegregation outright or having to choose between community control and desegregation goals.

The Ford Foundation, in its support of the community control experiments, followed the logic of these early African American community control activists. It carefully worked to reconcile its involvement in the community control project with its continued support for school desegregation and American racial integration. Early in Ford's involvement, staff member Richard Magat (1967) grounded the foundation's support in the democratic potential of community control, taking pains to distance Ford from the "militant" side of the movement. "The goal of a democratic society—and of public education as an instrument of society," he wrote, "is to *connect* various segments of society to the mainstream: it is the antithesis of separatism" (pp. 9-10. Emphasis in original).

Ford staffers and colleagues, most of whom were White, also reconciled their support of both community control and desegregated schooling by offering a critique of White leaders. They argued that the new demand for community control did not signal a turning away from integration by the Black and Puerto Rican communities that led the community control push. Rather, it represented a response to White leaders who themselves had turned away from the goal of integration. Ford's Mario Fantini and his colleagues (1970) wrote that those in communities like Ocean Hill–Brownsville and East Harlem who fought for community control had been "consistent fighters for integration" who had turned to community control as a "strategy of despair, a strategy determined by the broken promises of the white community" (p. x).

Some White community control supporters also balanced community control and desegregation goals by framing community control as an immediate alternative to the elusive goal of integration. For example, the initial April 1967 proposal for I.S. 201, submitted jointly by Yeshiva University professors Sol Gordon and Harry Gottesfeld, the I.S. 201 Coordinating Committee, the Ford Foundation, and the UFT, affirmed the ultimate goal of integration, but claimed, "[w]e cannot abdicate our role as educators in ghetto schools and wait patiently for integration before improving the quality of the schools" ("Proposal for Academic Excellence," 1967, p. 9). Similarly, a Ford staff member affirmed the foundation's commitment to integration, but wrote of community control as an immediate intervention for quality education. "It is our strong belief," she wrote, "that full integration of schools in this city is unlikely to happen in the near future, and the most important item on the agenda is to get quality education to every child regardless of where he lives and goes to school" (Feldstein, 1969, p. 2).

A growing number of African American leaders—both local and national—expressed explicitly that community control *should* replace school integration as a current strategy for racial equality and African American empowerment. Carmichael and Hamilton, in their groundbreaking 1967 articulation of Black Power ideology, wrote that integration was "a subterfuge for the maintenance of white supremacy" (p. 54). Using East Harlem's I.S. 201 as an example, they wrote that "Black parents should seek as their goal the actual control of the public schools in their community" (p. 167). Unlike those who at least initially rhetorically worked to reconcile support for both desegregated schooling and community control, Carmichael and Hamilton replaced a faith in the equalizing power of integrated education with a commitment to the building of alternative institutions by and for African American communities.

Yet Carmichael and Hamilton, like most community control supporters, did not support permanent and enduring separatism. Black Power theorists and community control supporters varied in the extent to which they advocated independence from American institutions. Many proponents of community-controlled schools argued that separate schools would allow for an opportunity to gain strength and "academic excellence" in "preparation for eventual integration" (Harlem Parents Committee, 1965, p. 5). As Carmichael and Hamilton (1967) wrote: "The concept of Black Power rests on a fundamental premise: *Before a group can enter the open society, it must first close ranks.* By this we mean that group solidarity is necessary before a group can operate effectively from a bargaining position of strength in a pluralistic society" (p. 44. Emphasis in original). They believed that only from this "position of strength" could African Americans enter and meaningfully participate in American institutions and political processes.

Similarly, James Farmer, a founder of CORE, wrote during the community control conflict:

> I see decentralization and community control as really being a forerunner to integration; and, in a larger sense, a partner to integration. . . . Control of the schools, an exercise in populist democracy, is essential for developing the self-image and self-respect of the black community. Only after the full flowering of the black self-image and after the elimination of cultural biases from all our institutions, can there be complete integration. (quoted in Perlstein, 1994, p. 281)

Ocean Hill governing board chair Reverend C. Herbert Oliver also echoed Carmichael and Hamilton, saying: "We feel that unequals cannot really be integrated anyway, so that there must be power in the black community; then we can really talk about integration" (quoted in Perlstein, 2004, p. 111).

Defending Desegregation

On the other side, some African American supporters of desegregation did not believe that simultaneous support for community control and desegregation could be reconciled. They, therefore, felt they could not support the community control effort. These leaders, many of whom were labor activists, did not see community control as a viable answer to desegregation frustrations. They echoed the concerns of White critics, from the labor movement and elsewhere, who believed that school decentralization and community control were threats to the future of desegregated schooling (Fein, 1970; Goldbloom, 1968; Kemble, n.d.; United Federation of Teachers, 1967).

A group of African American trade unionists, for example, responded to the dismissal of the 19 Ocean Hill–Brownsville teachers and administrators by linking due process rights to integration concerns. The full-page advertisement in the *New York Times* read:

> If due process is not won in Ocean Hill-Brownsville, what will prevent white community groups in Queens from firing black teachers—or white teachers with liberal views? What will prevent local Birchites and Wallaceites from taking over *their* schools and using them for *their* purposes?

> In this context, we must ask: Will decentralization lead to *apartheid* education or to maximum feasible integration? (A. Philip Randolph Institute, 1968, p. 39. Emphasis in original)

Bayard Rustin, head of the organization that sponsored this statement, was one of the most prominent African American leaders to oppose community control. He believed that racial integration in schools was an important goal (Rustin, 1969) and had worked with Reverend Galamison to organize his boycott in support of integrated schooling in 1964. He knew, as well, that school desegregation alone was not an effective solution to systemic racial inequality. He did not, however, believe that community control of schools was a comprehensive or a progressive alternative (Rustin, 1976). He felt that community control sanctioned and sustained school segregation (Anderson, 1997; Perlstein, 2004). He also did not believe that a focus on Black control of segregated schools was an adequate alternative, because he did not believe that a focus on *schooling*, itself, was adequate: "Unless there is a master plan to cover housing, jobs, and health, every plan for the schools will fall on its face" (quoted in Perlstein, 1993, p. 49).

Another prominent African American community control critic and integrationist, who was not affiliated with labor, was Kenneth Clark. The psychologist's research on the negative psychological impact of segregation had featured prominently in *Brown* (Clark, 1969; Kluger, 1975). As a new member of the New York Board of Regents, the body that oversees education in New York state, Clark had been involved in the early negotiations over I.S. 201 (Magat, 1967). Clark criticized the community control movement as an outgrowth of a misguided Black Power movement that "basically rejects the goals of integration and somehow attempts to seek racial justice through an intensification of racial segregation" (1968, pp. 98, 192).

Symbolic Politics

As participants considered their position on desegregation, New York's community control movement also provided a site to renegotiate the symbols of the civil rights struggle. Strikingly, both sides of the community control debate invoked George Wallace, who became the governor of Alabama in 1963 and a presidential candidate in 1968. Wallace was a consummate symbol of segregationism, as embodied in his 1963 proclamation of "segregation now, segregation tomorrow, segregation forever" and his attempt to "stand in the schoolhouse door" to block the integration of the University of Alabama.

Those who supported community control likened those who opposed it to Wallace and his Southern supporters. Scholar Maurice R. Berube (1969b) wrote:

> Who supports the UFT? . . . Quite a coalition. Certainly the larger segment would most probably support local control in the white South, but not

the urban black North. This is the audience [UFT head Albert] Shanker addresses himself to, in a tone, [New York columnist] Jimmy Breslin observes, that is but "an accent away from George Wallace." (p. 147)

But those who backed the UFT likened community control supporters to George Wallace. They argued that community control of New York schools would cement racial segregation and, therefore, its proponents might count among their allies those who supported local control of schools for the maintenance of White supremacy and racial segregation in the South. Labor activist Michael Harrington (1969) wrote:

> Most of the decentralization panaceaists are . . . devoted partisans of social justice. But it should give them pause that a George Wallace has similar ideas about local control in order to build white power. (p. 135)

The fact that both advocates and opponents of community control invoked Wallace is indicative of the fact that both sides of the community control debate were grappling with how to make sense of school desegregation as a strategy. The fact that it was not clear *who* represented George Wallace, standing in obstruction at the schoolhouse door, illustrates the complexity of the politics of the African American freedom movement at this time and the extent to which those concerned with African American educational equality struggled with old symbols and the memory and legacy of the civil rights movement.

AMERICAN PARTICIPATION AND INTERRACIAL PARTNERSHIP

Public school community control was a site to debate the continued possibility and potential of school integration. It also, more broadly, provided a space to define what it meant to opt out of desegregated institutions and to embrace self-determination. This meant that participants worked to redefine their relationship to mainstream American institutions and reforms. This redefinition occurred largely over the question of the continued efficacy of coalitional work and partnerships with White-controlled organizations.

As noted in Chapter 2, the relationship between African Americans and America has been a central debate of African American integrationists and nationalists for centuries. In the latter half of the 1960s, critics of the civil rights movement argued that this movement had not been sufficient to overcome deeply rooted and enduring racism, racial violence, and racial inequality. They questioned the legitimacy of America and American institutions and worked to redefine the place of African Americans in the country. In a debate with another African American man in Chicago who maintained that he *was* American, Malcolm X asked, "Why do you call yourself an American?" The man responded, "Because I was born here in this country." Malcolm X retorted, "Now look, if a cat has kittens in the oven, does that make them bisquits [biscuits]?" (quoted in Farmer, 1971, p. 577). This assertion that accident of birthplace rendered no binding connection between African Americans and America struck a cord with many African American activists and writers in the late 1960s (e.g., Cleaver, 1968).

While critical of and advocating a certain independence from American mainstream institutions, community control supporters also appealed to the very Americanness of their strategy. As Clarence Funnye (1967), former chair of New York CORE, wrote of parental and community control of schools: "This is as American as apple pie or violence. It is no more of a privilege than is already enjoyed by the typical white American parent" (n.p.). Some urged that they wanted nothing more than the freedom enjoyed by the average suburbanites of Long Island or Westchester. New York suburbs like Scarsdale were invoked frequently to underscore that community control was an uncontested privilege of the American White middle class (e.g., Cunningham, 1968; "Open Letter," 1968; Urban Coalition, 1968).

The Question of White Participation

Related to this issue of the relationship between African Americans and America was the question of the importance of coalition-building and the relevance of White people in movements for African American freedom. These were significant questions by 1966, when the flagging civil rights movement was rife with racially charged interpersonal tensions that left some Whites feeling hurt and abandoned by Black allies and some African American activists feeling frustrated, angry, misunderstood, and betrayed by White activists.

The question of continued White participation became central to many Black nationalist organizations and their leadership and created ideological schisms within and between organizations. Malcolm X had grappled with, and ultimately reversed, his position on the ability and sincerity of White people to be of any use to Black liberation struggles (Malcolm X & Haley, 1964). Yet, after his death and two particularly tense interracial summer projects, SNCC debated whether Whites could remain involved in the organization (Forman, 1985; King, 1967; Matusow, 1972). CORE, too, moved away from its multiracial civil rights base. By 1965, most of its members and leaders were African American, and, in the summer of 1968, it explicitly barred White membership (Van Deburg, 1992). The Black Panthers, on the other hand, supported working with White allies in their own organizations and "derided those who would 'quibble about color' in matters such as the use of white defense lawyers in court cases" (Van Deburg, 1992, p. 164).

With varying degrees of ambivalence and skepticism, Black nationalist leaders spoke of alliances with national and international groups of color and with White radicals who, working in their own organizations—such as the Weather Underground (Ayers, 2001; Jacobs, 1997)—could participate in revolutionary race and class struggle (Allen, 1990; Forman, 1985). Many Black nationalist leaders of the time agreed that coalition-building was possible and necessary. But they maintained that equal and effective national and international coalitions could only come once African American communities were independently organized and powerful.

At a time when many of the central civil rights organizations were struggling with the question of White participation and interracial organizing, the New York clash between community control supporters and the mostly White union dramatized this question and came to symbolize the answer for many. This clash was not simply a standoff between professional interests and community interests. It also was a meeting of competing ideologies of antiracist struggle (Perlstein, 2004; Podair, 1994; 2002).

In New York, the issue of White participation arose in the hiring of teaching and administrative staff for the demonstration districts. Increasing the numbers of educators of color was a key demand of community control advocates. Ocean Hill and Harlem educators focused, as well, on the importance of African American, especially male, leaders and role models (Isaacs, 1969; Isaacs et al., 1970; Negro Teachers Association, 1967). Between 1967 and 1970, just 4% of the city's public school principals were African American, while African Americans were 100% and 61% of the principals in the I.S. 201 and Ocean Hill districts, respectively (Gittell, 1971).

Yet the unit administrators of the demonstration districts also hired a significant number of White teachers, and they did so with apparently little conflict or opposition (Eisenberg, 1971; Gordon, 2001). At the beginning of the 1968–1969 school year, for instance, Ocean Hill–Brownsville unit administrator Rhody McCoy recruited 350 teachers to replace those who were striking to oppose the May staff dismissal. A significant majority of these new teachers was White, and many of these White teachers were Jewish (Ferretti, 1969; Ravitch, 1974). Many of these young White teachers had been VISTA or Peace Corps volunteers and were leftists who also were actively involved in movements for systemic change (Ford Foundation, 1969; Gittell, 1971; Gordon, 2001; Isaacs, 1969; Perlstein, 2004). An advertisement in the *New York Times* by Ocean Hill teachers provided these numbers to rebut charges of anti-Semitism in the district: 70% of the 541 teachers within the Ocean Hill–Brownsville demonstration district were White, and 50% of these White teachers were Jewish ("Anti-Semitism?" 1968). Even at J.H.S. 271 in Ocean Hill, where there was some movement for an all-Black staff, at the end of the 1968–69 school year, the staff was 60% White and 40% African American (Ford Foundation, 1969).

White supporters of community control, particularly teachers who had replaced striking UFT members in Ocean Hill, made sense of their involvement by endorsing Black self-determination and the need for African American leaders and role models in the school (Sleeper, 1990). Said a White teacher at one of the Ocean Hill junior high schools: "I'm here to teach math. I'm not here to set a moral or religious example, or to be the kind of symbol that Les Campbell [an African American Ocean Hill teacher] is. This, black people do by themselves." (Isaacs et al., 1970, p. 322). Even if they "could never aspire to more than guest status in the black struggle with which they aligned and identified themselves" (Perlstein, 1994, p. 163), many White teachers negotiated a supporting role in the movement for community control and recognized the power and legitimacy of Black teachers and leaders in sustaining this struggle.

Critique of Ford's Support

African American community control activists generally accepted the participation of sympathetic young, White teachers who seemed to understand the importance and legitimacy of Black leadership and control. Yet they grappled with the role of White allies through their negotiations with ostensibly sympathetic but external funding institutions. In New York, community control advocates wrestled particularly with the Ford Foundation's involvement as a funder of the demonstration projects. Ford provided the bulk of the private support for the demonstration districts in New York City.[2] Community control advocates accepted the financial support and the regular involvement of the foundation while many simultaneously questioned the politics of Ford's backing. Some viewed Ford's involvement as cooptive and disingenuous. Yet they also relied on Ford for the very survival of the project. Given the city's refusal to contribute any additional funds, the community control "experiment" would not even have begun without the foundation's technical and financial backing and institutional clout. Community control supporters remained dependent on an institution of which they were highly critical and that many saw as emblematic of American colonialism and White privilege.

Critics questioned whether Ford was committed to social change or was simply siphoning off dissent in an attempt to uphold the racial and economic status quo (Forman, 1985; Sweezy, 1970). African American writer and sociologist Robert L. Allen (1990), in the most extensive treatment of the Ford Foundation and the politics of Black nationalism, argued that the foundation funded programs to achieve "urban pacification" (p. 144) rather than encourage local initiative. Through the support and cultivation of local Black leaders, who were beholden to their White establishment funders, Ford maintained its control. Allen wrote of Ford: "To come to the point, the Ford Foundation has shaped itself into one of the most sophisticated instruments of American neocolonialism in 'underdeveloped nations,' whether abroad or within the borders of this country" (p. 76). He held a similar critique of Ford's leader, Bundy, arguing that Bundy supported opening up the New York school system just enough to divert and quell the anger of African American parents and their supporters. Echoing this critique, a member of the Ocean Hill–Brownsville governing board, Clara Marshall, wrote in 1968:

> The Personnel Committee also feels that the Ford Foundation has not fulfilled its commitment to the project on two accounts. First, of personnel choice which would have made the project succeed [sic]. This leads us to wonder whether Ford really wants to see our children succeed, or was the original money "cool off" money for last summer. (p. 4)

She shared the skepticism of some Black leaders at the time that large, White-controlled organizations were truly prepared to offer genuine support for African American liberation.

Through the way in which they chose participants and allies in the New York movement and the way in which they framed the politics of their movement, community control participants negotiated a politics of African American racial justice and equality. They grappled with the extent to which they viewed opting out of existing American institutions as efficacious to African American freedom. They simultaneously critiqued and sought precarious company with American mainstream reforms and reformers.

SCHOOL CHOICE IN THE POST-*BROWN* MOMENT

At a particularly charged time in African American race politics, as the civil rights movement contended with a challenge from Black Power, community control of public schools in New York City (then elsewhere) became a site to negotiate these politics. Community control advocates and detractors debated the ultimate utility of integrating American institutions and working in cooperation with broad coalitions for social justice. But, contrary to the findings in much of the literature on community control, there were also a number of internal political battles. For the most part, African American community control advocates did not simply reject integration of schooling or American life, nor did they simply eschew political partnerships with White allies.

Community control of public schools was the first of a number of school choice reforms in the post-*Brown* era through which African Americans debated and reconsidered the strategies and tactics of the civil rights movement. As the next chapter will show, African American independent schooling was another.

CHAPTER 4

Independent Schooling as Civil Rights Alternative

Civil rights–era strategies of racial justice relied on the use of public institutions and resources to redress inequality and the view that assimilation into these institutions was the most effective means to racial equality. African American independent schooling of the 1970s represents, in many ways, the starkest rejection of these strategies. But, even with this reform, we see African American activists and educators grappling with the question of how to relate to the state and its institutions. African American independent schools of the kind I examine here also represent a strong rejection of the educational status quo. But this must not be read as a rejection of schooling as an institution. Despite the commonly held view among African American independent school founders and advocates that American public schools were literally killing Black children and communities, these school advocates did not reject schooling as a liberatory institution. Rather, they combined a scathing critique of American public schools with a strong embrace of an alternative form of schooling as a means to cultural prosperity and racial justice.

FROM PUBLIC TO PRIVATE CONTROL

The short-lived community-controlled districts in New York City could exist, in large part, because of public support and the city's and state's experimentation with decentralization. The federal government even, in part, supported the staffing of these districts, by granting draft deferrals to young men working in urban public schools (Gittell, 1971; Shanker, 1970). Yet, as the New York City community control labor confrontation wore on, a growing number of community control activists began to question the extent to which publicly funded schooling could meet the educational, social-emotional, and political needs of African American students.

Facing an uncooperative Board of Education, regular confrontation with the teachers' union, and media scrutiny, some community control practitioners and advocates grew frustrated with the experimental nature of the public demonstration districts. Because the city's central Board of Education ultimately granted authority and autonomy to these districts, the community districts were subject to the whims of the central Board. Many felt that the Board had set them up for failure and had little investment in the community-controlled districts (Fantini et al., 1970; McCoy, 1970).

Furthermore, some saw the fact that the community districts were established as "demonstration" projects as evidence of the extent to which professional educators and bureaucrats were willing to "experiment" with the education of students of color. "For the most part," community control leader and Ocean Hill–Brownsville teacher Leslie Campbell (later known as Jitu Weusi) asserted, "the devil has only used our children for experimental purposes. . . . When the devil's plan has failed he often phases out the program, and then it's on to another experimental project" (1970, p. 28). Some felt that these short experiments provided simply a ready way to siphon off dissent and that they did not represent an interest in genuine power-sharing on the part of the Board (Gittell, 1971; Rogers, 1968).

As an alternative, an African American independent school movement developed and flourished in the 1970s. A 1992 report on the "historically Black independent school" defined it as "nonpublic, precollegiate, self-governing institution that is not financially dependent on a larger public or sectarian organization" and that also "serves an African American community, and has a governing board that is majority-African American" (Foster, 1992, pp. 189–190). By the end of the 1980s, there were an estimated 200 to 250 schools meeting this definition.

In part due to the frustration with public governance that it uncovered, the New York movement for public school community control contributed significantly to the development of this independent school movement. For example, after his involvement in the public school community control movement, Weusi founded the independent Uhuru Sasa Shule (translated as "Freedom Now School") in Ocean Hill in 1970, and he later became involved in national independent school organizing, as the first national executive officer of the Council of Independent Black Institutions (CIBI) (Hotep, 2001; Shujaa & Afrik, 1996). He wrote of the importance of financial and political independence for Black community institutions, citing the need to separate from New York's central Board: "The Ocean Hill–

Brownsville experimental project and the experimental project at I.S. 201 are doomed to failure unless they can obtain financial independence from the devils at 110 Livingston Street [the address of New York City's Board of Education] and elsewhere" (Campbell, 1970, p. 30).

There were other organizational ways in which the New York community control movement contributed to the growth of an African American independent school movement. The African-American Teachers Association (ATA), a New York-based organization that had been an active and adamant supporter of public school community control in New York, helped to found CIBI in 1972, a core organization of the growing movement for African American independent schooling. The first convention of the ATA in April 1972 in Brooklyn featured substantial debate on whether African Americans should continue to fight for public school community control or should redirect their energies toward the building of private school alternatives ("Black Teachers Hold 3-Day Meeting Here," 1972; Morrison, 1972; Shujaa & Afrik, 1996). Those who worked in and supported the latter course organized separately during the meeting. This organization was formalized later that year in a meeting in Frogmore, South Carolina, with a mission statement and a plan to develop independent schools across the country (Doughty, 1973; Shujaa & Afrik, 1996).

INDEPENDENT SCHOOL CONTEXT

In the late 1960s and early 1970s, CIBI schools were part of a growth of private, independent, community-funded private schools founded by African American, Chicano/Latino, and Native American parents (Wells, 1993; Stulberg, 2004). So, too, more generally, the number of public and private alternative schools grew significantly during the early 1970s (Graubard, 1972; Swidler, 1979).

This alternative school-building corresponded with a focus on school desegregation politics and policies, especially as school desegregation moved north.[1] In 1971, in its unanimous *Swann v. Charlotte-Mecklenburg Board of Education* decision, the Supreme Court established busing as an acceptable way to achieve school desegregation. The Court then made its first major ruling on Northern schools in its 1973 *Keyes v. School District No. 1, Denver* decision (Kluger, 1975; Orfield, 1978; 1996a). Following these rulings, the 1970s battles for school desegregation primarily revolved around busing as a means to achieve school integration in heavily segregated urban centers (Kluger, 1975; Orfield, 1978; 1981; Ravitch, 1981). A number of cities, as well, established voluntary desegregation programs in the form of magnet schools or voluntary school transfer programs aimed at busing urban students of color to suburban schools (Eaton, 2001; Rossell, 1990; Wells & Crain, 1997).

Throughout the 1970s, however, public schools were still highly segregated and unequal. School desegregation was hindered by a string of presidents who ranged from inactive to hostile on the issue. Richard M. Nixon made his anti-busing stance central to his presidency. He reduced federal oversight and enforcement, instructing the Department of Health, Education and Welfare (HEW) to curtail its investigations of and penalties for districts that violated *Brown*. He also, in 1972, recommended a "moratorium" on all busing plans and threatened to push for a constitutional amendment against busing (Kluger, 1975; Orfield, 1981). During Nixon's second term, with his four Supreme Court appointees installed, Nixon's anti-desegregation position was bolstered by the quick political retreat of the Court. After 1974, with the 5–4 *Milliken v. Bradley* ruling that struck down a lower court's metropolitan desegregation plan for Detroit and its suburbs, the Court proved less willing to take an active role in advancing Northern school desegregation (Kluger, 1975; Orfield 1996b).

Nixon's Republican successors were similarly opposed to school desegregation and its achievement through busing, and public attention turned away from the issue after the mid-1970s (Orfield, 1981; 1995). By the middle of the 1980s, the schools were barely more integrated than they had been in 1974 (Orfield, Monfort, & Aaron, 1989).[2] The segregation in large city schools, particularly in the Northeast and Midwest, proved the most intractable (Orfield, 1996a; Ravitch, 1981).

Through the 1970s and early 1980s, as American cities wrestled with desegregation, it became clear that school desegregation was often slow, cumbersome, and disproportionately taxing on students of color (who, for example, often were subject to long bus rides each day to schools far away from home) (Willie, 1989). There was, consequently, some disillusionment with school desegregation among African American leaders, scholars, and parents. In public opinion, busing for the purpose of desegregation was never strongly endorsed by African Americans, and support for both school desegregation and its achievement through mandatory busing declined among African Americans in the 1970s (Schuman, Steeh, & Bobo, 1985). African American elected officials and school administrators also did not show marked enthusiasm for busing as a means to racial equality.

Politically, many African American leaders during the 1970s and 1980s moved from their place outside of public systems to vie for and occupy new positions within these systems. During this period, electoral politics became a primary site for African American activism, as African Americans sought elected leadership and control through national office and through local public bureaucracies such as school boards and city councils (Henig, Hula, Orr, & Pedescleaux, 1999; Marable, 1991; 1992; Smith, 1996).

At first, those who focused on electoral politics as a means to racial justice spanned the ideological spectrum. In the latter years of the 1960s and very early 1970s, as Black nationalist organizations flourished, they combined a strategy of community-building with simultaneous critique of and involvement in electoral politics (Gurin, Hatchett, & Jackson, 1989; Smith, 1996). Black Power advocates and Black nationalists worked with African American elected officials and civil rights leaders to build this strategy.

In the years that followed, there was a substantial rise in both local and national elected Black leadership. The voting drives begun by civil rights groups in the South in the early 1960s, and boosted by the passage of the Voting Rights Act of 1965, produced an expanding Black electorate (Marable, 1991). This constituency elected African American leaders in growing numbers. In 1967, Richard Hatcher of Gary, Indiana, and Carl Stokes of Cleveland, Ohio, became the first African American mayors of large cities. In subsequent years, many of America's largest cities elected African American mayors, school board members, superintendents, and city councilmembers.

As African American activists turned increasingly to electoral politics, they focused on the schools as a way to increase local elected political power and control within local bureaucracies. Schools were sites of racial politics to the extent that they became the focus of "black administrative control" (Henig et al., 1999, p. 52). Jeffrey R. Henig and his colleagues (1999) argue that school bureaucracies were among the first local administrative bodies to gain African American representation and leadership. African Americans entered and led school boards and school districts more readily than they did, for example, police and fire departments. White city leaders were "willing to cede schools to black control" while they focused on retaining control of economic decision making and law enforcement (p. 26).

THE CIBI MODEL

As many African American elected leaders and bureaucrats fought for access to and reform of public institutions from *within* the system, African American independent schools were located fairly far to the margins of African American political participation of their time. They provided an alternative form of African American schooling and political participation not unequivocally grounded in desegregation, integration into American mainstream institutions, or electoral politics. As a way to respond to public schools' failure to adequately serve many African American students and as a way to channel frustration with the pace of change and rate of success of public school movements for community control and civil rights politics, African American independent school-builders carved out an alternative view of racial equality and of quality schooling.

The New Concept Development Center (NCDC), a CIBI school in Chicago founded in the early 1970s, provides an apt example of this broad understanding of the role of schooling in African American communities and national politics. It was a small school located in the southside, a majority–African American neighborhood of South Shore. The school was built, according to cofounder Carol D. Lee, by a group of middle-class "Black intellectuals," including a number of current academics such as Lee, Haki Madhubuti, and Jabari Mahiri (Lee, 1992; Mahiri, 1998; Peterson, 1976). Grounded in the Black Arts Movement, Lee, Madhubuti, and others came together to found an independent publishing house in 1967, called Third World Press (Van Deburg, 1992). From this work, the group began the school as part of a larger community-based organization, called the Institute of Positive Education (IPE). Although the school was IPE's first project, the organization eventually published a magazine, organized community lectures, and ran a food cooperative, a bookstore, and a typesetting business. The press and these other independent businesses, housed in one complex in South Shore, helped to finance the school and to provide independent, Black-owned and community-oriented businesses for the neighborhood (Brookins, 1984; Lee, 1992; Ratteray, 1986).

Placing the New Concept Development Center at the center of a community-run organization represented a fairly common model among CIBI schools. Weusi's school in New York, Uhuru Sasa, for instance, was also part of a community center in Brooklyn called The East, which hosted concerts and performances, founded a bookstore, and ran a restaurant called The East Kitchen. These community businesses helped to fund Uhuru Sasa (Hotep, 2001). A 1973 report found that, of 21 CIBI members, 10 ran bookstores, five operated grocery stores, and four ran clothing co-ops (Doughty, 1973).

CIBI member schools focused heavily on academic excellence and achievement, measured by both the schools' own assessments and the available standardized tests, and some CIBI supporters undertook research to document the extent to which their students outperformed their public school counterparts (Lomotey, 1992; Lomotey & Brookins, 1988). Of the 10 schools in a 1984 study, for instance, nine used standardized tests as one measure of student progress (Brookins, 1984). But CIBI advocates and practitioners employed a politicized understanding of school achievement (Ratteray & Shujaa, 1987). CIBI schools stressed individual and collective transformation through a focus on *culture*, making an explicit connection between developing racial identity, boosting academic achievement, and building and sustaining Black communities, histories, and traditions.

This cultural focus came from the social movements of the time, and social movement politics provided an important context for the African American independent school movement. Many of these schools had their ideological and organizational roots in African American racial justice movements and their corresponding push for public school community control, and, later, cultural nationalism, the Black Arts Movement, and pan-Africanism (Karenga, 1982; Smith, 1996; Van Deburg, 1992).

The Council of Independent Black Institutions has persisted beyond the heyday of these social movements. The organization, founded in 1972, still exists today. Recent analyses indicate that the number of schools that are members of CIBI has declined since the late 1970s (Walker, 2001), but that CIBI is still an active national organization. A 1997 report placed the number of CIBI members at 36 U.S. schools, 5 schools in the United Kingdom, and one in Ghana (West-Burns, 1997). A more recent count, according to the current CIBI website, put the number of CIBI member schools at 16, with eight full institutional members and eight associate members in the United States. Although I focus here primarily on the early, most active years of CIBI, it is important to point out that this organization persists and continues to engage with the politics of school choice (as I will discuss in Chapter 8).

SCHOOLING FOR SELF-DETERMINATION AND SURVIVAL

In response to the question "Why does this revolution start with the schoolhouse?", New York's I.S. 201 administrator during the community control years, Charles E. Wilson, responded: "Because Americans ask education to do all the things they used to pray to God for" (quoted in Mothner, 1969, p. 43). While social scientists in the mid-1960s questioned the ability of schools to close racial gaps in both academic achievement and life chances (Coleman, Campbell, Hobson,

McPartland, Mood, Weinfeld, & York, 1966), many African American leaders maintained that schooling was a legitimate and important site of social change. In the thinking of desegregationists, Black Power advocates, and cultural nationalists alike, schools were one of a few key institutions that must be changed as part of a comprehensive struggle against racial inequality. In both the community control and the independent school movements, African American activists and educators put their faith in school as a site of social change and cultural survival. At the same time that they provided a radical critique of American schooling and a recognition that schooling perpetuates existing inequality, they also believed that schooling—through these school choice initiatives—could be a site of liberation.

The Perils and Promises of Schooling

According to CIBI leaders and advocates, American public schools were oppressive, even deadly, to students of color and their communities. A group of African American community control supporters who met at Harvard in January 1968 wrote in their position paper of the high stakes of schooling:

> The single institution which carries the heaviest responsibility for dispensing or promulgating those values which identify a group consciousness of itself is the educational system. To leave the education of Black children in the hands of people who are white and who are racist is tantamount to suicide. (quoted in Haskins, 1973, p. 26)

Public and private school community control advocates were critical of the relationship between the American government and public schools that served Black students. Often, invoking the emerging Black nationalist language of the time, they understood this relationship in colonial terms. They framed community control as a way out of this colonial relationship, a form of educational self-determination that would disrupt American imperialism.

Given this view of schooling as a life-or-death institution, independent school activists looked to school choice plans as a matter of survival. CIBI activists believed that independent schools were part of a larger process of "decolonization," defined as "the acquisition of ownership and control by African people of the political, economic, social, and educational institutions that are rightfully their own" (Afrik, quoted in Shujaa & Afrik, 1996, p. 256). In this vision, these schools ultimately would exist as a critique of and with independence from White-controlled American institutions. The mission statement produced in the 1972 South Carolina CIBI meeting began by delineating this broad vision of schooling. It noted that the Council of Independent Black Institutions should:

> be the political vehicle through which a qualitatively different people is produced . . . a people committed to truth—in practice as well as in principle—and dedicated to excellence . . . a people who can be trusted to struggle uncompromisingly for the liberation of all African people everywhere. (quoted in Shujaa & Afrik, 1996, p. 259)

CIBI founders believed that schools could fuel political change to the extent that they aided personal transformation and facilitated the development of young leaders who were committed to social change and African American communities.

A Turn to Culture and Identity

For CIBI schools founders, this response to American educational institutions involved a focus on culture. CIBI schools were deeply rooted in a pan-Africanism and cultural nationalism that focused on the development of a racial self, family, community, and history. Many African American independent school founders and supporters held that American public schools at best ignored African American culture and history and at worst systematically rooted it out. Mwalimu J. Shujaa (1994), a cofounder of an Independent Black Institution (IBI) in Trenton, New Jersey, and the national executive officer of CIBI from 1990 to 2000, wrote: "There is much to suggest that one of the functions of schooling in the United States has been to effect a gradual destruction of the cultural identity of African-Americans" (p. 30).

IBI builders, those who built schools on the CIBI model, held an understanding of schooling that linked the survival of a people to the endurance of its culture (e.g., West-Burns, 1997). They believed that building, sustaining, and bequeathing African American intellectual and cultural identity was necessary to African American survival. The belief in schooling as a necessary tool of self-determination came with an understanding, as well, that survival could be denied or bestowed through schooling.

To these activists, self-determination meant the power to define and name oneself and build and control institutions in this name (Lomotey & Brookins, 1988). The concept of self-determination also was tied to the notion of nation-building: of political, economic, and sometimes territorial independence. For CIBI founders and participants, nation-building generally meant believing that African American communities comprised "a nation within a nation" and must develop and govern the relevant and important institutions within this nation (Lomotey & Brookins, 1988, p. 172). CIBI (2001) has more recently defined *nation-building* as "the conscious and focused application of our people's collective resources, energies, and knowledge to the task of liberating and developing the psychic and physical space that we identify as ours" (n.p.).

With the building of CIBI and its member schools through the 1970s, CIBI adopted and worked to institutionalize a kind of nationalism that many other Black nationalists found regressive for its limited attention to economic and political structures and solutions (Van DeBurg, 1992). Yet CIBI founders focused on culture in part because they understood schools to be cultural institutions that, by design, inculcated a specific set of values. They believed that schooling in America was never either culturally or politically neutral, generally orienting students toward "the White Anglo-Saxon Protestant Male (WASPM) value system" (Lomotey & Brookins, 1988, p. 165). In response, CIBI supporters envisioned themselves to be "cultural workers," building schools to be sites of cultural resistance and transformation (Madhubuti, 1994, p. 4). These sites, according to longtime CIBI activists Shujaa and Hannibal T. Afrik (1996), provided "'liberated zones' or 'free spaces' where the process of education would be insulated from the cultural assault of Western hegemony." CIBI supporters understood schooling, then, to be a struggle for "cultural liberation," through both personal and collective transformation (p. 260).

In the service of both academic success and collective African American liberation, CIBI schools focused on the development of racial identity and self-esteem-building, where the self was explicitly African/African American. In his dissertation on 10 CIBI schools, Craig C. Brookins (1984) found that all focused on building both "superior academic excellence" and "a strong Black identity and self-concept" (pp. 83–84). Most CIBI school-builders assumed a link between these two: that academic success could best be achieved through a centering of African and African American history, experience, and identity. In drawing the connection between cultural development and school achievement, CIBI schools adopted Maulana Ron Karenga's pan-African cultural nationalism. Karenga's system stressed reliance on his ostensibly African value system called the *Nguzo Saba*, the Seven Principles of Blackness.[3] Brookins (1984) reported that all 10 schools he observed used the Nguzo Saba, while Ina Walker reported in 2001 that all CIBI schools still use the Nguzo Saba.

CIBI founders and supporters chose a race-specific educational program, an African- or "Afrikan"-centered approach that developed and relied upon a particular conception of African values, history, tradition, and legacy (Akoto, 1994; Lee, 1994; Lomotey, 1992). Many of these schools began as a way to serve very young children in day cares or preschools (Sharp, 1976), and the institutional arrangement of CIBI schools varied. A few were public schools of choice, some were religious schools, and most were private, tuition-supported schools (Bowers, 1984; Cole, 1998). Yet they shared—and continue to share—a certain amount of programming and collective ritual, which has been documented by those participating in IBI-building. CIBI member schools celebrated certain African and African American holidays, focused on African and African American cultural and historical figures, and developed African/African American-centered school songs or pledges to begin and end the school day (Brookins, 1984; Hotep, 2001; Shujaa & Afrik, 1996).

For instance, all CIBI member schools are required to incorporate the CIBI pledge into every school day. Kofi Lomotey, the former director of IBIs in Oberlin and East Palo Alto and former CIBI national executive officer, said that he cowrote the pledge (with Hannibal Afrik) in 1980, and that it is now a mandatory part of the CIBI school day (Hotep, 2001). The pledge is a call to personal and political action in the name of African American freedom. It is:

> We are an Afrikan people struggling for national liberation.
> We are preparing leaders and workers to bring about positive change for our people.
> We stress the development of our bodies, minds, souls and consciousness.
> Our commitment is to self-determination, self-defense and self-respect for our race. (quoted in Hotep, 2001, p. 225)

This ritual, along with many others performed by IBI students, represents one of the ways in which CIBI has sought to build and affirm students' commitments to its political and cultural projects.

From the beginning, CIBI educators also concentrated on building schools that felt like extended families for their students. This notion of schooling sought to obscure the distinction between biological kinship and a fictive kinship based on race and commitment to African

American communities and children (Doughty, 1973; Lee, 1992). This kin-like connection was accomplished in part by the language used to describe the relationships of students and their teachers. Students at many CIBI schools called each other "brother" and "sister" and referred to their teachers by first name, preceded by the Kiswahili terms for parents, "Mama" and "Baba" (e.g., Lee, 1992; West-Burns, 1997). This fictive kinship feature of IBIs is central in many accounts of CIBI member schools and is among the most salient common characteristics of CIBI schools. Although not, of course, an explicit purpose of this conception of schooling, this focus on extended racialized family also served to downplay the class discrepancy between many middle-class Black educators who founded and ran these schools and the Black communities they served, many of which were fairly low-income (for a related point on the class politics of Afrocentrism, see Ginwright, 2004).

INDEPENDENT SCHOOLS AND PUBLIC EDUCATION

In their broad understanding of schooling as an institution of cultural repression and of personal and political transformation and cultural liberation for African Americans, African American independent school founders heaped a broad charge on schools. For these African American independent school-builders, the call for self-determination in schooling was grounded in the assumption that the existing institutions did not and could not, by design, serve the interests of African American people (Lomotey & Brookins, 1988). But, like their counterparts in the public school movement in New York City, independent school proponents believed that schools could be a crucial institution in the struggle for collective survival and growth.

As in the public school community control movement, the question of the legitimacy and openness of American mainstream institutions was also a very active one within African American independent schools. For instance, IBI educators rejected even the kind of coalition-building found in the public school community control movement. The IBI movement was not multiracial and, by design, it did not include White educators or activists (Bowers, 1984). In the CIBI case, most of the debate about American participation was manifest in the politics of private schooling and in discussions about IBIs' relationships to public schools and public school systems.

Opting Out of Public Schooling

Beginning in the later days of the New York City community control project, African American advocates of public school community control increasingly entertained the possibility of independence from public institutions and support. When the fifth Black Power conference, called the first Congress of African People, met in Atlanta in September 1970, school privatization was a significant topic of discussion. The Education and Black Students Workshop, chaired by community control advocate Preston R. Wilcox, produced a working session on "Independent Black Educational Institutions." This session was asked to "develop plans for establishing a parallel school system incorporating all legally, physically, and psychologically independent schools at every educational level into a national Pan African School System" (Satterwhite, quoted in Shujaa & Afrik, 1996, p. 257). Participants of the working group debated the extent to which public schools still had a place in this independent institution-building.

The growth and development of African American independent schools in the years following the public school community control movement signaled a serious questioning of the viability of public schooling and its ability to adequately serve African American students and communities. Even more so than the school choice movements before and after it, this private school initiative represented an opting out of the public system. Independent school proponents still saw schools as a crucial site of political change and social mobility. But they believed that these goals would be served best through a kind of privatization that took African American institutions out of the control of both White-led and multiracial public bureaucracies. These private school-building efforts took place at the same time as public policy debates on vouchers and tuition tax credits for private schooling, as I will discuss in the next chapter. But, by design, many of these school-builders had little to do with vouchers or other forms of public educational policymaking.

This kind of opting out of public reforms represented a response to inadequate public schooling for African American students (Hoover, 1992; Lomotey & Brookins, 1988). It also, more generally, reflected a growing frustration with mainstream politics and politicians. During the 1970s and 1980s, Americans' faith in government and public institutions waned, as did their faith in one of the government's key institutions: the public schools (Tyack & Cuban, 1995). The significant loss of confidence in public schools was exacerbated by the country's fiscal decline and its effects on school funding in the 1970s, leading education scholar David B. Tyack and his colleagues to report in 1984 that "[i]n recent years public education has suffered fiscal inflation and ideological deflation" (p. 210). African Americans' disillusionment mirrored that of the general public, even as Black leaders increasingly sought power through public office. In the area of public schooling, surveys found that African Americans and other communities of color were even more dissatisfied than their White counterparts (Schneider, 1988). African American parents acted on this disaffection by enrolling their children in private schools in increasing proportions during the 1970s and 1980s.[4]

The Politics of Funding

Some independent school models represented a rejection of public schooling and public government control of African American education. Some also represented a renegotiation with the public sphere and with American institutions more broadly. This renegotiation happened in a number of ways. Through the politics of funding, in particular, African American independent school leaders debated the extent to which they would accept public support and enter into relationships with public institutions. Many community-based independent schools, including a number that focused on African American children and African American community control, relied on public support for their survival. Often struggling financially, they drew funds from federal programs geared to specific populations, like Title I for low-income students, as well as local and state monies allocated for youth programming and for nonpublic schooling (Gittell, 1970; Parsons, 1970). While most charged tuition to supplement or eliminate the need for public support, some schools also relied on funding from large private foundations, such as Ford (Berube, 1969a; Institute for Independent Education, 1991).

African American independent schools worked to balance significant financial need with the desire to be independent and unencumbered by public politics or private foundations' demands. These schools differed in their funding philosophies, corresponding to a broader difference in ideology, on the extent to which they sought separation and independence from mainstream politics and institutions. Most members of the Council of Independent Black Institutions and a number of other African American independent schools across the country strove for complete financial independence from the state. CIBI schools thus primarily relied on tuition and private donations from

African American individuals and community-based organizations and businesses. Lomotey and Brookins (1988) found that tuition revenue made up 80 to 90% of IBI budgets. However, an earlier study reported that six of the existing 21 CIBI schools received "a significant portion of their funding from governmental sources" (Doughty, 1973, p. 256). This public support came in the form of food subsidies (Bowers, 1984) or state daycare funding (Forté-Parnell, 1998).

Although some IBIs did receive public support, Lomotey and Brookins (1988) asserted that IBIs' financial independence was a prerequisite to ideological, moral, and political independence:

> IBIs could, of course, receive federal, state, or local government funding, or they could receive funding from corporations and foundation [*sic*]; but the view is that since they have rejected the system in this country, it would be contradictory to seek funding from people who are supporting and perpetuating that same system. Generally, when you receive funding from someone, they attempt to control (at least in part) what you are trying to do. (p. 178)

In fact, this kind of financial independence became—and remains—one of the criteria for membership into CIBI.

As was the case in both the 1960s public school community control movement and, as we will see, the voucher and charter school movements of the past few decades, the issue of funding provided a key axis of institutional definition for these independent schools. In these cases, funding decisions presented more than a question of organizational solvency. They raised the issue of political legitimacy and ideological congruence. Lack of funding surely limited the goals and scope of independent institutions (Brookins, 1984). Yet IBI builders believed that reliance on public funding and support from mainstream foundations served to limit their independence and, therefore, to challenge their political and educational missions.

Relationships with Public Schools

CIBI educators generally rejected the notion that public schooling could ever sufficiently serve the academic needs of African American students or provide them with the tools of their own freedom (Doughty, 1973). Lee (1994) wrote that the public schools could go a certain distance toward preparing African American students for "economic self-sufficiency," by arming them with academic skills, a sense of the foundations of American democracy, and knowledge of their history. But "Even if public schools were to accomplish these things, the conditions necessary for African-Americans to achieve ethnic pride, self-sufficiency, equity, wealth, and power would not be met" (p. 308). Independent school advocate and scholar Joan Davis Ratteray (1986) agreed, chastising leaders and communities of color for their continued fidelity to and "unrelenting support" of public schooling (p. 7). For Ratteray and others, African American independent schools were the solution to the incorrigible public system, one that failed Black students by design.

But CIBI leaders sought to bring one aspect of publicness into independent schooling: access. Lee (1992) wrote of the CIBI school in Chicago that she helped to found that, in contrast to many private schools, "in its 20-year history NCDC has accepted every student who has registered to attend, and only two children have ever been asked to leave the school" (p. 175). Ratteray (1994) also noted approvingly that African American independent schools attracted and served families from a range of economic backgrounds, the majority of whom were not upper-middle-class or wealthy. Such schools sought the freedom of exclusivity in teacher hiring, administration, and governance. But they often sought to be accessible to all students, regardless of financial need and academic skill.

Many CIBI educators also actively sought a relationship with public schools out of the desire to effect change in African American schooling beyond the reach of their small, independent schools (Lee, 1992; Lomotey & Brookins, 1988), acknowledging that the majority of African American families still supported and sent their children to public schools (Lomotey & Brookins, 1988; Mahiri, 1998). CIBI founders envisioned that their small schools, which had more freedom to innovate than their public counterparts, could serve as models for public schools that wished to adopt a more culturally relevant, African/African American–centered curriculum. "Indeed," wrote Lee (1992), "IBIs represent the 'laboratory' schools for the development of pedagogy and projects that reflect African world views and interests" (p. 174).

Furthermore, this interest in public schooling was not simply ideological. CIBI's member schools often sent their students back to public schools for middle or high school. Because IBIs often sent older students back to the public school system, some oriented their curricula toward this system in an attempt to provide an "easy transition" to public schooling for their students (Bowers, 1984, p. 114). The New Concept Development Center (NCDC), for example, built its curriculum both from the standards of the Chicago public school system and the CIBI guidelines (Brookins, 1984). Lee (1992) wrote that NCDC and other independent Black institutions offered not "bastions of narrow, separatist, anti-American instruction," but a "promise of hope for public education" in the ways in which they prepared Black students to enter and succeed in Chicago public schools:

> Public school principals enthusiastically welcome NCDC graduates because they have come to expect these children to enjoy reading, patiently engage in mathematical and scientific problem solving, think critically about social issues, be well-rounded in their creative interests and talents, and behave well. (p. 174)

Some IBI leaders thus believed that this private education served as a temporary haven to ready young students, both academically and psychologically, to excel in public schools, despite the shortcomings of these schools (Brookins, 1984; Lomotey & Brookins, 1988).

HISTORICAL ROOTS OF MODERN CHOICE POLITICS

The debates on the limits of integrationism and the constraints of public schooling in the African American public school community control and independent school movements foreshadow the debates in recent decades on vouchers and charter schools. African American school choice politics, since the post-*Brown* moment when desegregation became the primary focus of race and school politics, has been a place to discuss and reconcile a range of racial justice strategies and philosophies. School choice politics since *Brown* also has been a site to debate and assess the extent to which American institutions— such as schools—can and will serve African Americans as equals.

Contrary to the framing in the mainstream literature on either community control or African American independent schooling, these reforms were neither marginal nor inconsequential to the race and school politics of their time. Even if they were small and/or short-lived, they were squarely at the center of the most important political questions of their day. Regardless of what one believes about their politics or their educational accomplishments, it is important to recognize these reform efforts as outgrowths of the social movements of their time and as significant sites of the politics of American participation and racial justice. As such, we can learn a lot from them that can be applied to current policies and politics. Understanding the meanings with which Jitu Weusi, Stokely Carmichael, Rhody McCoy, and Joan Ratteray imbued school choice after Brown helps us to raise critical questions about the complex politics of race and nation of current choice reforms.

CHAPTER 5

Vouchers, Race, and the American Welfare State

Publicly funded education vouchers are, in many ways, the ultimate public school opt-out. They are an exit from public schooling on the public's dime. They imply government-funded dissatisfaction with an institution that is virtually entirely monopolized by the state. But, in fact, voucher politics reveal a debate about the extent to which the welfare state can and should serve all of its people through one of its key institutions: the public schools. Vouchers raise the question: What can we expect from the state?

This is a question that clearly has a lot to do with African Americans. And, in fact, African Americans always have been central to American voucher debates. This has been true especially since the first true publicly supported voucher program began in Milwaukee in 1990. Pick up any *New York Times*, *Newsweek*, or *Washington Post* article about vouchers now, and you are likely to see featured an African American voucher-hopeful parent (almost always a mother) struggling to find and finance a quality education for her children. The media portrayals of African American parents and children as desperate and satisfied voucher customers are joined with headlines such as "Free at Last: Black America Signs Up for School Choice" (Shokraii, 1996), "Minorities Flock to Cause of Vouchers for Schools" (Brooke, 1997), "Black Parents at Heart of Tug of War" (Archer, 1998), and "The New Politics of Education Casts Blacks in a Starring Role" (Staples, 1998).

Despite this recent press attention, we know far too little about the range of ways in which African Americans have been part of voucher debates. In this chapter, I argue that, since *Brown v. Board of Education*, vouchers have been a site of the central questions of the day with respect to African American educational and racial equality. These include the question of whether an integrationist or nationalist strategy better serves African American communities. But, even more prominently, voucher politics reveal a long-standing conversation about the proper role and shape of the American welfare state. This is a particularly charged conversation when it involves questions of race, and, more specifically, when it involves African American survival, well-being, and equality.

THE CURRENT STATE OF VOUCHER REFORMS

Though American educational vouchers have been debated at least since the *Brown* decision, publicly funded voucher programs were politically untenable and virtually nonexistent until 1990. The current voucher push has roots in two very different sources. First, it owes its viability in part to a reinvigorated scholarly debate, due primarily to the 1990 publication of John E. Chubb and Terry M. Moe's *Politics, Markets and America's Schools*. In this formative work, Chubb and Moe cited unions, public bureaucracy, and the fact that public schools are subject to democratic decision making as reasons to opt for "market alternatives" in schooling. They claimed that public school failure could be traced to the very fact that public schools are democratic institutions. They proposed, instead, "[s]ome sort of voucher system, combining broad democratic guidance with a radical decentralization of resources and choice" (Chubb & Moe, 1988, p. 1085). In a frequently quoted passage of their 1990 book, they wrote enthusiastically on the importance of choice: "we think reformers would do well to entertain the notion that choice *is* a panacea. . . . . It has the capacity *all by itself* to bring about the kind of transformation that, for years, reformers have been seeking to engineer in myriad other ways" (p. 217. Emphasis in original).

The current voucher movement also owes its birth to a push for more independence and control in schooling by African American activists in Milwaukee. In 1987, long-standing frustration with the city's troubled desegregation program (see Dougherty, 2004) and with recent findings on the underachievement of African American students in the district led a group of African American lawmakers, parents, community leaders, and academics to propose the creation of an independent district of approximately 6,000 students. Rejecting a desegregation program that placed undue burden on students of color and failed to deliver academic results, the group proposed an experiment in community control and choice: a cluster of nine schools with 97% African American enrollment that could be opted into or out of by parents (Bell, 1989; Carl, 1996; McGroarty, 1996).

This community control plan was rejected by the state legislature. But it increased attention to the issue of African American achievement in Milwaukee schools (Carl, 1996; George & Farrell, 1990). It also served as a direct precursor to the voucher movement in Milwaukee. African American state representative Annette "Polly" Williams and Howard Fuller, the secretary of the Wisconsin State Department of Employment Relations in Democratic governor Tony Earl's administration in the mid-1980s and the eventual superintendent of the Milwaukee Public Schools, were two primary backers of the 1987 proposal. They sought support for the independent district from Republican governor Tommy G. Thompson, a White voucher proponent who had unsuccessfully proposed a "parental choice" plan to the state legislature in the same year. Although the governor did not ultimately support the independent district, he began to work with Williams to craft voucher legislation for the city. Williams and others supported a voucher plan for the same reasons that they had proposed the independent African American district: frustration with the way in which the public schools in the city were underserving Black students and dissatisfaction with the city's busing program (Apple & Pedroni, 2005; Carl, 1996; Fuller, 2000; Holt, 2000; McGroarty, 1996).

In May 1990, with the passage of the Wisconsin Parental Choice Plan and the strong support of both Governor Thompson and Williams, Milwaukee became the first city in the country with a publicly funded voucher program that included private schools. This initial program allocated state funding for up to 1% of the city's public school students, or almost 1,000 students, to attend any participating private, nonreligious school in the city. To be eligible to receive the $2,500 voucher, students had to be from low-income families (Wilkerson, 1990). In 1995, the legislature raised the cap on participation to 15% of the district's students and included parochial schools in the program (Walsh, 1998a). The plan has withstood a number of court challenges, the most significant of which came in November 1998, when the U.S. Supreme Court let stand a Wisconsin supreme court ruling that the inclusion of religious schools in the voucher program did not violate the separation of church and state mandated by the First Amendment (Lewis, 1998).

The successful passage of the Milwaukee voucher plan marked a new political willingness to consider vouchers that was largely absent even through the politically conservative 1980s. Other states began to consider—though generally they rejected—their own voucher programs. In Colorado, in 1992, and in California, in 1993, voters rejected state voucher plans by decisive margins (Associated Press, 1993; Brooke, 1997).

The next successful voucher proposal was a Cleveland plan similar to Milwaukee's. Backed by White Republican governor George Voinovich and passed by the Ohio state legislature in March 1995, the Cleveland voucher program at first provided approximately 2,000 K–3 students with vouchers worth up to $2,250 (Dillon, 2005; *Zelman v. Simmons-Harris*, 2002). Priority was given to low-income students. Unlike Milwaukee's initial plan, the program included religious schools, and most recipients used their vouchers to attend such schools. Support for the Pilot Project Scholarship Program among local African American leaders was unclear. Some voucher supporters claimed that Cleveland's voucher plan was driven by an African American city councilor, Fannie Lewis, who launched a grassroots campaign among parents in her district to pass the Ohio law (Dwyer, 1997; Shokraii, 1996). Some voucher opponents, however, argued that the voucher plan passed without significant support among African American leaders (Murphy, Nelson, & Rosenberg, 1997). In fact, the *Plain Dealer* reported that all 12 African American members of the state House of Representatives, all Democrats, raised opposition to the voucher plan when it came before them as part of a Republican-backed budget proposal, noting that the plan threatened to deprive Cleveland public schools of much-needed funds (Suddes, 1995).

After Ohio established vouchers for Cleveland, a number of states considered their own voucher plans. Generally, these failed to garner legislative support or voter endorsement, as was the case in legislative battles in Texas in 1996–1997, the District of Columbia in 1997–1998, and Pennsylvania in 1998, and in ballot initiatives in Oregon in 1990, Colorado in 1992, California in 1993 and 2000, and Michigan in 2000. A December 1997 *New York Times* article reported that "voucher proposals are being prepared in about half of the nation's 50 states. The plans run the gamut from bills in state legislatures to proposals for state constitutional amendments to initiatives by local school boards" (Brooke, 1997, p. A1). Public voucher proposals have been joined by a number of private voucher plans, which provide "scholarships" for students to attend private schools and are largely funded by wealthy individual donors. In September 1997, the *New York Times* reported that there were more than 30 such programs nationwide (Dao, 1997).

In 1999, under the leadership and strong support of new Republican governor Jeb Bush, Florida passed the first statewide voucher plan in the country, geared to students in "failing" public schools. Students were eligible for state-supported vouchers to purchase nonreligious or religious private school education if they attended a school that earned a state grade of "F"—based on student test scores—for 2 out of 4 years in a row. In the first year, just 58 students from the only two qualifying schools in the state participated in the program (Associated Press, 1999b; Raspberry, 1999).

Legally, voucher proponents earned a significant victory in June 2002, when the Supreme Court ruled, in *Zelman v. Simmons-Harris*, that Cleveland's voucher program did not violate church-state separation by including religious schools. Proponents likened the Court's decision to the *Brown* desegregation ruling in its scope, legal importance, and impact on educational equality (see Stulberg, 2006). They predicted that, with the First Amendment issue settled by the Court, the ruling would open the door to voucher proposals across the country.

Proponents are still waiting to realize this goal. Since *Zelman*, just a few other states have passed voucher plans, including a program for special education students in Utah and a program deemed unconstitutional in Colorado. Ohio implemented a statewide Florida-like voucher program in the 2006–07 school year, which makes vouchers available to up to 14,000 students who attend or have been assigned to public schools that rank in the lowest two categories on a statewide assessment for 2 of the last 3 years (Townsend, 2006). Washington, D.C., is the only other city to have enacted a Milwaukee-like program in the past decade. The U.S. Congress, after unsuccessfully debating vouchers in the District of Columbia for many years, implemented and funded a voucher program for the district in 2004, which is also limited to low-income students.

Furthermore, in early January 2006, the Florida state supreme court ruled that the Florida voucher program was unconstitutional, not on First Amendment grounds but because it violated the state constitution's mandate that "[a]dequate provision shall be made by law for a uniform, efficient, safe, secure and high quality system of free public schools" (quoted in Dillon, 2006, p. A16). The court ruled that the program, which served 730 students, must end after the 2005–06 school year (Dillon, 2006).

The number of students currently taking advantage of the country's public voucher programs also is still relatively small, despite the enormous amount of attention that vouchers attract in education policy circles and in public debate. A July 2005 article estimated that a total of just 36,000 students participated in the voucher programs in Cleveland, Milwaukee, Florida, and the District of Columbia (Dillon, 2005). The pro-voucher Institute for Justice estimated this number to be approximately 38,000, or less than 0.08% of all students nationwide (cited in Toppo, 2005, p. 9D).

African Americans' opinions about vouchers always have been divided. Voucher proponents today often assert African American voucher support as if it is an established fact and common wisdom. This is more self-serving than it is true. The best data here come from the nonpartisan think tank the Joint Center for Political and Economic Studies, which has conducted multiple nationwide polls containing a voucher question. These data reveal that African Americans, in general, now tend to support school choice of various kinds, but that this support certainly is not decisive or overwhelming.

VOUCHERS AND A LOCAL STATE

Voucher programs always have been controversial—despite their small size and their political marginality—because they raise fundamental questions about the nature of American participation and the limits and possibilities of the American welfare state. In fact, when vouchers were first introduced after *Brown*, they were a way for local governments to assert themselves against what they believed was a meddling federal government. This struggle between local and federal control was about race, as it has been so many times in American history. In particular, it was about school desegregation.

When Southern states argued against school desegregation in the *Brown* cases, they stressed the necessity of local control and "states' rights." In his argument before the Supreme Court on how the Court should implement its desegregation decision in the states, Texas attorney general John Ben Shepperd exemplified this position. Noting that "Texas loves its Negro people . . . and Texas will solve their problems in its own way," Shepperd urged: "We see no reason to pluck local affairs out of local hands. . . . Our argument may be summed up in eight words . . . : It is our problem—let us solve it" (quoted in Kluger, 1975, p. 734).

After *Brown* became the law of the land in 1954, opponents of federal intervention and of racial desegregation sought a way around the Court's order. As *Brown* mandated the removal of legal barriers to public school desegregation, segregationists devised ways to assert local control and undermine the ruling by removing White students and resources from public schools. Segregationists in many Southern states introduced voucherlike publicly funded tuition grants to White students only, which could be used to purchase a segregated private education in all-White "academies." These programs allowed White students to avoid desegregated schooling and condemned African American students to intractable segregation in public schools. Proponents wrongly reasoned that these private options were legally untouchable.[1]

The *Washington Post, Times Herald* reported, in December 1964, that a total of eight Southern states had tuition-grant programs (Chapman, 1964), while the paper reported that, by 1968, "about 200 private schools [serving approximately 40,000 students] have been established in recent years as escapes for whites from desegregated public schools" (Jacoby, 1968, p. B3). Often, this public funding of private education required state constitutional amendments. For instance, in Virginia, in a move that gained wide national attention, voters passed a measure in January 1956 that changed the constitution to allow for state-supported tuition grants to public schools (Baker, 1957). This was an explicit maneuver to avoid school desegregation. The group that proposed this constitutional amendment, the Gray Commission, noted that "tuition grants are vital to the prevention of enforced integration" and proposed "legislation to provide that no child be required to attend a school wherein both white and colored children are taught" ("Gray Report Text," 1955, p. A15).

Virginia's private school plan received the most national attention, in large part because Virginia contained the only county in the country to shut its public schools entirely in an effort to evade desegregation. Beginning in the fall of 1959, the Prince Edward County school board (one of the initial defendants in the set of cases that comprised the *Brown* decision) closed the public schools to the county's approximately 1,500 White and 1,700 African American students rather than comply with a pending desegregation order ("Virginians Plan," 1959). To ensure that White students were provided with schooling during these closures, a tuition-grant program that largely reimbursed White families for the cost of private schooling was first privately funded and then, by 1960, supported by state and local funds (Gates, 1962; Henig, 1994; Muse, 1961). Most of the Virginia county's White children took advantage of this program (Sitton, 1961).

The NAACP represented the primary public African American response to this antidesegregation tactic. It successfully challenged the Prince Edward County school closings (Phillips, 1961) and the use of tuition grants in the county (Douglas, 1964), then in the state as a whole (Chapman, 1964). Eventually, Southern tuition grant programs were deemed unconstitutional in Supreme Court rulings against the Virginia program in 1964 and similar South Carolina and Louisiana programs in 1968 (Dewar, 1968; "Tuition Aid," 1968).

This school desegregation debate, in the first decade after the *Brown* ruling, included a significant discussion about the proper role of the federal government, a rehashing of American debates that were at least as old as the Civil War. Vouchers became one means through which Southern states reasserted local and state power over racial segregation in their public schools.

VOUCHERS AND A MINIMAL STATE

Maintaining segregation by defending local control was one purpose of early voucher-like reforms. Another purpose was a kind of school privatization that shrank the role and responsibility of all government. This was the original intent of the father of 20th-century American education vouchers, conservative economist Milton Friedman. Since Friedman, vouchers have served as a site to debate the scope of state involvement in the provision of social services.

Friedman introduced a voucher proposal in a 1955 book chapter, then in his 1962 book, *Capitalism and Freedom.* His plan was driven primarily by free-market assumptions that competition and choice would produce a higher-quality educational product. Friedman recommended that parents be given a choice to spend in private schools the equivalent of the funds spent on their child in their local school district. The state's role would be nominal. It would disburse funds and ensure simply "minimum standards." Friedman's primary concerns were with efficiency and freedom of choice, and he did not have a particular focus on equity.

Friedman's voucher proposal was not implemented in the decades following its introduction. But his philosophy of small government and his belief that vouchers could serve as an alternative way for the state to deliver schooling reemerged during the Reagan era. As governor of California from 1967 through 1974, Ronald Reagan supported vouchers for the state (Stevens, 1971). As a presidential candidate in 1980, Reagan supported both vouchers and tax credits for private school tuition (Morgan, 1980). President Reagan's voucher and tax credit support was part of a larger program of privatization, grounded in free-market thinking and small government (particularly federal government) ideology (Cohen, 1981; Henig, 1994; Kirp, 1982a).

Friedman's and Reagan's focus on a minimal state found a counterpart in a community control argument for vouchers. Friedman himself invoked this rationale in the early 1970s. A February 1970 article reported that "Dr. Friedman considers the voucher system as 'the only way to have effective community control over schools.'" It continued by quoting Freidman: "Community control comes through decentralization, and the only effective way to decentralize is to bring decisionmaking directly to the individual" (Leedom, 1970, p. 6).

In a 1973 piece, Friedman argued specifically that vouchers would bring community control to African American parents. Here, echoing an argument that would be made by many people 3 decades later, Friedman hinted that Black leaders were out of sync with Black communities and did not necessarily have community interests in mind when they opposed vouchers. He condemned Black leaders for rejecting the voucher option in a power play for the public schools:

> Their constituents would benefit from it most; it would give them power over the schooling of their children, eliminate the domination of both the citywide politicians and, even more important, of the entrenched bureaucracy. Black leaders themselves frequently send their children to private schools. Why do they not help others to do the same? My tentative answer is that vouchers would also free the black man on the street from domination by his leaders, who correctly see that control over local schooling is a powerful political lever. (1973, p. 65)

Friedman claimed that vouchers would provide a more authentic form of community control to African American families, in that they would remove some power from government and from those who governed.

Some African American voucher advocates through the years have agreed with Friedman's rationale. They have supported the minimal-state reform because they believe that vouchers promote a community-controlled remedy to a failing state: an American government that has failed, consistently, to provide quality and equality in schooling for African American children. Some African Americans have been willing to embrace vouchers because they believe that public schools in urban areas are in dire condition and they doubt that these schools will ever adequately serve Black children and their families. As African American columnist William Raspberry, long a "voucher agnostic" (Raspberry, 1987), wrote in 1998: "If I find myself slowly morphing into a supporter of charter schools or vouchers. . . . [i]t is because I am increasingly doubtful that the public schools can do (or at any rate will do) what is necessary to educate poor minority children" (1998b, p. A27).

Some African American educators, parents, and politicians have recognized that vouchers may not be a systemic solution to the massive problem of urban public schooling, but—using language of rescue and survival, and likening vouchers to "life vests" (Raspberry, 2003b) and "lifeboats" (Raspberry, 1998a; Staples, 2002)—they have supported vouchers as at least a small way to "save" some young people from these public failures. As African American voucher supporter and former Democratic U.S. representative from New York City, the Reverend Floyd Flake, said: "If an airplane crashes, you don't take the position that there are no survivors. . . . You try to save as many people as you can" (quoted in Archer, 1998, p. 15).

In the context of this failure of public schools to serve many Black children and communities—a form of state failure—some African Americans have embraced vouchers because they require relatively minimal state involvement in the delivery of education and they provide a degree of community control that is not possible in most public schools. For example, the *Bay State Banner*, an African American newspaper in Boston, reported in 1970 that parents had formed a group to explore the voucher option (Bordett, 1970; "Parents Ponder," 1970). The *Banner* reported, in 1973, that African American state representative Mel King, of Boston's South End neighborhood, supported vouchers for their community empowerment potential (Bellamy, 1973). Similarly, Willie Brown, a longtime Democratic member of the California Assembly and, eventually, the first African American mayor of San Francisco (from 1996 to 2004), voiced support for vouchers as early as March 1971 as a means of "total community involvement" ("Voucher System," 1971, p. 6).

This kind of community control rationale for vouchers has been most pronounced in the past 15 years, particularly in Milwaukee. For example, Milwaukee voucher activist Williams (1998) cast her support of vouchers as a way to gain freedom from the welfare state, as a tool of self-determination: "We are sick and tired of dependency on social programs that take away all of our will, motivation, and drive. We want what everybody else wants. We want to be self-sufficient" (p. 6). In Milwaukee, as well, veterans activists like Fuller and journalist Mikel Holt have embraced vouchers less as a school privatization reform and more as a tool of African American self-determination and social justice (Fuller, 2000; Fuller, personal communication, September 2006; Holt, 2000).

This approach to vouchers as a tool of African American political and educational self-determination is quite controversial. Over the years, there have been important disagreements about the extent to which African Americans should give up on the state as the primary provider of schooling and other services. Some African American voucher skeptics have couched their distaste for vouchers in an opposition to the notion of a minimal state. For example, Newark NAACP education chair Terence Baine asserted that vouchers signal a renunciation of the responsibility of the state, noting: "It's really like a way of government walking away, giving up. Disgusting" (quoted in Wilgoren, 2000, p. A16).

Other African Americans have opposed vouchers because they believe that vouchers signal a loss of a vital public institution, an institution that is very important for African Americans. For instance, in 1981, James Comer, an African American psychiatrist and school reformer at Yale, wrote that he opposed vouchers in part because of the upward-mobility value he believed that public schools held: "My mother was a domestic worker and my father was a steel-mill laborer and janitor. Had it not been for the existence of a good public-school system, my opportunities, and those of many blacks and whites like me—many now middle-class and willing to 'write off' today's poor— would have been far fewer" (p. E15). Similarly, Vernon Jordan, a lawyer and longtime civil rights leader, who became executive director of the National Urban League in 1972, asserted the importance of schooling to Black children and communities and raised suspicion that vouchers were yet another untested fad: "Black people have a tremendous stake in education—it will literally determine our survival. . . . Black people have to insure that new educational experiments will not become yet another means to rob black kids of the schooling that is their ticket to survival" (1972, p. 8).

On the other end of the spectrum in this debate over the extent to which the state should be involved in education, others, still, may believe that vouchers do not provide *enough* of an opt-out from public policy and public control. For instance, in the late 1960s and early 1970s, despite an active voucher debate, the voucher option did not attract the attention of many Black nationalists and others who were building educational alternatives through independent, community-controlled private schools. I could not find any evidence that founders, leaders, or members of the Council of Independent Black Institutions (CIBI) took public positions on the voucher proposals of this period or throughout the organization's history, even when the debate over charter schools became such a divisive issue within CIBI (see Chapter 8). In many ways, this makes sense, given that vouchers are still a public policy solution, requiring public dollars and government involvement. With publicly funded vouchers, the state's role may be relatively minimal, but it is not nonexistent. Some voucher advocates, even those who identify with Black nationalist goals, have been willing to accept state aid if it brings with it increased choice and control over the individual decision of where to send one's children to school. For others, vouchers do not fit with a program of complete self-determination.

VOUCHERS AND A PROGRESSIVE STATE

Vouchers have been part of various efforts to shrink the federal government's role in education and, more generally, to minimize public control of education. They also have been envisioned to accomplish quite the opposite, as a mechanism for increasing the state's role in redistributing educational resources and in ensuring the delivery of an equitable education for all Americans. The voucher program proposed and partially implemented by White liberal sociologist Christopher Jencks in the late 1960s and early 1970s exemplifies this approach.

By the late 1960s, scholars, educators, and policymakers on the political left began to take on school privatization in new ways, envisioning some form of privatization as a potential solution to persistent educational inequality by race and class (see Forman, 2005). As I have discussed in Chapter 4, during this period, African American educators and other activists began to turn to small, independent schools as means to educational and political community control. So, too, policymakers and others began to consider school privatization as a response to the failures of urban public schools for students of color.

Jencks was instrumental in shifting the school privatization conversation. In a 1966 article titled "Is the Public School Obsolete?", Jencks condemned the organization of city schools, arguing that many urban public schools were dull, oppressive, and uninspired, and were undeserving of additional financial support. The fact of centralized public governance itself, coupled with a shortage of resources, fostered stagnation in public schools. In this early piece, Jencks began to articulate an argument for tuition vouchers for low-income urban students, asserting that failing public schools survived only because they had a monopoly on education for those who could not afford private schools. Given a choice, families would take their business elsewhere, joining or creating schools that would have to be responsive to their needs in order to retain a clientele. Jencks also contended that these private alternatives might be more racially and economically integrated than their public counterparts, since they would not be neighborhood-based.

A few years later, Jencks endorsed "an independent black school system" for New York City. He published an article entitled "Private

Schools for Black Children" in the *New York Times Magazine* in November 1968, in the midst of the labor-community clash in Ocean Hill–Brownsville. Jencks proposed a publicly funded private alternative not because he felt that private schools could do a better job of educating Black children or because he believed that academic achievement within these schools would help African Americans to reach economic, social, and political parity. At the time, Jencks did not have much faith that schools—public or private—could mitigate racial and economic inequality (Jencks, Smith, Acland, Bane, Cohen, Gintis, Heyns, & Michelson, 1972). Rather, Jencks (1968) supported these private initiatives as a *political* solution, as a way to meet the demands of African American political leaders, recognizing that schools represented a significant political site and played an important part in African American social movements of the day.

Jencks, then, in a 1970 piece in the *New Republic*, proposed a heavily regulated national voucher plan aimed at low-income students and designed to equalize schooling by increasing access to private school alternatives and by making it possible for students to opt out of failing public schools (Areen & Jencks, 1972; Jencks, 1970). The Nixon administration gave Jencks the opportunity to implement his voucher plan under a pilot program funded by the Office of Economic Opportunity (OEO). Richard Nixon, as a presidential candidate in both 1960 and 1968, had supported some form of public aid to private schooling (Garinger, 1971; "Nixon Asks," 1968). His OEO backed the Harvard sociologist through Jencks's Center for the Study of Public Policy.

The Jencks plan received a significant amount of national media attention and was incredibly controversial. School districts were offered initial funding to conduct "feasibility studies" for pilot voucher programs and a number of primarily urban districts considered these. However, only a handful of school districts took the step of conducting such studies, including Gary, Indiana; Seattle; San Francisco; Alum Rock, California; San Diego; Rockland, Maine; and New Rochelle, New York (Feron, 1973; Stevens, 1971).[2] These districts had to contend with an image problem. Vouchers, until Jencks's proposal, were identified with either Friedman's privatizing impulses or with virulent post-*Brown* segregationism. As Jeffrey R. Henig (1994) notes: "The sense that vouchers represented a political potato too hot to handle was so widespread that local school officials almost uniformly resisted the OEO's advances, even though the project would presumably have provided both additional federal resources and a reputation for innovation" (p. 66).

In the end, only one district in the country, Alum Rock, agreed to implement a voucher-like program, beginning in the fall of 1972. A Northern California district of 16,000 students and 24 elementary and middle schools near San Jose, Alum Rock had a student population that was approximately 48% Latino and 11% African American in 1972. It received federal support through 1976, drawing funds to establish public "minischools" of choice within existing schools. These schools had more freedom than their district counterparts to devise and fund their own curriculum and programming. Participating students received "vouchers" approximately equal to the per-pupil spending in the district (with low-income students' vouchers worth an additional one third), to choose one of the participating minischools. The program did not include private schools, because there was not sufficient state legislative support for this controversial move. Thus, the Alum Rock program was not much more than a public school choice plan that brought additional resources to participating public schools (Bulman & Kirp, 1999; Feinberg, 1972; Wells, 1990).

Teachers' unions, civil rights organizations, and others concerned with achieving school desegregation and retaining public school constituencies opposed the inclusion of private schools in the Alum Rock experiment. The American Federation of Teachers president Albert Shanker was quoted in June 1975 in the *New York Times*: "He said he did not care much about Alum Rock because it involved only public schools, but was afraid the experience there would be used in a 'national sales campaign' for vouchers. 'We oppose any public funds for non-public schools,' he added" (Reinhold, 1975, p. 18). Locally, NAACP leaders were skeptical of the experimental nature of the untested plan, but they seemed to soften their opposition after the first year of the program (Lublin, 1973).

The Jencks experiment was relatively short-lived. By 1976, the Alum Rock program was over, and vouchers had lost both visibility and interest as a politically and educationally viable education reform (Hechinger, 1975). Although the Jencks reform was not, ultimately, politically feasible, it demonstrated a way in which vouchers were envisioned as a mechanism to redistribute educational resources, via the state, to educationally underserved students and communities.

VOUCHERS AND A DIVIDED STATE

School desegregation was a primary concern in the Jencks-era voucher debates. The timing of Jencks's voucher plan and the Alum

Rock program coincided with a shift in the way that lawyers, courts, civil rights activists and opponents, and school districts thought about school desegregation. As discussed in Chapters 3 and 4, until the early 1970s, desegregation efforts were largely contained to the South, as desegregation was legally defined as the removal of legal barriers to integration, or *de jure* segregation. Jencks introduced his voucher plan just as the North began to combat *de facto* segregation through busing, and desegregation became legally defined as a more affirmative process. It is not surprising, then, that as the country reconceptualized desegregation, voucher politics became a site to grapple with school integration policy and politics. Since *Brown*, voucher politics also have become a site to debate the racially divided state: the extent to which the state has a role to play in either the maintenance or the mitigation of racial segregation.

While the segregative intent of the Southern tuition grant plans after *Brown* was indisputable, the segregative impact of Alum Rock–like vouchers was debatable. Some voucher supporters during this time argued that school vouchers were not a means to evade desegregation but actually offered a more meaningful and effective route to true desegregation. This is an argument that is common in today's voucher debate (for discussion, see Stulberg, 2006).

In the early 1970s, both Jencks (1970) and Friedman (1973; 1975) helped to introduce this pro-voucher rationale. For instance, Friedman argued that, by limiting government's role in school assignment, his plan provided what he considered to be a desirable *voluntary* "gradual transition" from racially "nonmixed" to "mixed" schools (1955, p. 131). In the mid-1970s, at the height of the school busing controversy in the North, Friedman argued against government-sponsored "forced busing" for desegregation purposes, writing that what was needed, instead, was "freedom of choice." He wrote that a voucher plan "might well lead to more busing than now, but it would be voluntary, not forced. It would promote racial tolerance by leading to the choice of schools on the relevant ground of the interests and aptitudes of the students, not the irrelevant ground of the color of their skin" (1975, p. 73).

Voucher skeptics also have invoked desegregation concerns, as they had for tuition grants in the years following *Brown*, fearing that vouchers would exacerbate existing racial and economic segregation in schools. In June 1970, the *New York Times* published an editorial that opposed Jencks's voucher plan. It raised the concern that vouchers could promote racial segregation: "Even though the planners of the demonstration projects are making some provisions to prevent it, the danger remains that the vouchers could become instruments of White segregation or black separatism" ("The Wrong Prescription," 1970, p. 36). The *Christian Science Monitor*, cautiously supportive of Jencks's plan in a July 1970 editorial, also raised the segregation concern: "One fear is that the vouchers could become a bonanza for the segregation academies in the South" ("Worth a Try," 1970, p. 12).

The question of the impact of vouchers on school segregation was reopened in the early 1980s by an academic study that received popular attention. James Coleman, a White sociologist who had directed the momentous school equality study, *Equality of Educational Opportunity* (the Coleman Report), in the mid-1960s, was an avowed desegregationist (e.g., Coleman, 1981). By 1981 and 1982, he and his colleagues concluded that private schools were better suited to meet the "twin goals of quality and equality" (Coleman, 1994, p. 237). They supported school choice and tuition vouchers as a means to realize these goals. They rested this claim on the key finding that students in private schools performed better on most academic subject tests and made larger academic gains than their public school counterparts, even when controlling for a number of family background variables. They also found that the racial and economic test-score gap was narrower in Catholic schools than in public schools. Arguing that the differences lay in the organization of public and private schools, Coleman and his coauthors asserted that the large size and unwieldy organization of public schools rendered them less effective at providing the consistent discipline, rigorous academics, and demanding expectations necessary for student achievement. They also made another controversial finding, concerning racial segregation in schools. They found that private schools were more "internally" racially and economically integrated than public schools (Coleman, Hoffer, & Kilgore, 1982; Coleman, 1994).

As early as 1967, it was reported that Coleman supported some form of school privatization—here, in the form of performance contracts (Maynard, 1967). By 1978, there were media reports of Coleman's direct support for tuition credits and vouchers (Feinberg, 1978). The *Chicago Tribune*, in a September 1978 editorial, called for an alternative to "forced busing" for racial integration that could "achieve the same goals: upgrading educational opportunities for minority children and achieving peaceful and voluntary integration." It cited Coleman as a proponent of choice measures (including vouchers) for these purposes, noting that his willingness to try alternatives to desegregation "is all the more significant" because the Coleman Report of 1966 supported integrated education ("A Better Option," 1978, p. B2).

Since the post-*Brown* tuition grant programs, vouchers have been linked to the politics of racial desegregation—the politics of a divided state. Recently, these conversations about the continued relevance and desirability of school desegregation played out in the response to the Supreme Court's *Zelman* decision, as the ruling on the constitutionality of vouchers in Cleveland was likened to the *Brown* decision in its significance and scope (for discussion, see Stulberg, 2006). As I will illustrate in the next three chapters, these conversations about desegregation and school choice are still quite active. In the 1990s and beyond, school choice policies have been rich sites through which to debate the politics of desegregation at a moment of significant shift in these politics.

VOUCHERS AND THE STATE OF BLACK POLITICS

Race always has been a feature of post-*Brown* voucher politics, if sometimes quite implicitly. But, since the 1990 Milwaukee plan became law, African Americans have become central to voucher conversations *and* vouchers have become an important part of current African American political debates. In particular, voucher politics has become a place to debate the question of who "authentically" represents diverse African American communities and interests. This question raises others that are debated through voucher politics: With whom should African Americans partner to achieve power and equality in America? And how should "civil rights" and equality be defined in the post-civil rights era?

Voucher politics since 1990 provide an important site to define and debate Black politics, at a moment when these politics are particularly contested. Some have indicated that intra-racial disagreement over issues such as vouchers might be a signal of a new stage of African American politics. For instance, when the Urban League of Greater Miami made headlines by supporting a voucher program in its state, although the National Urban League opposes vouchers, the president of the local organization remarked: "Isn't that healthy? . . . We are not bound by color the way we used to be bound, where people said, 'You can't think that way because you're black'" (quoted in Holmes, 1999, p. 17). The latest iteration of school choice has arisen at a time when African Americans are more extensively represented among elected leaders and are incredibly politically diverse and divided. In this context, vouchers provide a ready site to reassess what it means to continue to vie for power in America. The voucher debate is also now a place to define what it means to fight for racial justice at the turn of the millennium, particularly in the absence of a broad social movement.

Political Partnerships

The partisan politics of the most recent voucher push are messy. African American Democrats and members of the civil rights left, who traditionally seek *public* solutions for social problems, fall on both sides of the voucher debate. So, too, do Black and White Republicans and White conservatives, who traditionally seek small government solutions but who may see vouchers as a solution to a school quality problem (largely in urban and low-income areas) that does not directly impact their own children. The civil rights establishment still tends to oppose vouchers. The NAACP consistently has opposed the policy since it challenged Southern tuition grant programs following *Brown*. Among its concerns, the civil rights group worries that vouchers deflect resources and attention from needy public schools (Nakamura, 2004). The Reverend Jesse Jackson opposes vouchers, as does Eleanor Holmes Norton, the District of Columbia's delegate in the House of Representatives (Jackson, 2004; Magnusson, 2003). But the voucher plan for the District of Columbia has the support of some of the city's leading African American Democrats, including recent district mayor Anthony A. Williams and former city councilor Kevin P. Chavous (Raspberry, 2003a; Schemo, 2006a). A number of new African American groups also have formed to support private school choice. Nationally, the group that has received the most attention is the Black Alliance for Educational Options (BAEO), founded by Howard Fuller of Milwaukee in 2000 (Apple & Pedroni, 2005; Henry, 2001; Reid, 2001a).

With a voucher politics that does not organize neatly along party lines, and with the advent of new African American–centered voucher organizations, African American voucher supporters often now find themselves in coalition with those with whom they share little else politically. These odd alliances raise the question of what it means for the cause of African American freedom and equality to form political partnerships that are more expedient than they are based on shared worldview. This is a question that also arose through school choice debates in the 1960s in, for instance, the debate about the Ford Foundation's support of New York's community control movement (Allen, 1990).

The "strange bedfellows" created by the current voucher movement have been the subject of some academic consideration (Apple & Pedroni, 2005; Bulman & Kirp, 1999; Carl, 1996; Pedroni, 2005; Wolfe, 2003). In particular, recent attention has focused on the extent to which White liberal criticism of these alliances smacks of a kind of paternalism or racism, in that it portrays African American voucher advocates as if they do not know their own best interest or cannot legitimately critique longtime allies and exercise agency in seeking new partnerships (e.g., Apple & Pedroni, 2005; Pedroni, 2005). This view is an important one. But these alliances remain a sociological and political puzzle to be scrutinized, in part because they do seem to draw together such disparate interests with respect to race politics. Exemplary cases of this include the partnership between African American Milwaukee activists (including BAEO) and anti-affirmative action, anti-busing conservative legal groups like the Institute for Justice and the Center for Equal Opportunity, and largely White conservative funders like the Bradley Foundation, which (as is widely noted) helped to support the publication of Richard Herrnstein and Charles Murray's *The Bell Curve*.

Voucher supporters on both sides of these odd partnerships explain them as fueled by mutual self-interest. Polly Williams, of Milwaukee, has argued of the partnership between conservative, White, well-off voucher supporters and their Democratic, African American, urban, low-income allies: "They needed us to legitimize them," she said, and "[w]e needed them because they control the media, they control the money, they control everything" (quoted in Belluck, 1998, p. A12). Similarly, conservative White lawyer Clint Bolick of the Institute for Justice said of his alliance with Cleveland's Fannie Lewis: "School choice has not succeeded anywhere except where we're able to put together that kind of alliance." He continued: "In every battle, it's vitally important to work with people who can vividly illustrate a theme. . . . We're very conscious about being out-of-towners" (quoted in Stephens, 2002, p. A1).

BAEO activists, in particular, have been careful to downplay the negative impact of their connections to White conservatives, noting that only *some* of their backing comes from conservative forces (Raspberry, 2001a), that they are not beholden to conservative interests simply because they receive funding from conservatives (Reid, 2001a), and that their fundamental interests are not threatened by these alliances. As Fuller noted: "I recall something else we used to say in the '60s: 'No permanent friends, no permanent enemies, just permanent interests.' You can deal with all sorts of people if you keep your permanent interests, your fundamental purpose, in mind" (quoted in Raspberry, 2001b, p. A15). Holt (2000) of Milwaukee echoed this sentiment, arguing that the Bradley Foundation provided key financial support without infringing on governance in the Milwaukee voucher push. He reasoned that, because these financial backers were relatively hands-off, the support of White conservative organizations did not threaten the organizational or political independence of African American voucher activists.

Despite voucher proponents' view that these alliances serve African American interests, some Black voucher opponents have been highly skeptical of these partnerships. For instance, at the NAACP's annual convention in Milwaukee, in July 2005, chairman Julian Bond spoke of Milwaukee's Black voucher proponents, arguing that they are being duped by the Bradley Foundation and are little more than puppets for White conservatives. "Like ventriloquist dummies," he charged, "they speak in their puppet master's voice, but we can see his lips moving" (quoted in Kertscher, 2005, n.p.).

Post-Civil Rights Era Politics

The latest iteration of educational voucher politics uncovers a debate about African American political partnerships and allies. It also reveals a debate about the goals and tactics of racial justice efforts in the post–civil rights era (Holt, 2000). This is true, as well, of the current charter school movement, as I discuss in more detail in the following chapters. Some see vouchers as a next phase of the civil rights movement and as a break with what they view to be outdated, civil rights-era tactics, which focused on integration of American institutions and on *public* remedy to social inequalities. They acknowledge that Black politics looks different in the new millennium from how it looked in the 1960s: Some of the structural barriers to racial equality have fallen, but racial parity has not yet been achieved. Fuller noted of this shift: "I remember the old days when we were marching and holding up signs calling for Power to the People. Well, a lot of the people who were holding those signs are now a part of the bureaucracy, and they no longer want the people to have power" (quoted in Raspberry, 2001b, p. A15). The pro-voucher Reverend Flake (1998b) similarly noted of this political change: "the NAACP has been wed to its notion of civil rights based on the needs of the past—prior to 1964-65. . . . They have not found the need to reassess their historical positions, deal with the reality of the failures, and come up with new ideas" (p. 19).

At a moment of particular shift in the politics of race, as the next chapter discusses in detail, key political and philosophical questions are again up for grabs. So, too, is central racial symbolism. Voucher proponents now sometimes paint civil rights groups and other African American leaders who oppose vouchers as traditionalists, standing, like George Wallace, at the door of "revolution" against the interests of their constituents (Center for Education Reform, 1999; Moe, 1999). As in the late-1960s community control debate, George Wallace stands in as a particularly racially charged symbol of those who oppose change. Those on both sides of the voucher debate claim that *they* are the true proponents of racial equality and justice, the true agents of racial change.

In recent years, disagreements among African Americans about the meaning of and means to racial equality occur particularly by political party affiliation, generation, and class position. Voucher politics has become a site for revealing, exploiting, and negotiating these divides.

With respect to party, African Americans, especially younger people, are now less inclined to identify themselves as Democrats, and some feel that their support has been taken for granted by the Democratic Party (Clemetson, 2003). Vouchers have become one political issue that Republicans have used to attempt to garner African American support for their party (Wolfe, 2003), at a time of high-stakes party politics and narrower-than-ever electoral victories for the GOP. In 1998, for example, the executive director of the Christian Coalition, Randy Tate, identified vouchers as an issue with which the Republican Party could attract voters of color. He suggested that vouchers provided a way that conservatives could "go forward in reaching out to minorities on the critical issue of educating their children. All conservatives have to do," he wrote, "is to get their feet off the brakes" (p. A29).

Voucher politics now also reveal a generational divide among African Americans. Younger African Americans tend to be significantly more supportive of the voucher concept. A 2001 editorial by Joint Center analyst David A. Bositis noted: "Three-quarters of African-Americans younger than 35 supported vouchers, as did 62% of those between 35 and 50. However, blacks older than 50 oppose vouchers by 48% to 44%" (p. A23).

A few young African American politicians over the last decade symbolize this generational divide, and it is not surprising that they often break with their elders on the subject of vouchers. Cory Booker is exemplary here. The Newark city council member was in his early 30s when he challenged the longtime Newark mayor Sharpe James, who is also African American. Booker's 2002 mayoral bid was unsuccessful, but he became Newark's mayor 4 years later, after James decided not to seek reelection. During these two high-profile mayoral races, Booker gained national attention as an Ivy League–educated Rhodes scholar who had grown up middle-class in the suburbs of New Jersey, a child and beneficiary of the civil rights movement (Benson, 2006; Cave & Benson, 2006b; Tepperman, 2002). As an African American Democrat, Booker made news by supporting school vouchers (Cave & Benson,

2006a). For example, under the headline "Young Blacks Turn to School Vouchers as Civil Rights Issue," the *New York Times* featured Booker as "part of a growing cadre of young blacks who have embraced vouchers, and school choice more broadly, as a central civil rights issue for their generation" (Wilgoren, 2000, p. A1). Booker, a member of BAEO's board (Reid, 2001a), noted of the possibility of vouchers: "It's one of the last remaining major barriers to equality of opportunity in America, the fact that we have inequality of education. . . . I don't necessarily want to depend on the government to educate my children—they haven't done a good job in doing that" (quoted in Wilgoren, 2000, p. A1).

So, too, vouchers reveal a class split among African Americans. According to the Joint Center, in 1997 and 1999, approximately 70% of African Americans with annual incomes of under $15,000 supported vouchers, as compared to 50% of those earning over $35,000 a year in 1997, and as compared with 60% of African Americans in general in 1999 (Brooke, 1997; Wilgoren, 2000). This difference speaks to a broader theme in voucher politics: Vouchers are framed as an opportunity to close the choice gap, a way to provide school choice to lower-income families who cannot afford private school tuition or to make residential choices based on school quality. As columnist Raspberry (2003a) concluded: "As a middle-class parent whose children attended both public and private schools, I can't see anything particularly noble about denying that same choice to children whose parents are poor" (p. A23).

Some have asserted that vouchers have divided African American leaders from their constituents, that most Black leaders and elected officials oppose vouchers while poll data indicate that the majority of Black Americans support them (Henry, 2001; Owens, 2002; Shokraii, 1996). This gap between leaders and constituents largely can be explained by the generational and class divide on the voucher issue (Brooke, 1997). As Bositis suggested in 2001: "Virtually all black leaders oppose school vouchers. Conservatives often suggest that these leaders are out of touch with the black public. That is certainly not true if you limit the black public to those who tend to vote, an older group" (p. A23).

SCHOOL CHOICE AND DEBATES ABOUT THE STATE

Questions about state power often have been inflected with questions about race: the role the state should play in mitigating racial inequality and combating racism, the proper scope of state power when it comes to legislating racial equality or even racial contact, the limitations of the state in successfully balancing competing interests while still protecting basic human rights. Vouchers provide a racially charged challenge to the welfare state. They offer a state-funded way to opt out of one of the most significant public institutions. They do so in the context of the failure of public schools to adequately and equally serve many African American children and communities. Vouchers also provide a solution that is relatively outside of the public system, challenging the civil rights tradition of fighting for solutions through public means, like the law, the ballot box, and the schools.

Few African American leaders over the past 50 years have been free-market ideologues in the mold of Milton Friedman. For the most part, African American voucher participation and advocacy has been strategic. Since *Brown*, most African Americans who have supported vouchers have made tactical calculations that vouchers, at particular historical moments, can serve as a means to providing long-denied quality schooling for African American children and to gaining school resources and choices, local power and control, and political leverage. So, too, although vouchers are only worth enough to provide limited educational choices, they do open up access to parochial schooling, which is a huge beneficiary of the current voucher program. For example, the Supreme Court noted in its *Zelman* decision that in 1999–2000, an astounding 96% of the more than 3,700 students participating in the voucher program used their vouchers to attend religious schools.

As African Americans have entered into and, in some cases, led voucher debates and pushed policies forward, vouchers have become a site to grapple with the power, potential, and limitations of the American welfare state. As we will see in the following chapters, charter schools, as well, have provided such a site in the past 15 years.

CHAPTER 6

The Founding of the West Oakland Community School

Charter schools are a prolific form of federally sanctioned public school choice, yet they are a relatively new reform. Their educational successes and long-term impacts on the landscape of American schooling cannot yet be determined. Charter schooling is, however, a significant political and educational strategy of the past 15 years that has impacted school ecology and economy in cities and towns, state and national school policy, and political debate from mayoral to presidential campaigns.

Charter schools emerged in a changing landscape of race in the 1990s. Nowhere were these shifting politics more evident than in California, where schools and universities have been *the* site for the renegotiation of the gains and strategies of the civil rights movements of the 1960s and 1970s. In just 3 years, the state saw the 1995 annulment of affirmative action at the University of California by its governing body; a similar reversal of affirmative action in the state, with the passage of Proposition 209 in November 1996; and the virtual elimination of bilingual education with Proposition 227 in June 1998. California has proven to be an unfortunate beacon for the nation. In the late 1990s, a number of cities and states followed suit, as they began to revisit and revoke their affirmative action and school desegregation laws.

It is in this moment that the West Oakland Community School (WOCS) was born in Oakland, California. After the passage of Proposition 209, a group of educators, nonprofit workers, and youth activists came together to found a charter school dedicated to serving African American students. The group convened out of common concern for the future of equal educational opportunity in the absence of affirmative action and in the face of sobering recent findings on the educational achievement of African American students in Oakland's schools. The West Oakland Community School marked a strategy of quality schooling and racial justice at a time when the very definitions of educational quality and equality were under substantial review.

Charter schools like WOCS have become a response to unequal educational opportunities for a number of underserved student populations. These schools have been the subject of significant academic study, popular press, and political rhetoric. Charters that particularly serve students of color receive enthusiastic support from politicians—such as Oakland's recent mayor Jerry Brown on the left and President George W. Bush on the right—eager to showcase their educational successes. Much of the academic debate on charter schools and racial equality has centered around the extent to which charters are an extension of or a retreat from the *Brown* decision: the extent to which they provide for or detract from equal educational opportunity and the possibility of integrated schooling (Elmore & Fuller, 1996; Frankenberg & Lee, 2003; Fuller, Elmore, & Orfield, 1996; Grove, 2004; Nathan, 1996a; 1996b; Orfield, 1998; Parker, 2001; Stulberg, 2006; UCLA Charter School Study, 1998; Wells, 2000a; 2000b; 2002).[1] Neither proponents nor critics, however, as they stake their ground in this highly polarized area of study and public debate, adequately treat the relationship between the race politics and school politics of the charter reform (Stulberg, 2004). There is little discussion of the breadth of the educational and political challenges that charter schools like WOCS raise.

The West Oakland Community School provides a site to confront the shifting politics of race and schooling at the turn of the millennium. Like other African American school choice initiatives before it, WOCS is an active terrain for debates about the nature of racial equality and the limits and possibilities of American institutions. In this chapter, I tell the story of the founding of WOCS, focusing on its 3-year planning phase, from 1996 to 1999. I examine WOCS as an African American charter school responding to changing California race politics and persistent educational inequities, and as a product of local and national race politics and an opening in current education reform.

POLITICS OF SCHOOLING AND RACE IN THE 1990s

The Birth of Charter Schools

The late 1990s, like the late 1960s, marked the beginning of a time of significant political flux in both school and race politics. In schooling, challenges to Progressive-era centralized education reached new heights. Public education became increasingly decentralized and privatized, through renewed enthusiasm for school choice and local control. School choice scholar Amy Stuart Wells and her colleagues (1999) write of this moment in school history: "the foundation of public education has perhaps never before been shaken in quite the way it is today by various reform movements designed to undermine the bureaucratic structure and cultural hegemony of public education" (pp. 178–179). At the same time, educators and policymakers increasingly focused on student and school "standards," graduation exams and requirements, and statewide testing. This culminated in the national No Child Left Behind Act of 2001, which mandated state testing and particular kinds of reporting of test data and attached consequences to schools' poor performance.

In the late 1980s, both liberal and conservative politicians turned their attention to school choice, as part of a broad debate on school quality and equal access. Along with political attention, popular focus on school choice has been extensive. A growing public school choice movement accompanied vouchers and other private initiatives. Some of these public alternatives, like the controlled-choice plans of Berkeley and Cambridge, focused specifically on maintaining and advancing racial desegregation in schooling. Others emerged from a call for innovation, equity, and increased local control in the face of stagnant and ineffective city bureaucracies. These new public plans, policy analysts Robert C. Bulman and David L. Kirp (1999) argue, constituted a "quiet revolution in American education" (p. 44).

Charter schools are one such public choice innovation. They, like vouchers, developed as a response to failing district schools. Unlike vouchers, however, charters were envisioned by early supporters as a vehicle for racial desegregation in public schooling. Generally, charter schools are independent public schools, chartered by the state for a fixed amount of time. Although these schools have substantial autonomy from state and local school bureaucracies, they are held accountable for demonstrating academic achievement and the fulfillment of their particular missions (Nathan, 1996a). Some charters are "conversion schools," existing schools that have become charter schools, while most are start-up schools, developed and managed by groups of parents, community leaders, teachers, or educational nonprofits or for-profit companies. Because charter schools have some autonomy in terms of governance and curriculum, these mission-driven schools range from arts to math and science academies, to college preparatory schools, to programs focused on particular racial/ethnic or language groups, to schools that look programmatically very similar to their traditional district counterparts.

Charter schools were introduced in Minnesota in 1991, on the heels of a 1988 proposal by Albert Shanker, the president of the American Federation of Teachers and the symbol of opposition to the public school community control movement in New York City in the late 1960s (Bulman & Kirp, 1999; Shanker, 1988). A Minneapolis policy group published a report in November 1988 that called on Minnesota legislators to authorize "chartered schools" in Minneapolis and St. Paul. The report detailed the ways in which such schools, developed by teachers, districts, and parents, could benefit Minnesota public education (Bulman & Kirp, 1999; Nathan, 1996a). The Citizens League grounded its endorsement of this reform in two concerns: quality schooling for all and meaningful racial integration in schools. As a vehicle for expanded educational opportunity and access to quality schooling, charters offered a "more sophisticated response" to racial segregation in schooling, a very explicit tool of desegregation (Citizens League, 1988, p. 17).

Bulman and Kirp (1999) argue that while this charter reform proliferated quickly, it did so without a "grand theory," such as that provided by Milton Friedman and Christopher Jencks for vouchers (p. 52). Yet, they argue, charter schools benefited from the discursive reframing of school choice as a strategy for educational equity and the reshuffling of traditional educational alliances brought about by voucher politics of the early 1990s. With this new ideological and political space, and with the help of high political visibility and federal sanction, the number of charter schools has grown quite quickly. As noted in Chapter 1, charter laws have now passed in 40 states plus the District of Columbia. As of September 2007, there were an estimated 4,147 charter schools serving more than 1.2 million students (Center for Education Reform, 2007).

California became the second state to pass charter legislation, in 1992. Facing an impending voucher initiative, Proposition 174, state legislators proposed the new reform as an alternative to vouchers. The charter legislation passed in September 1992 and was signed into law by Republican governor Pete Wilson, authorizing 100 new charter schools for the state (Bonsteel, 1997; Hart & Burr, 1996). The voucher initiative was easily defeated in November 1993. But charter schooling has grown significantly in California. In May 1998, Governor Wilson signed an expansion bill that had bipartisan support in the state legislature. This bill substantially raised the number of charter schools allowed in the state (Bulman & Kirp, 1999). As of September 2007, according to the Center for Education Reform (2007), there were approximately 710 charter schools in operation in California, serving an estimated 238,593 students.

Race and Charter Schooling

National school choice advocates have linked choice rhetorically to civil rights and a broad notion of racial equality in schooling (Nathan, 1996a; 1996b; 1998; Salisbury & Lartigue, 2004. For a discussion, see Stulberg, 2006). For example, one vocal voucher and charter school advocate, the Reverend Floyd Flake, often publicly connects school choice, in its significance to African American education, to the school desegregation movement of the 1950s. He also has argued that "[t]he next wave of the civil rights movement will be a demand for choice in schools" (quoted in LaCayo, 1997, p. 74; see also Flake, 1998a; "We Cannot Afford to Wait," 1998).

Among those who agree that public and private schools of choice offer a next step in the civil rights struggle, there is no uniform vision for how individual schools should fulfill this charge. By design, the many kinds of choice schools differ substantially from one another in their mission and character. Even among those with predominantly African American student bodies and with a particular concern for African American equal educational opportunity, few schools of choice have chosen an explicit focus on race. In the past 15 years, some of the strongest examples of African American–centered schools of choice have come from community-sought district initiatives. Milwaukee became the focus of intense debate when the school board created two "African American immersion schools" in the fall of 1990. In response to data on academic achievement and experience, these public schools of choice focused specifically on African American boys. Other cities, such as Detroit, proposed and piloted similar schools, both public and private (Hopkins, 1997; Lawton, 1990). Of the few *charter* schools that focus on race through an African- or African American-centered pedagogy and curriculum, many are schools that began with ties to the African American independent school movement of the 1970s. While these schools have since become charters, they sometimes retain their connections to the Council of Independent Black Institutions (CIBI).

Demographically, charter schools tend broadly to reflect the racial makeup of their districts. In fact, in many states, including California, this demographic reflection is required by law (Parker, 2001). The 2000 national charter school study found that 69% of charter schools mirror—within 20%—their district's racial/ethnic demographics, while approximately 17% serve a higher proportion of students of color than their districts (RPP International, 2000). However, a more recent study of 2000–2001 data by the Civil Rights Project at Harvard found that African American students are overrepresented in charter schools nationwide, whereas White students are underrepresented. The study found that 33% of charter school students nationwide are African American, compared to just 17% of other public school students. This is not surprising, given the study's finding that charter schools are disproportionately located in urban areas. These patterns vary significantly by state. In California, both White and Black students are overrepresented in charter schools: 18% of charter school students in the state are Black, while 42% are White (Frankenberg & Lee, 2003).

The Harvard study also concludes that students are substantially segregated in charter schools. It finds that charter schools in many states tend to be more "intensely segregated" than other public schools, defined as having student bodies that are more than 90% Black or Latino (Frankenberg & Lee, 2003, p. 40). In California, "black charter school students are attending intensely segregated charter schools at rates almost two times higher than black [noncharter] public school students" (p. 42).

Affirmative Action and Desegregation Reconsidered

The range of public and private school alternatives that developed in the 1990s coexisted with massive continuing inequities in schooling. State spending on education in California was among the lowest in the country ("The Schools We Get," 1997). There were also, to quote Jonathan Kozol (1991), "savage inequalities" in spending between districts within California, as there were between urban and suburban schools throughout the country. These inequities came with huge gaps in achievement within and between schools, while race and class disparities in the kind of education students received translated into achievement gaps nationwide (Jencks & Phillips, 1998).

Educational inequalities persisted in the context of a significant shift in race and education politics, particularly with respect to two strategies and legacies of the civil rights movement: affirmative action and school desegregation. During the 1990s, affirmative action was, in the words of desegregation scholar and advocate Gary Orfield (1999), "hanging on by a thread" (p. B7). The country saw almost a decade of reconsideration of the policy in higher education, jumpstarted by the elimination of affirmative action in the University of California school system and in the state (Chávez, 1998). Eight years later, in the summer of 2003, the Supreme Court handed down two major decisions on affirmative action in higher education. The rulings involved two challenges to the University of Michigan's affirmative action admissions plans. They upheld, but narrowly delimited, the use of race in college and graduate school admissions (Greenhouse, 2003). Three years later, however, in November 2006, voters in Michigan passed a Proposition 209–like ballot measure, which virtually eliminated affirmative action in education and employment in the state. The passage of the Michigan initiative prompted its backer, California anti-affirmative action activist Ward Connerly, to happily predict: "I think the end is at hand for affirmative action as we know it" (quoted in Paddock, 2006, p. B1).

Legal challenges to school desegregation policies also reflected a larger shift in the politics of race in the 1990s. Even as schools remained substantially race- and class-segregated (Frankenberg & Lee, 2002; Orfield & Yun, 1999), courts ended desegregation orders that had been in place for decades. Cities that have revised their desegregation plans in recent years include some of the country's most prominent symbols of school desegregation, such as Little Rock, Arkansas, and the site of the country's first Supreme Court-approved busing plan, Charlotte-Mecklenburg, North Carolina (Hendrie, 1998b; 1998d).

Similarly, during the 1990s, the politics of desegregation and affirmative action met in magnet schools, which use race as one of many admission factors in order to achieve racially diverse student bodies. As cities were being released from prior court desegregation orders, magnets faced new legal challenges. These challenges often came from White—and sometimes Asian American—parents, who claimed that their children were denied equal access to competitive magnet schools by virtue of their race/ethnicity (Hendrie, 1998c; Walsh, 1998b). In San Francisco, for example, a suit brought by a group of Asian American parents against one of the city's top magnet schools led to a settlement in which the district proposed to end a 15-year-old desegregation consent decree and eliminate race as a category by which to assign students to its schools (Associated Press, 1999a; Guthrie 1999).

Just as in the late 1960s the symbol of George Wallace was up for grabs in the fight for community control, so was "civil rights" in the 1990s. As was exemplified in the fight over Proposition 209 (also named the California Civil Rights Initiative), those who advocated both "race consciousness" and "color-blindness" claimed to hold their position in the name of civil rights. So, too, "racism" in the 1990s was sometimes just as likely to connote anti-White attitudes and behavior to many (particularly White) people as it was to imply prejudice and discrimination against people of color. For example, during the Proposition 209 fight, the *San Francisco Chronicle* published poll results indicating that 24% of White male respondents, as compared with just 27% of men of color, reported that they had "personally experienced racial bias" (Wilson, 1995, p. A8). The unequivocal phrases of a generation ago became open to redefinition, indicating the state of political flux with which we entered the new millennium. It is within this context of the changing politics of race and schooling that the West Oakland Community School emerged.

POLITICS OF SCHOOLING AND RACE IN OAKLAND

In December 1996, as the WOCS group was just beginning to envision its school, Oakland Unified's Task Force on the Education of African American Students drew national attention with its ostensibly radical solution to unequal schooling in Oakland. Offering data that suggested that Oakland's district schools failed to serve its African American students adequately, the Task Force proposed, through the now infamous "Ebonics" resolution, that schools give new attention to African American language and culture as a means of improving academic achievement (for documents and discussion, see the edited volume by Perry & Delpit, 1998).

The Task Force did not, as many enthusiastic skeptics claimed, endorse the teaching of "Black English" in Oakland's public schools. Rather, it recommended the recognition of "Ebonics" as a distinct language that deserved preservation through Oakland's schools (Applebome, 1996; Diringer & Olszewski, 1996; McWhorter, 1997; Page, 1996; Perry & Delpit, 1998). It called, in part, for the implementation of programs that would help teachers understand and appreciate the "primary language" of African American students and facilitate the teaching and learning of "English" to Black students ("The Oakland Ebonics Resolution," 1998).

Not only was Oakland the first district to pass such a resolution (Sanchez, 1996), but its timing lent itself to the media frenzy that followed its unanimous passage. Introduced just a month after the passage of the anti-affirmative action Proposition 209, it provided yet another example from California of the controversy surrounding an explicit attention to race in educational policy. It was an example, over the sleepy holiday season, for the entire nation to see. For both advocates and opponents, it provided fuel for an already active fire.

While the findings that accompanied the "Ebonics" proposal were eclipsed, the Task Force provided new evidence of the ways in which the district's schools underserved African American students. The Task Force found, for example, that while 53% of Oakland Unified's students were African American, 71% of students assigned to special education classrooms were African American. Additionally, 80% of students who received suspensions in Oakland's schools were Black, and the average grade point average (GPA) for Black students was 1.80 —the lowest among the racial/ethnic groups recorded in the district (Task Force, 1996).

Charter schools were born in Oakland in large part as a response to the district's failure to adequately serve many of its students. Charter schools in the city also emerged in the context of the local politics and rather unusual history of race and schooling. As Kirp (1982b) argues in his analysis of the politics of race and schooling in the Bay Area, Oakland never attempted or achieved significant school desegregation, and grassroots enthusiasm for it was limited. The short movement for desegregated schooling was led by the NAACP in the early 1960s, in response to an assignment plan for a new school that exacerbated high school segregation in the city. This movement had faded by the mid-1960s. Also, despite considerable racial segregation in the schools, the district was never compelled by court order to integrate its schools.

By the time that desegregation came in earnest to the North in the late 1960s, Oakland's White population was in significant decline (Kirp, 1982b). In these years, the city also gained a number of prominent African American leaders and activists. Many of these leaders acquired local power through the War on Poverty programs, which had begun in the 1960s and were backed by both federal funds and private foundation support, like that of the Ford Foundation (Kirp, 1982b). Marcus A. Foster, Oakland's first African American school superintendent, took office in 1970. By the early 1970s, other Northern cities, by political pressure or court mandate, had implemented some form of school desegregation as a route to equal educational opportunity for students of color. But Foster and others in Oakland brought, instead, a new focus on school decentralization, resource redistribution, and African American participation and leadership to the district ("25 Years Later," 1998; Kirp, 1982b).

School desegregation has never been the policy against which most of Oakland's leaders have measured educational or political progress. Rather, Oakland often has turned to alternative strategies for quality and racial equality in the city's schools, such as the "Ebonics" resolution or the 1992 establishment of a semi-autonomous Afrocentric Academy at the failing McClymonds High School in West Oakland (Ginwright, 2004). Charter schools like WOCS have emerged as a legacy and active site of these race and school politics.

THE WEST OAKLAND CONTEXT

The WOCS founding group chose West Oakland as a home for its charter school, both for the community's historic ties to African Americans and for the ways in which its African American residents were underserved economically and educationally. Its location on the San Francisco Bay made West Oakland, historically, a major site for transportation and industry. In 1869, the neighborhood became the western end of the U.S. transcontinental railroad, and many African Americans who served as Pullman car porters settled there. Industrial growth during World War II also brought a large Southern migration of African Americans into West Oakland. During this economic boom, West Oakland became a vibrant cultural center as well. However, when World War II ended, shrinking defense-related industries brought significant economic decline. This was exacerbated, in the 1950s and 1960s, when two major highways were built in such a way that they cut off West Oakland from the rest of the city. Still, the area retained an active social, political, and religious life. The Ford Foundation targeted West Oakland for its community participation programs of the early 1960s, nurturing local leadership (Kirp, 1982b). West Oakland was also one of the cradles of the Black Power movement, as the site of the founding of the Black Panther Party and the Panther's Oakland Community School (for this history, see Ginwright, 2004; Noguera, 1996; Oakland Citizens Committee for Urban Renewal, 1998).

West Oakland's rich history underlies a present marked by excessive poverty, racial segregation, and poor school performance. West Oakland reported the lowest median household income in Oakland in 1990 (Noguera, 1996; Urban Strategies Council, 1996). According to the 1990 census, the data available when the WOCS founders convened, West Oakland had a disproportionate number of African American residents and young people in school. These data revealed that 77% of West Oakland residents were African American, as compared to 43.9% of Oakland residents as a whole (Urban Strategies Council, 1995). In the 1996–1997 school year, when the WOCS founding group began to meet, 51.9% of students enrolled in Oakland Unified's schools were African American. Yet African American students made up 76% of students at Lowell Middle School, one of the two district middle schools in the neighborhood, and 80% of students at McClymonds, the only public high school in the neighborhood (Oakland Coalition of Congregations, 1997).[2]

The schools in the neighborhood woefully underserved their students. According to district data for the 1996–97 school year, at Lowell Middle School, just 28% of eighth-grade students performed near or above proficiency in reading on the district's standardized test. In math, this number was 20%. The average eighth-grade GPA was 1.10 in English and 1.46 in math classes (Oakland Coalition of Congregations, 1997). At the high school level, the data were even more disheartening. At McClymonds, one article reported that, of an entering class of about 300 freshmen, only 50 were likely to graduate (Ruenzel, 1998). In 1996–97, just 11% and 5% of McClymonds 10th graders were near or above proficiency in reading and math tests, respectively. Only 60 students took the SAT in the spring of 1997, scoring an average composite score of 730 (as compared to a state average of 1010). Also, of the just 29 Advanced Placement tests taken at the school in 1997, no student received a score of 3 or above (Oakland Coalition of Congregations, 1997).

THE WOCS FOUNDING GROUP

The West Oakland Community School was the brainchild of Marjorie D. Wilkes, an African American woman who was in her mid-30s when she brought the WOCS founding group together. Wilkes began her career in New York City at the teachers' union and moved to the Bay Area to work with an education-focused nonprofit in West Oakland. Her involvement in a project to increase parental input in Oakland middle schools, for which she and parents received a chilly reception from many school administrators, convinced Wilkes that West Oakland needed an alternative school. As she began to dream of starting this school, she envisioned an institution with enough freedom to try its hand at educating the students who are typically underserved by Oakland's public schools. In this regard, she held a particular interest in African American students.

In the spring of 1996, Wilkes put together a group of 14 friends and colleagues, all of whom worked in the Bay Area. She chose a group that she felt shared a concern for African American students and for social justice. The group was predominantly African American, and included one Asian American member and, initially, two White members—including me. (The other White member dropped out of the group after its first two meetings.) The group was also relatively young, with the oldest members in their 40s and early 50s and most in their

20s and 30s. The group also had substantial academic credentials. A significant number of its members held degrees from Ivy League and other prestigious public and private universities, such as UC-Berkeley. The members of the "working group," as it was known, included a few full-time public and independent school teachers, a number of professionals who either ran or worked with nonprofits focused on education and community development, and a few graduate and undergraduate students who were affiliated with local youth-focused nonprofits.

Akiyu Hatano, for instance, later became the charter school's director. In May 1996, when Wilkes convened the WOCS group, Hatano was a public middle school teacher in San Francisco. She had known Wilkes for years. They became friends in New York City through educational foundation work. Hatano, like Wilkes, was Ivy League–educated—she at Harvard and Wilkes at Princeton. Hatano was in her late 20s when the charter school working group convened, and she was initially the only Asian American member.

Wilkes also asked other teachers to join the founding group, including two or three young African American men and women who were involved in African American independent schools in Oakland. Wilkes included in the working group, as well, an African American woman in her 50s who had spent much of her career at an alternative public school in Oakland. She was also a former member of the Black Panthers who had been active in the West Oakland Panther school in the 1960s.

From her work in nonprofits, Wilkes included in the WOCS group Greg Hodge, a longtime West Oakland resident, a graduate of Northwestern University in Chicago, and an African American man then in his mid-30s. Hodge was active in leading a number of community- and citywide organizations and he was the executive director of the Urban Strategies Council, the nonprofit for which Wilkes worked. Eventually, Hodge would go on to serve as Oakland Unified's school board president and to run for mayor of Oakland in 2006. Wilkes also included her then-husband, Anthony Reese, an African American man who was an associate director for an economic and community development nonprofit in San Francisco and had a degree from Harvard's Kennedy School. I also was part of this initial group and had been brought in after I had become friends with Wilkes through my work at one of West Oakland's middle schools and, then, at the program Wilkes ran through the Urban Strategies Council.

Under Wilkes's leadership, this founding group came together out of frustration and anger over the educational realities and the political potentials of the day in California. The group saw a city and a state that were perpetually unresponsive to the needs of students of color and increasingly willing to take away old civil rights-era remedies. It saw, as well, the way in which profound racial and economic segregation informed the schooling experience of West Oakland students. In a very explicit response to educational inequality and the sense that African American educational opportunity was constricting rather than expanding in Oakland and in the state, the group wanted to design a school that could provide an academically rigorous and politically and culturally engaged education for African American students.

"RACE VERSUS PLACE"

For the West Oakland Community School, the question of how to build a charter school in the service of African American equality arose first in the question of whether and how to focus explicitly on race in building the mission of the school. Members of the founding group believed that they were building the school to address a need for quality schooling in West Oakland. WOCS founders, like those involved in the other choice efforts in this book, felt very deeply that this education was a matter of survival for African Americans in what they perceived to be an increasingly hostile California. In the very first meeting, Reese said, "No one except Native American people is in as bad a shape as we are. We are a race fighting for survival. Will Black people survive all the attacks, pathologies, unemployment, etc., that are threatening our survival?" For many, the affirmative answer to this question meant an explicit focus on serving African American students and their families.

In its first 6 months of planning, the founding group worked to negotiate a race-specific remedy to educational inequality at a time when the rhetoric of color-blindness was taking new hold in public policy and debate. The question of the relevance and viability of an explicitly racialized solution to public school inequities was central to the founders' mission-building process. At the second meeting of the group, Reese said that "it is appropriate to apply race-specific remedies within the context of a racist society." The group questioned, however, whether this concern for "race" also corresponded with a concern for the community of West Oakland.

This question became known in the group, from its very first meeting, as the issue of "race versus place." The distinction was predicated on the assumption that, despite continued racial and economic segregation, "race" did not necessarily equal "place" in the context of a changing West Oakland. The founders acknowledged that in 1996, West Oakland was predominantly Black, and so it would be easy to tie race to place in a vision of the school. But the group also discussed the fact that West Oakland was gentrifying, and it was very possible that its demographics by race and class could shift significantly in just a few years. If the group, therefore, professed a concern for "place," it might, with time, serve fewer and fewer African American students. The group also worried that an articulation of a race-specific mission might be a political liability and might hurt its chances of being granted a charter from the district or the state, particularly in the shadow of Proposition 209. A focus on geographical space seemed less risky.

The working group went back and forth for almost 6 months about whether it should include race as an explicit piece of its mission. Finally, the group scheduled the discussion to decide this question for November 6, 1996, one day after the California elections. On November 5, Proposition 209 passed, and, the next day, the WOCS group voted unanimously to privilege "race" over "place" in the articulation of its vision. On this day, Wilkes asked each member of the working group to weigh in individually. Every person in the group expressed concern about current California race politics and acknowledged that they intended WOCS to be a response to these politics. This response, the group argued, required a specific focus on African American students. As the meeting summary read:

> Our discussion was framed and impacted by the passage of Proposition 209 yesterday, signaling a trend of reversals of civil rights gains. The election cast a shadow on our discussion and, we agreed, makes our work seem all the more urgent.

Although the nine founders who voted to privilege "race" over "place" agreed unanimously to do so, there was some self-selection in this group already. The decision to articulate this mission in the school's public documentation was not made formally until the end of 1996. But from the group's first meetings, driven by Wilkes and her selection of a founding team, there was a presumption that the school would exist primarily to serve African American students and their families.

In addition, two key participants in the school's planning process joined the group after the November 1996 decision to focus on "race" over "place." Derek Peake, a young African American and Filipino man, was a friend of Wilkes's at Princeton. He and his partner, Ted Uno, a young White and Asian American man who graduated from UC–Berkeley and subsequently taught at a public high school in the South Bay, had founded Quilombo, a West Oakland neighborhood-based nonprofit that focused on youth leadership and community development. They joined the WOCS group in early 1997, and both believed that if they had been part of the initial "race versus place" discussion, they would have pushed for a focus on place, or on race *and* place, and both were troubled by what they viewed as the founding group's decision to set race *against* place in its mission.

In November 1996, however, the existing founding group was united in its desire to explicitly focus on race as a strategy of equal schooling. This decision was bolstered by the support of a number of local African American educators and leaders, including the West Oakland City Council representative and local pastors and community activists (West Oakland Community School, 1998b). Perhaps most significantly, WOCS also received the enthusiastic support of key members of Oakland's school administration. By the beginning of 1997, WOCS founders were engaged in discussions with district personnel and board members as to how to put together a successful charter proposal. Oakland's school board had a record of receptivity to charter schools (Schorr, 1999i). Furthermore, in the context of the failed "Ebonics" resolution, the WOCS charter school took on new meaning, particularly for the district's African American leadership.

Weeks after the "Ebonics" resolution, WOCS members met with an African American district administrator who was also a member of the Task Force on the Education of African American Students. She suggested that the board was not fazed by the media attention surrounding its actions and would probably be receptive to another effort to increase academic achievement specifically for African American youth. In fact, some of the board's African American senior members stepped up enthusiastically to support WOCS. Some felt that they had lost on the "Ebonics" resolution and saw the WOCS charter petition as a worthy next endeavor in the education of Oakland's African American children. Leading this charge were the board's West Oakland representative, Lucella Harrison, and her colleague Toni Cook, who was also a forceful leader of the Task Force ("Opening Pandora's Box," 1998).

This board support for an explicitly African American school was particularly mobilized during the March 10, 1998, hearing of the Curriculum and Technology Committee, a three-member board committee that had to recommend that the WOCS charter petition be considered for approval by the entire board. This committee, comprised at the time of Harrison, Cook, and Jean Quan, met a week before the entire board was scheduled to vote on the charter petition. During this meeting, the only non–African American committee member, Quan, raised a series of technical questions and concerns about the petition, particularly about the school's budget. Cook objected that Quan's level of scrutiny represented a departure, a standard to which she believed no previous charter applications had been subjected. Quan asked for some additions to the proposal and the committee scheduled a special hearing, a day before the full board vote. At this special hearing, with little comment from Quan, the committee quickly passed the WOCS proposal. The following day, on March 18, Harrison presented the charter petition to the entire school board. She spoke in first-person plural, urging, "I truly hope you'll support us in this effort." Following her, Cook spoke enthusiastically on the school's behalf. Directly linking the "Ebonics" resolution to the West Oakland charter school effort, she said: "I'm particularly touched that someone heard our clarion call of almost a year ago." With these comments, and a few others from supportive board members, the board unanimously approved the WOCS charter petition.

RACE AND QUALITY SCHOOLING, BROADLY DEFINED

The "Ebonics" resolution and the controversy surrounding it, coupled with the rolling back of affirmative action in the state, made highly salient the question of explicitly race-based solutions to unequal schooling. Through building the West Oakland Community School, African American educators and their partners grappled with a definition of *racial equality*, ultimately choosing to focus explicitly on race as a strategy to combat racial inequality in schooling. In this way, the group shared an approach with those who proposed and supported the "Ebonics" resolution and affirmative action, rather than those who urged a more "race-neutral" approach to mitigating racial inequality and closing the academic achievement gap. WOCS founders asserted a solution that supporters of Proposition 209 found outdated: an affirmative attention to race and African American students, and an explicit focus on combating racism and racial inequality in schooling.

Like many of their predecessors in other choice initiatives featured in this book, WOCS founders built their school on a broad understanding of educational excellence that linked school success to community development and racial identity-building. Also like their predecessors, WOCS leaders felt that a response to the achievement gap between White and African American students required building an explicit connection between racial identity and academic success. In this response, WOCS presented a rethinking of the meaning and purpose of public schooling: a reassertion of race in an understanding of quality schooling and a reenvisioning of the role of public schools in building and sustaining African American communities.

Schooling for Community Building

WOCS founders held a broad view of the purpose of schooling that understood schools to be integral parts of communities and community-building. In this vision, they explicitly linked charter schooling to similar movements before it, noting that charter schools were, according to Wilkes, the "latest chapter in community control over schools." The vehicle through which the WOCS group hoped to achieve this connection between school and its surrounding community was first known as the Village Center and was later renamed the Youth & Family Center. Modeled on recent school-based community center models in New York and San Francisco, called Beacon Centers, the WOCS Village Center was designed to provide a range of educational, social, and health-related services for WOCS students and their families. In their charter application, founders described WOCS as "a multi-service community center with an innovative school at its heart." They envisioned that the school would, in effect, be a center of community life:

> We will operate year-round, Monday through Saturday, from early morning until late evening. Our lights will flicker on at seven thirty in the morning, when parents can bring their children for breakfast, tutoring and other morning activities. The last lights will go off as students, parents and other community members head home after an evening of tutoring and homework help, basketball, African dance, GED, ESL or adult literacy classes. (West Oakland Community School, 1998a, p. 2)

WOCS members viewed this kind of school as a potential vehicle for economic, social, and political "community revitalization" and growth in West Oakland (West Oakland Community School, 1997, p. 3; 1998a, pp. 1–2).

The charter school's leaders believed that WOCS had an active role to play in the well-being of West Oakland. As part of linking the school to its geographic community, WOCS founders envisioned forming partnerships that would bring new actors into public schooling, many of whom either purposefully stood outside of public school constraints or were left out of traditional public school collaborations. These partners included a local church, where the school was housed, and youth-focused nonprofits in Oakland.

These collaborations, in part, grew from the founding group's need to develop organic connections in the West Oakland community. Although the founders worked *for* the West Oakland community and were of the same racial background as the majority of West Oakland residents, they were not initially predominantly *from* or *of* the community, in that many did not live in the neighborhood. Founders worried about appearing to be "carpetbaggers," and building partnerships with community groups helped allay this concern. While they shared middle-class status with many of the founders of the New York community control movement of the 1960s and the Independent Black Institutions of the 1970s, they were generally even less initially tied to the geographic community they served than many of their predecessors.

In this context, "community-building" meant designing a school that had as its mission absolute accessibility and responsiveness to the community it served, through which West Oakland residents could convene to define and meet their own needs. Community-building also meant bringing in new West Oakland residents and activists, specifically African American middle-class educators who became increasingly tied to the neighborhood through their involvement with WOCS. A number of WOCS founders and subsequent staff members made it their goal to personally move into and become active in West Oakland. Some WOCS founders envisioned that the school could draw them and others like them to "serve as positive, accessible role models for the community's youth, providing day-to-day examples of neighbors who are well-educated, well-employed and committed to uplifting the community" (West Oakland Community School, 1999a, p. 3).

In linking the school's essential function to community building, WOCS founders also believed that student academic success would be served best by drawing an explicit connection between academic achievement, racial identity, and community development. They felt that schools should not, as they often do, stand apart from their communities. Rather, they should be an active part of growth and revitalization in African American neighborhoods. They believed that students would do best if their communities thrived and if their schools paid attention to the "broader social and economic challenges that shape their lives" (West Oakland Community School, 1998c, p. 3). So, too, WOCS leaders believed that students' success in communities like West Oakland should not have to be defined by leaving the community, but by living and thriving within it, understanding it, and working to change it. To implement this vision, WOCS staff members worked to link the school to West Oakland by bringing the community's adults into the school as teachers, mentors, and board members, and by making West Oakland's history and present a part of the school's curriculum (West Oakland Community School 1998a; 1999b).

Academic Achievement and "Knowledge of Self"

WOCS founders also agreed that a focus on academic rigor and achievement had to be a significant part of serving African American children. Some, like Wilkes, expressed that it was important that WOCS students be able to stand up to any standard measure of academic success, including scoring high on the SAT and speaking so-called "standard English" in job or college interviews. Academic success, traditionally defined, was important to the group as both an educational and political goal. WOCS leaders believed that such success would provide a strong response to the data on how Oakland's African American students fared in district schools and in admission to the area's top colleges, in the context of debates over "Ebonics" and affirmative action policies.

WOCS leaders built their curricular standards so that they aligned with the new Oakland and California academic standards, aware that WOCS students would, by law, take the standardized tests that assessed this body of knowledge. Hatano, who became the instructional leader of the school, drew up subject-based academic standards or goals, reflecting a move in many charter schools toward the concretization of school mission through student and teacher performance standards. To the district and state standards, and the standards culled from subject-specific academic professional associations, Hatano and others added a specific focus on West Oakland and on the history and experience of African American communities (West Oakland Community School, 1998c).

The WOCS founding group also believed that "knowledge of self" was an important aspect of the school's educational mission, and this "self" was explicitly racialized. Like their earlier counterparts in the public school community control and independent school movements, WOCS founders understood academic excellence to include necessarily a focus on building a healthy self-concept, including a strong sense that African American identity encompassed physical beauty, purposeful and collective action, and academic success. The school's charter renewal application read: "Students will exhibit a healthy, vibrant spirit, and develop a strong and positive self-concept. Students will know their family, community, and cultural histories, and will understand that they are heirs to a glorious legacy of African American achievement" (West Oakland Community School, 2003a, p. 8).

WOCS members combined this attention to racial identity with a focus on students' emotional and physical health. As the charter application noted:

> Our vision for our students is three-fold. First, they will be *healthy and whole*. They will maximize their physical, mental, spiritual and emotional potential. They will have a strong respect for themselves and others. They will value a life dedicated to the pursuit of racial and economic justice. (West Oakland Community School, 1998a, p. 2. Emphasis in original)

In this focus on nurturing the "whole child" (West Oakland Community School, 2003a, p. 4), WOCS founders blended cultural nationalism with a progressivist language and understanding of education common to many free schools of the 1960s and 1970s (Wells, 1993).

Schooling for Social Justice

Finally, in defining *quality schooling*, WOCS builders reasserted a role for public schooling in struggles for racial and economic justice. As Preston R. Wilcox (1969), in 1960s New York, imagined community members serving meals and working construction in the schools of Brooklyn and Harlem, WOCS founders envisioned that the school itself could be an agent of change in the community, as a social center and eventually an economic asset, bringing jobs, people, and resources. WOCS founders also envisioned that the school could reach beyond the West Oakland community through the legacy of its students. Founders hoped that WOCS could serve as an agent of broad social change by training its students to see the need for change and to have the desire and capacity to realize it.

In their vision of schooling as a site for social change and leadership development, WOCS founders explicitly viewed themselves in the tradition of community control and other school-based movements for African American freedom and social justice. They drew on West Oakland's rich history of African American activism, linking their efforts to those of the Black Panthers and their Oakland Community School. WOCS leaders also found inspiration in other activists of the past, including those in the civil rights movement who built Freedom

Schools and who, like Ella Baker, nurtured youth leadership. Through these historical referents, WOCS leaders fashioned a politicized understanding of African American schooling at a historical moment of particular urgency for the group. As a WOCS funding proposal read:

> While these [academic] problems are urgent and complex in and of themselves, they become increasingly so in the current political environment—with the rollback of affirmative action, the massive changes in public welfare, and the growth of prison construction. Two facts are clear and irrefutable: (1) the consequences of educational failure are increasingly costly to both the individual and to society; and (2) disproportionate numbers of African American children continue to experience educational failure. (West Oakland Community School, 1999a, p. 2)

WOCS founders linked past movements for social justice and movements that viewed schools as sites of community-building with the current reform strategy of charter schooling. In so doing, they grounded their work in an expansive definition of quality schooling and a broad vision of the role of public schools. The ways in which WOCS leaders were able to institutionalize this expansive vision, and the barriers to doing so, are the subject of the next chapter.

CHAPTER 7

Politics, Successes, and Challenges of the West Oakland Community School

The West Oakland Community School's first class of sixth graders gathered for its first "morning ritual" on September 7, 1999. Students stood in new school uniforms, anxious and giddy, as they met their new classmates. Their director, Akiyu Hatano, led the students in reciting the words with which they would begin every school day, "A Pledge to Myself," written by Mychal Wynn in his book, *Empowering African-American Males to Succeed: A Ten-Step Approach for Parents and Teachers*:

> Today I pledge to be the best possible me. No matter how good I am, I know that I can become better. Today I pledge to build on the work of yesterday, which will lead me into the rewards of tomorrow. Today I pledge to feed my mind: knowledge, my body: strength, and my spirit: faith. Today I pledge to reach new goals, new challenges and new horizons. Today I pledge to listen to the beat of my drummer, who leads me onward in search of my dreams. Today I pledge to believe in me. (as recorded in West Oakland Community School, 1999c)

Fifty young African American voices, some strong, some still tentative, began their school year affirming themselves in the recreational hall of the Lutheran church that housed their new school.

From 1999 to 2006, WOCS enrolled and successfully graduated two cohorts of middle school students. Yet, seven school years after this first earnest group of sixth graders uttered the WOCS pledge, the school closed its doors. In its short life, this small charter school experienced both significant successes and substantial hurdles. In this chapter, I examine the ways in which these successes and challenges were situated in the local and national education and urban politics of their day, as well as the local and national politics of race and class. I argue that even though charter schools are given some autonomy and programmatic leeway, they certainly are not immune to the effects of their political contexts, and we cannot fully understand or judge them without understanding the politics in which they are situated.

CITY AND SCHOOL POLITICS IN OAKLAND

During the life of the charter school, there were substantial changes in Oakland city and school district politics. Most significantly, the politics of race and schooling was dominated by declining school enrollments and an ensuing fiscal crisis, resulting in a state takeover of Oakland Unified. So, too, the district experienced simultaneous centralization of power and decentralization of schooling.

On the decentralization side, perhaps prompted by the growth of charter schools, and explicitly in response to the race- and class-based achievement gap, the district developed an entity called the New Small Autonomous School in May 2000. These schools were designed as a kind of in-district charter school alternative, and they were supported by a partnership between a community organizing group, Oakland Community Organizations (OCO), and a progressive school reform group, the Bay Area Coalition for Equitable Schools (BayCES). The initiative allowed for the creation of small schools of choice that would have the autonomy to develop their own missions, curricula and programming, and to hire their own credentialed, unionized teachers (Oakland Unified School District, 2000).

So, too, Oakland Unified has supported decentralized schooling through charter schools. When the West Oakland Community School's founding group convened in May 1996, Oakland had only one functioning charter school. Since the Oakland school board voted to approve WOCS's charter in March 1998, charter schooling has grown substantially in the district. The June 1998 election of Mayor Edmund G. "Jerry" Brown was significant here (Schorr, 1999c). The former California governor and three-time presidential candidate replaced Elihu Harris, who chose not to run for a third term. Brown was elected by a huge margin, with 59% of the vote against 10 opponents. One reporter called his win "one of the most lopsided victories in the city's political history" (DelVecchio, 1998b, p. A1). The racial politics of the election were not unsubstantial. Brown's win, the first for a White candidate in 20 years, along with the recent replacement of the African American school superintendent, signified to many a loss of Black leadership in the city (DelVecchio, 1998a; Dillard, 1998; Lerman, 1999; Payton, 1998). Mayor Brown was reelected in March 2002, also by a very large margin. As the *San Francisco Chronicle* reported on the day after his reelection: "Oakland Mayor Jerry Brown was re-elected last night in a landslide that surpassed his lopsided victory four years ago" (DeFao, 2002, p. A17).

As a candidate in 1998, Brown gave attention to the public schools primarily through his enthusiasm for charter schooling. Charter schools seemed to be, in fact, his only education platform. As the *Chronicle* reported: "Oakland Mayor Jerry Brown's education policy can be summed up in two words: charter schools" (Olszewski, 1999a). Brown seemed drawn to charter schools for their localism and for the opportunity they seemed to present for small community groups to gain control of failing schools from centralized and unresponsive governing bureaucracies (Bailey, 1998; Brown, 1998; Olszewski, 1999a; Stinnett, 1999).

Since Brown was elected mayor, there has been a substantial surge of charter school activity in Oakland. By the end of the 2005–06 school year, 26 charter schools were active and operating in the city (California Department of Education, n.d.). Charter schools are relatively abundant in Oakland (Rauh, 2006; Sturrock, 2005). As of September 2006, approximately 7,000 students, or 14% of the city's school-age children, were enrolled in charter schools in Oakland (Rauh, 2006; Oakland Unified School District, 2005). Mayor Brown, himself, backed two charter schools in the city: an arts-themed school and a highly controversial military school (Brown, 2001).

With this decentralizing move toward small, alternative schools has come the opposite tendency toward centralization in the district. Once Mayor Brown was elected, he also backed city receivership of the school district that would give him power to appoint a trustee of the system, in the model of Chicago's Mayor Richard Daley (Schorr, 1999f; 1999k). He did so amid an early 1999 investigation of financial misconduct by the school superintendent, Carole Quan (Locke, 1999; Schorr, 1999g; 1999h; 1999l), and a very public spate of in-school violence and racial tension at one of the district's high schools in the fall of 1998 (Reynolds, 1998). In December 1999, to much criticism, the city council followed Brown's urging and put an initiative on the March 2000 ballot that created three new school board seats that Brown had the power to fill (Johnston, 1999). This initiative passed by a small margin, creating a 10-person "hybrid" board of elected and appointed members, and Brown gained increased mayoral control of Oakland's public schools (DeFao, 2001; Gewertz, 2000).

In the years that followed, Oakland Unified began to demonstrate slow gains in student achievement under popular superintendent Dennis Chaconas (May, 2003; Murphy, 2003). But, at the end of 2002, district administrators announced that Oakland Unified was in significant debt (a debt later calculated to be $53 million; see Johnson, 2004b). Chaconas and his staff attributed the district's financial troubles to the loss of students due to the increasing number of charter schools in the city and shifting demographics that resulted from steep housing prices that drove families with school-age children from the city (May, 2002; Oakland Unified School District, 2005). Enrollment had declined considerably, as the district lost nearly 10,000 of its 43,000 students in a 5-year period (Gehring, 2005; Johnson, 2004a; Oakland Unified School District, 2005). Many analysts also attributed the district's debt to financial mismanagement and internal accounting problems. Noted one report: "Experts say Chaconas' successes were undercut by a 4,300 enrollment drop as students switched to charter schools, a 24 % teacher pay raise and an antiquated budgeting system that miscalculated overspending in nearly every department" (May, 2002, p. A1).

Ultimately, the district's debts resulted in state bailout and state takeover. As the *Chronicle* reported on December 8, 2002, "California's sixth-largest school district is broke and headed for the most expensive takeover in state history" (May, 2002, p. A1). In May 2003, California's state legislature voted to provide a loan of $100 million to Oakland Unified and to take control of the district (St. John, 2003). Once this loan was approved by Governor Gray Davis, the state superintendent placed Oakland's schools in the hands of a state administrator, Randolph E. Ward, who was charged with returning the district to financial solvency. This state takeover forced the resignation of Chaconas, who had been in office for 3 years, and took power away from the Oakland school board, turning it from a governing body into an advisory one.

Charter schools have played an interesting role in the politics of the fiscal and governance crisis and in the ensuing belt-tightening that has included district school closings (Oakland Unified School District, 2005). On the one hand, they have gained attention as part of the problem: They draw students from district schools at a time of already-declining enrollment and resource scarcity. On the other hand, Ward and his administration framed charters as part of the solution to failing district schools (Gehring, 2005; Rauh, 2006), proposing (as is one of the possibilities under No Child Left Behind) to convert these schools into charter schools (Gammon, 2005). Ward's administration included charter schools as part of the systemwide reform effort, writing in April

2005: "It is obvious that the growth of charter schools within and near Oakland are [sic] a significant factor in OUSD's [Oakland Unified School District's] recovery, whether the district manages their participation or not. OUSD intends to proactively manage its relationship with charter schools as a component of its renewal" (Oakland Unified School District, 2005, p. 64).

WOCS's SUCCESSES

Amid this district and city activity, WOCS stood as a small school trying to survive. In many ways, the school succeeded in implementing much of the broad vision of schooling developed by its founders. It combined a small, safe, caring, supportive, African American–centered environment with a rigorous, college-preparatory, social justice–minded program that drew students from West Oakland and elsewhere in the East Bay. It served its students fairly well, particularly compared with the most relevant district school alternatives.

Culture of Academic Achievement

Some of the school's success can be measured in student achievement data. WOCS students performed significantly better on standardized testing measures than their counterparts at the neighboring middle school, Lowell, and, in many cases, they outperformed students in Oakland Unified as a whole. The California Department of Education (2001) indicates that the best way to compare student scores on the nationally normed tests is to compare the percentage of students scoring at or above the 50th percentile (the National Percentile Rank, or NPR). On this measure, from 2000 to 2004 (WOCS students did not take the test in 2005), a higher percentage of WOCS students scored at or above the 50th NPR each year in both reading and math tests than did middle school students at Lowell. On all but two tests given in these 5 years (the 2001 and 2002 math tests), a higher percentage of WOCS students also scored at or above the 50th NPR than students in the district as a whole. Similarly, California has a statewide measure of academic performance, known as the Academic Performance Index (API), which is a scaled score from 200 to 1,000, and a statewide decile rank of 1 to 10 based on performance on the state's standardized tests. This provides another way to measure schools' growth and to compare schools' performance. On this measure, as well, WOCS students fared well when compared with other students in Oakland and with

African American students in the city and the state. Its statewide rank consistently placed it in the top five middle schools in the district, out of approximately 20 schools each year. Although there are limitations to what these data tell us,[1] they give us a very broad sense that WOCS students were outperforming their peers in West Oakland and, in many cases, in the district as a whole.

Alongside standard measures of educational achievement, WOCS founders and staff were successful in building a school around a broad understanding of educational success. As discussed in the previous chapter, WOCS leaders built their school on an understanding of school quality that linked school success to community development and racial identity-building. WOCS leaders felt that a response to the achievement gap between non–African American and African American students required developing an explicit connection between African American identity and academic achievement. This was to counter the view in the academic literature (Fordham & Ogbu, 1986; Fordham, 1988) and elsewhere that there is a disconnect between strong racial identity and academic identity and achievement for African American students. As the WOCS renewal application document stated as one of WOCS's three "core values": "Low-income African American students suffer from unique educational challenges often rooted in low self-esteem and in the mistaken belief that 'Blackness' and educational success are antithetical" (West Oakland Community School, 2003a, p. 2).

The culture of the school clearly valued academic achievement, and this was evident in the ways in which the students genuinely and enthusiastically supported each other when they were recognized for their academic accomplishments. Academic success was something that students generally felt they could celebrate.

In June 2002, for example, WOCS held its annual end-of-year "closing circle," in which students and staff sat in a circle in the school's main hall. The closing circle began with the regular "morning ritual," during which students raised their hands to do "positive recognitions." Then, students were asked to fill in the following three statements one-by-one: "my biggest challenge this year was . . . ," "my highlight of the year was . . . ," and "one thing I love about myself is. . . . " There was a heavy focus on academics in students' comments. Most of the students' positive recognitions went to teachers and to the school's directors, Hatano and Marjorie Wilkes. Students thanked teachers for pushing them, for putting up with them, for listening to them, even for giving them detention (as one boy said: "I'd like to thank Baba S.[2] for giving me numerous detentions." To which Baba S. responded with amusement: "I like your use of 'numerous.'").

The celebration of academic accomplishment was a regular occurrence at the school, not something simply reserved for special events. During my visit to the school in February 2005, a small group of students participated in an oratorical competition in the city. Four students returned to campus around lunchtime, practically bursting to share the news with staff that they had won three first-place and one second-place medals in the competition. They showed off their medals to students and staff, receiving enthusiastic hugs from the school's director and administrative assistant.

WOCS was successful in connecting African American identity and academic identity and achievement, in part because students received such positive, warm reinforcement for their academic accomplishments. The school also was successful in this regard because it defined educational attainment as a *communal* accomplishment, rather than simply an individual one. Thus, students did not have to feel a tension between individual academic achievement and identifying with their families and communities (Fordham, 1988).

This communal framing of educational achievement was particularly evident at eighth-grade graduation. At the school's first graduation, on June 20, 2002, 15 graduates—dressed in suits, dresses, a piece of kente cloth around their necks, and a purple cord for honor-roll recipients—were honored by a large group of family members, current and former WOCS staff, and WOCS board members and founders. The ceremony opened with the then-chair of the WOCS board, Greg Hodge, who welcomed students and poured libation, a ceremonial honoring of God and of ancestors that is practiced in some African American and other communities. For centuries, Hodge said, African/African American people had risked a lot to give and receive education. As he poured libation, he asked people in the audience to shout out the names of ancestors, relatives, and others who had been important to their education. Throughout graduation, in numerous ways, education was recognized as a family and community affair, where the community was often defined by race.

African American–Centeredness

This connection of racial and academic identities and achievements was part of a broader set of WOCS's accomplishments over the years. WOCS succeeded in carrying out its mission to focus explicitly on serving African American students. This focus, however, did not come primarily through curricular or pedagogical innovation. In some respects, as discussed in the previous chapter, the WOCS curriculum was fairly traditional. It drew heavily on California state academic standards. WOCS also did not veer far from established and emerging educational practices in the way in which it approached the core academic subjects. The school integrated math and science courses and language arts and social studies courses in "block" scheduling. To this core, WOCS added a range of supplemental curriculum and programming over the years. Depending on what was financially possible from year to year, the school offered various iterations of leadership development, enrichment, academic literacy, and physical education courses (West Oakland Community School, 1999b; 2003a; 2003b).

Despite the relatively traditional curricular focus and the variation in the leadership development and enrichment programs, which represent the pieces of the school day that could focus more heavily on African American history and culture, WOCS was successful in creating a school *culture* that centered a particular kind of African American tradition. This tradition was the kind of cultural nationalism or pan-Africanism that was (and is) also central to many African American independent schools. One of the ways in which WOCS served African American students and centered their experience was by connecting them to pan-African traditions and a set of values described and understood as particularly pan-African.

In this way, WOCS seems to be a direct descendent of African American independent schools that are part of the Council of Independent Black Institutions (CIBI). For example, WOCS celebrated Kwanzaa through an annual December student performance and dinner marking the end of the fall semester. Decorating the walls of the school as guides to student conduct were lists of the Nguzo Saba, the seven principles celebrated through Kwanzaa, and the Virtues of Maat, defined by WOCS as "the foundation of the ancient civilization of our ancestors in the Nile Valley" (West Oakland Community School, 2003b, p. 14). Also like CIBI schools, there was a heavy focus on ritual (such as pledges and daily "morning rituals") as a form of community-building at WOCS.

Like Family

Finally, perhaps one of the most striking aspects of WOCS and one of the ways in which the founding group stuck closest to its mission, is that it succeeded in creating a school that many experienced as an extended family. This fictive kinship-building was one of the three "core values" of the school, as written into the school's charter: "A small school, purposefully designed to feel as much like a village of extended family members as a place of learning, can better meet the needs of low-income students living in communities like West Oakland" (West Oakland Community School, 2003a, p. 2).

As part of establishing who constituted the school's relevant community, WOCS founders built a fictive kinship around both racial identity *and* mission. This was evident in the planning phase of the school, as well. Many members of the working group were good friends, and connections among founders deepened over the years, especially as many of the founders joined the school's board and worked together for almost a decade. These close relationships reflected that many founders saw the process of building the school as a very personal endeavor.

Like their counterparts in the CIBI network, WOCS founders and leaders were quite successful in instilling a sense of family in staff and students and their families. WOCS used some of the same strategies as the CIBI schools to build a familylike community at the school. Like CIBI member schools, WOCS used the Kiswahili "honorifics," the familial titles "Mama" and "Baba" for teachers and other adults affiliated with the school, referring, for example, to Wilkes as "Mama Marjorie" and Hatano as "Mama Akiyu."

The culture of the school was very familial as well, exhibiting the kind of "institutional caring" that historian Vanessa Siddle Walker (1996a) found to be present in a pre-*Brown* segregated African American school in North Carolina. The language arts/social studies teacher who later became the school's executive director, for instance, was strict with her students in her classroom but also was quite loving. She hugged and laughed easily with students during class as she worked with them. Staff called students "baby," "brother," or "sister," invoking familial terms and terms of endearment regularly. Staff members also were very accessible to students, and students responded to this. The language arts/social studies teacher mentioned above hosted a "girls' night out" for eighth-grade girl graduates, a slumber party on the night of the 2002 graduation. Some students I spoke with noted this accessibility, mentioning to me that they could and did call teachers at home if they had homework questions. Both boys and girls naturally put arms around their male and female teachers when they talked to them, easily giving hugs and other signs of affection. Students also said that teachers always knew what was going on socially with students. Students were very comfortable with teachers, but not in an inappropriate way. As teachers maintained a sense of authority and respect, they also cultivated a sense of care and of proximity and accessibility.

One parent of an eighth-grade boy at WOCS with whom I spoke in February 2005 also used the word *family* to describe the relationship she and her son had with school staff, noting the accessibility of WOCS teachers. She mentioned that a WOCS teacher called on a Sunday and spoke with her for an hour about her son's work, that teachers sometimes called just to report *good* news and offer praise for her son, and that the director of the school took a lot of care and time to help with high school placement for her son. She believed that both student accomplishment and disciplinary issues were communal affairs at WOCS. The culture of the school allowed her son to thrive in a way that she thought would have been impossible at any other school in the area.

WOCS's CHALLENGES

The West Oakland Community School had some substantial and poignant successes, and it had a reputation as a very successful Oakland school. WOCS also faced significant hurdles. Many of these are reflective of the challenges facing similarly situated urban charter schools (UCLA Charter School Study, 1998). I have labeled these challenges of *student achievement, external relations, mission maintenance*, and *sustainability*.

Student Achievement

Compared with the neighboring school and with other public middle schools in Oakland, WOCS served its students well. Test performance was relatively good, but there was certainly significant room for growth throughout the years. WOCS struggled with other areas related to achievement as well.

In particular, WOCS faced significant challenges with its student retention and graduation rates. WOCS began its first year with 50 sixth-grade students. Due to space and resource constraints, WOCS did not add a new class of sixth graders every year, as founders initially had planned to do. Rather, the school just served one grade at a time, following each cohort of sixth graders through eighth grade.

By the time the first cohort was at the end of its eighth-grade year, 34 students remained. Wilkes and Hatano felt strongly that the school should not practice "social promotion," and that only those students who met WOCS's high academic standards should graduate. This class of eighth graders, by December of their eighth-grade year, had an average overall GPA of 1.68 in their core classes. Of 38 students, 24 were on academic probation (West Oakland Community School, 2001). By the end of the school year, in this first cohort of 34 remaining students, only 15 students received WOCS diplomas. The second cohort, too, had approximately 34 students remaining by the end of eighth grade, and just 16 of these students participated in the graduation ceremony in the spring of 2005 and received WOCS diplomas. Those who completed eighth grade but did not officially graduate were those students deemed not to have adequately met the academic and/or service and leadership requirements of the school.

Hatano and Wilkes felt a regular sense of pain and conflict about this performance data. They knew that they and WOCS teachers held high standards and that these standards were designed, in contradistinction to the district schools in the area, to provide students with academic preparation to succeed in high school, college, and beyond. But they also were regularly disappointed that they lost students who could not meet these high standards or whose parents decided that the school was too academically demanding for their children. This conflict became a regular conversation about whom the school could best serve. When Wilkes convened the initial working group, she had in mind that the school would serve the neediest and most challenging students, those left behind by the traditional schools in the district. She also knew that charter school opponents often accused charter schools of "creaming" the top students from the existing population, and she had no desire to do this. Rather, she wanted to design a school for those students who were falling through the cracks at the local middle school, those who needed the *most* support.

But, with scarce resources, WOCS leaders and staff found it extremely difficult to serve the students for whom they had built the school. The first cohort of students had significant needs. Many were students whose previous schools were not serving them well. In a 2003 interview with me, Shawn Ginwright, a WOCS founder and former chair of the school's board, a Berkeley Ph.D. who wrote a book on an Afrocentric school reform effort in Oakland, and a faculty member then at Santa Clara University and now at San Francisco State, talked about "the sobering reality of what the young people bring to the school":

> I think after the second year, we really had to make a decision as a board to look at our recruitment strategy . . . because the students who were coming . . . essentially overwhelmed the capacity of the school itself. . . . Students had sexual abuse, and violence, and depression . . . and their parents weren't as involved in their children's education. . . . We set out with the dramatic

notion that we could open a school for the most disenfranchised students, and we realized early on that that shit is hard, that shit is hard. . . . It's a matter of resources and energy.

WOCS board members and staff quickly learned that the school had limited capacity to serve these students well.

After the first cohort of students graduated, in the spring of 2002, WOCS leaders took a different approach to recruitment and admissions. By law, the charter school could not accept or reject students based on academic criteria, and it had to admit students on a first-come, first-served basis or by lottery of interested students. But, within these parameters, there was room for directing the admissions process. Wilkes noted that the application for the second cohort looked much more like a private school application. It included a student statement and a parent/guardian statement, a letter of recommendation from an applicant's former teacher, a parent/guardian interview, an orientation, and a diagnostic test. By contrast, applicants for the first cohort needed simply to attend one information session to qualify for admission to the school.

This new process yielded a second cohort that was still entirely African American and predominantly low-income and West Oakland–based. But the second cohort, according to Wilkes, had fewer low-income students, many fewer students from single-mother homes, fewer students from West Oakland (Wilkes estimated that 70% of the first cohort and 50% of the second cohort lived in the neighborhood), and more students with families that WOCS staff members reported to be actively involved in their children's education.

Some attributed this shift from first to second cohort to a lack of capacity and a change in recruitment and admission strategy. Some also attributed this shift to the fact that, by the time the school was ready to enroll its second cohort, it had built a reputation as a school with strong academics and high expectations. This resulted in a self-selection that was not present with the first cohort of families who were simply looking for an—or *any*—alternative to their existing school. Dirk Tillotson, an attorney who is now a charter school advocate in New York, was a member of the WOCS board, served as the president of the board of the American Indian Public Charter School in Oakland, and founded and ran a charter school support group in Oakland called Oakland Charters Together. He reflected, in a 2003 interview: "We had a lot of agonizing discussions at times about some of the kids that the school maybe just didn't have the capacity to serve." He continued, in discussing the change from first to second cohort: "I think there are definitely more people who *chose* the school now, rather than, I think the first round was kind of just scooping up kids who were there." Celsa Snead, a founding board member, an attorney, and a longtime friend of Wilkes's, also noted in a 2003 interview that the shift was, in part, due to self-selection: "More people recognize the school as an opportunity, you know, people who were really into making sure their kids get a college-prep middle school education."

The retention challenge and the shifting demographics of the school provided perhaps the single largest sense of failure for some WOCS founders. Many times over the past several years, Wilkes and Hatano expressed concern and regret about whom the school could realistically serve. The fact that the school could not adequately serve all of the neediest students in the neighborhood, grouped here with a set of challenges around student achievement, raised questions for some WOCS founders about the school's core principles, making it a particularly painful shortcoming.

External Relations

The second broad set of challenges facing WOCS relates to the school's external relationships, with the district and the school's relevant communities. WOCS faced a variable, but not particularly supportive, relationship with Oakland Unified. In my observation and the view of many founders, this was characterized by obstructionism, relatively benign neglect, and, more recently, increased oversight without much accompanying support. Early on, when the district was fairly new to charters, it was quite open to the reform, as evidenced by the number of school groups to which it granted charters. But this early openness did not translate into facilitating WOCS's work. WOCS founders reported that, early on in the charter school's relationship with the district, Oakland Unified sometimes did not process the school's paperwork or disburse state finances in a timely way. At first, the district did not have even one person dedicated to working with the city's charter schools. Now, there is one charter school coordinator at Oakland Unified, with a staff of two, who handles charter school communication and business (Rauh, 2006). For a number of the early years, WOCS school leaders felt that the school was generally left alone to do its work, without either much support or much intrusion from the district. As Hatano said in a 2003 interview, the district "gave us lots of leeway to just do things the way we saw fit."

But, with the fiscal crisis and ensuing state takeover, as well as the statewide and national culture of accountability created by No Child Left Behind, WOCS school leaders felt more scrutiny from the district and less support. Hatano noted in 2003: "The [district's] charter schools coordinator was at WOCS yesterday looking through personnel files and making sure everybody was fingerprinted and had an appropriate credential. . . . They *never*, ever, ever have done that before." She concluded: "Money is tight, people are looking over their shoulders." Hodge, well positioned to speak to charter-district relations in Oakland as a member of the founding team and board of WOCS and as a member and then the president of the Oakland school board, said, in a 2003 interview, that the district's financial crunch resulted in its shifting its approach to charter schools. While the district office, he said, used to be supportive of charter schools and charter applicants, helping with technical assistance and the charter application process, this changed when resources became scarce: "People on the board and in the administration began to be less interested in supporting the charter development, as much as saying, 'we have limited resources, and we don't want to help with that.'"

A number of WOCS founders and leaders mentioned in interviews with me in December 2003, 6 months after state administrator Ward came to Oakland Unified, that charter schools were not likely to benefit from the district's fiscal and leadership troubles. Tillotson said to me that he believed charter schools were particularly vulnerable during the district's fiscal crisis. There was a perception, he said, that charters "drained revenues from OUSD," and, "as the deficit rose, the charters became a scapegoat."[3]

As WOCS negotiated its relationship with Oakland Unified over the years, it also struggled to build community relationships. This was a particular vulnerable area for WOCS, since it claimed to be a community and community-building institution, with *community* defined by both race and place. Early on, during the charter application phase, Wilkes and others sought the trust and support of some long-standing West Oakland leaders, some of whom seemed wary of relative newcomers. Many of these activists had long histories in local and national African American freedom struggles and seemed to be natural allies for the school. But, once the charter was approved, WOCS staff members quietly went about the business of opening the school and serving small cohorts of students. Faced with all of the challenges of starting a new institution, school staff often could not prioritize cultivating these relationships.

Over the years, some WOCS leaders expressed that they believed that this community-building piece of WOCS's mission needed work. Hatano, who worked tirelessly as the instructional leader for the school, talked in 2003 about the fact that the school had not developed the connection with community advocates and activists that she had envisioned:

> We just have not had a lot of larger community support in West
> Oakland. . . . I think that in the beginning we had some promise
> that there might be community supporters who really advocate
> on behalf of the school and maybe even raise funds and keep the
> school kind of on a higher profile in the community. None of that
> has happened. I wish it had. . . . It just has not worked out the
> way that we had hoped.

Hodge, too, said that WOCS was so small that it was "kind of a quiet place in terms of the landscape of what happens in West Oakland in general," that it was not yet a real "player in the neighborhood." The West Oakland Community School also had not formed significant partnerships with the neighboring district schools, Hodge noted: "There is still a lot left to be desired, I think, in terms of the community-building aspects that have been part of WOCS's vision." This shortcoming speaks to the fact that the daily challenges of running a new school on scarce resources are so great that WOCS staff members often felt pulled inward rather than out toward community members and institutions.

Mission Maintenance

Though the years, WOCS also faced a broad challenge of how to remain true to its mission. The three pieces of the school's mission remained *leadership development, college preparation,* and *African American history and culture.* The challenge of mission maintenance arose particularly around the school's focus on race. As mentioned above, through the school culture and the ways in which school staff tied academic achievement to racial identity, the school was very successful in instituting a focus on African American students, communities, culture, and history. But this focus was not particularly well defined or institutionalized through curriculum or programming.

During the school's planning phase, the working group had a number of conversations about whether the school would be explicitly "Afrocentric." Many shied away from this term, noting that it was very politically loaded in an Oakland that had just experienced the "Ebonics" resolution and a failed, explicitly Afrocentric reform effort at the local West Oakland high school (Ginwright, 2004). Many in the group also felt that the term was not precise enough and did not help to describe a particular approach to serving African American students. Ultimately, the founding group decided not to use the word to describe its focus on race. But, when these same founders talked about how to focus on African American history and culture at WOCS once the school was up and running, they often used the term *Afrocentric* to describe the question of what the school should be with respect to its focus on race.

Both Ginwright and Hatano, in grappling with this question in 2003, mentioned the cultural and ritualized aspects of the school as areas of success in fulfilling the school's mission to focus on African American students. Ginwright said, "Everybody at the school calls each other Mama and Baba, they do morning circle. And so there's still a lot of focus on traditional African ideas and themes." Hatano, however, acknowledged that these aspects alone did not necessarily constitute an Afrocentric or African American-centered program. She mentioned a lack of specific programming and a lack of clarity about how to fulfill the school's African American-centered focus: "I just think back to the race versus place conversation; it was much more clear then in the planning stage. Now I'm not sure where we are."

When the school experienced a financial crunch, the focus on African American history and culture was the first piece to face downsizing. For the 2003–04 school year, the decision was made to eliminate the position of Student Life and Leadership Coordinator, filled by a popular leadership teacher, Baba D., whom many in the school community saw as the person who pushed for and seemed to "carry" this part of the school's mission. His leaving concerned a group of parents. These parents indicated that they had chosen WOCS for its explicit focus on African American students, history, and culture, and they urged the school to increase its commitment to this piece of its mission. When board members talked with me in December 2003 about the extent to which the school had fulfilled its mission, many mentioned the leaving of this teacher, the impact it had on parents, and the questions it raised about how the school should define and implement the race-specific piece of its mission.

The African American-centered piece of the school's mission was culturally institutionalized, but because it was definitionally unclear and was not programmatically institutionalized, it became defined by a few individuals and was largely dependent on them for its existence and for the shape it took from year to year.

Sustainability

Finally, WOCS faced a range of serious challenges around sustainability. Its sustainability issues fell into two broad, and related, categories: *resource* challenges and *leadership* challenges. These were not unique to WOCS. WOCS faced many of the same challenges as other schools that some in the WOCS group called "mom and pop" or (referring to Hatano and Wilkes) "mom and mom" charters, those that are not supported by a nonprofit charter management organization (CMO) or well-resourced for-profit chain. These sustainability issues were often the topic of conversation among WOCS board members, including Wilkes, Hodge, and Ginwright, who had significant training in nonprofit management.

On the resource side, WOCS faced a constant struggle to remain financially solvent, and this impacted every aspect of the school and its ability to fulfill its mission. This was, in large part, a function of the school's location in a state and a city that do not adequately support public schools. Generally, WOCS's budget in its last few years was somewhere between $600,000 and $650,000 per academic year (though this dipped to $450,000 in 2004–05), and generally less than half of this money came from the state. WOCS had to raise between 40 and 60% of its budget in the form of individual donations, private foundation and corporate money, and public grant funds. This imperative required a constant attention to fundraising, a significant staff energy drain and source of perennial stress and urgency. Said Hatano, during the school's fifth year: "At this point, we're still kind of, . . . year-to-year, just chasing money."

The fact that WOCS was always financially strapped meant that it had to make difficult choices about curriculum and programming. This resource challenge, therefore, is closely linked to mission maintenance. For instance, as another example of the ways in which the school's mission was compromised by its financial pressures: WOCS initially envisioned itself as a community institution, a gathering place that served as both a school and a community center and learning space for West Oakland's adults. Its proposed Youth & Family Center was never implemented, in large part because it was just too expensive. WOCS rented a small space from a church, and expanding to enroll more students or to serve the community's adults required more space and more staff resources than it could secure. The fact that the school could not open this community center, could not serve the adults in the community, and could not provide before- and after-school programming for young people impacted the extent to which the WOCS staff could really have an effect on students' lives.

Another, related resource challenge for WOCS was that the school always struggled to maintain its desired enrollment of 50 students. It began with 50 students in the fall of 1999, the maximum number of students it felt it could serve in its small facility. But the school regularly lost students over the years and had a difficult time filling their spots. The decision to serve just one grade level at a time also limited enrollment to a maximum of 50 students and meant that WOCS could only recruit students from one grade at a time in any given year.

Declining enrollment was an issue that received significant board and staff attention. By the third year of the school, December 2001, when the school served its first cohort as eighth-grade students, a memo prepared for a WOCS board meeting announced: "The sobering news is that our enrollment continues to decline. We started this school year with 44 students (34 returning students and 10 new students), and our enrollment currently stands at 38 students, the lowest it has ever dipped." The board memo indicated that the staff believed that enrollment had declined for four reasons: Academic standards presented a "challenge" to students and families, new students sometimes had a difficult time adjusting to a school in which most of the students had been together for years in a very close-knit community, the school did not receive support from the district for special education services, and some students faced family "crises" that resulted in their leaving the area and the school (West Oakland Community School, 2001, p. 2). This struggle to retain students had a significant financial impact on the school, as every student loss resulted in the loss of much-needed state revenue.

Related to these financial pressures, the second significant sustainability issue for WOCS was the challenge of school *leadership*. This was one of the defining and most difficult issues for the school. Wilkes and Hatano served as the school's first beloved, trusted, tireless, and highly effective leaders. As founders of WOCS, they felt complete ownership over the school, and their own sense of professional and personal accomplishment was intricately connected with WOCS's success. They were also both charismatic leaders who embodied the familylike culture of the school. They were almost always accessible to staff, parents, and students, and they provided a structured, efficient, affectionate, and loving environment for everyone involved with the school. They embodied the school and all that it stood for.

Eventually, however, they needed a break. They had sustained the school for a number of years, through its planning phase and the heady first years of its existence, and they were both exhausted. As Wilkes said, "I have found that launching a charter school has consumed every bit of physical, mental, emotional, and spiritual stamina that I possess" (quoted in King, 2004, p. 182). Despite their need for a break, Wilkes and Hatano knew that their leaving would have a significant impact on the school, and they approached the search for new leadership extremely carefully. They and the board searched for and found a new director, an African American woman in her 30s who had experience running nonprofits and had no prior relationship with WOCS.[4]

The new director was, in short, a mismatch for the school. Some board members believed that she did not feel the same sense of personal investment in WOCS or seek to build the same familylike connections with the school's leaders or staff, and that she treated her position at WOCS more like a job than a calling. She entered the difficult position of filling the shoes of two beloved and sorely missed leaders, and I think that she felt the weight of a board—comprised mostly of school founders—that still operated with a strong sense of ownership and mission. Ultimately, she did not make it through her first academic year with WOCS. After clashes with staff, Hatano and Wilkes, and the board, she resigned in the middle of the 2003–04 school year, and her position was filled by the existing language arts and social studies instructor, also an African American woman, who remained in the executive director's position through the 2004–05 school year.

As Oakland Unified faced its own crisis of leadership, the shift from the founding directors to new leadership was a blow to WOCS from which the school could not, ultimately, recover. The legacy of this leadership decision changed the course of the school. The leader who replaced Wilkes and Hatano did not fulfill her fundraising duties, leaving the school even more financially strapped than usual. By the middle of the 2004–05 school year, the board faced the prospect that it could not afford to keep WOCS open.

THE CLOSING OF WOCS

During the 2004–05 school year, the WOCS board made the difficult decision to close the school for a year to regroup. The current cohort of students would graduate in June 2005, and school leaders would need to recruit a new class of sixth graders for the following school year. So, in some ways, it was a natural time to take a break. Board members just could not envision a way in which the school could remain financially solvent, and they did not want to enroll a new class of students that they could not guarantee they could serve through eighth-grade graduation.

But after the board made this decision, an 11th-hour opportunity arose to keep the school open. Two African American mothers in Oakland had sent their daughters to a predominantly White boarding school in Woodstock, Connecticut, called the Hyde School. Hyde was founded in 1966 in Bath, Maine, by Joseph Gauld, with a heavy focus on character development, parental involvement, and "family education," a model that appears fairly therapeutic in its language and focus (Hyde Schools, n.d., n.p.). Hyde now has private, boarding campuses in Connecticut and Maine, as well as three urban day school campuses: a magnet school in New Haven, Connecticut, and charter schools in Washington, D.C., and the Bronx, New York (Associated Press, 2006; Hyde Schools, n.d.).

The two Oakland parents, along with other African American families who had sent their children to Hyde boarding schools, were interested in starting a Hyde campus in Oakland, designed to serve students like their children: African American students who wanted and could benefit from an alternative to traditional district schooling. They began conversations with some members of the WOCS board in the spring of 2005 and, by the summer, it was decided that the umbrella organization that oversees and raises money for the Hyde schools would provide finances and leadership to assume WOCS's charter.

The school would remain open, but under new management. During a July 2005 board meeting, many of the founding WOCS board members resigned and were replaced with Hyde staff and other trustees chosen by Hyde. Hyde staff recruited teachers and a new class of sixth graders for WOCS, and they brought in their own leadership team. Hyde assumed WOCS's charter, which had been renewed in 2003 through the 2007–08 school year, agreeing to carry out the goals established in the charter. After 2008, Hyde staff and WOCS board members understood, Hyde would have the option to make significant changes, either by applying for its own charter with a different mission and different set of goals, amending the existing charter at renewal time, or giving up its charter status.

The Hyde organization had grand plans for WOCS. In a press release posted on its website, it wrote that "the newest member of the Hyde family of schools—the West Oakland Community School (Hyde-Oakland)" had opened with 34 sixth-grade students in the fall of 2005. It estimated that the school would grow to become a K–12 school serving 1,100 students (Hyde Leadership Public Charter School, n.d.).

However, the school only survived for 1 year. At the end of the 2005–06 school year, the same summer that Hatano very suddenly and unexpectedly passed away, Hyde closed the West Oakland Community School.

After 7 years, WOCS's leadership problems and resource needs eventually overcame the school. WOCS was sustained, year to year, by leaders who were incredibly committed to the institution and its success. Because they were so personally invested, they weathered WOCS's financial challenges and they, somehow, opened the school doors each September. Ultimately, the school could not survive the leadership void created when Wilkes and Hatano left the school. Their leadership was not sufficiently institutionalized, and these founding codirectors could not find replacements who felt as connected to the school and its vision and who were willing to work as tirelessly to make sure that the school remained solvent.

My fieldwork was complete by 2005, and I did not have access to the school during the year that it was run by Hyde. Therefore, I cannot say what factors led the new board to decide to close the school. I can say, however, that the shift in management in the last year of the school, and the fact that the struggling school ultimately closed its doors, speaks to many of the challenges faced by urban charter schools today.

CHARTERS AND THE POLITICS OF URBAN SCHOOLING

Charter schools, as public schools, are not isolated from the politics of funding, of class, of race and space, and of schooling that inform so much of public school policy. As others have argued (Anyon, 1997; Henig et al., 1999; Noguera, 2003), public schools are intricately connected to urban politics and conditions. We see that charter schools are not exempt from these politics simply because they have some freedoms that district schools do not. As I have demonstrated in this chapter, WOCS faced many of the internal challenges of other community-based charters, particularly challenges of leadership and mission maintenance. But these internal challenges were quite related to the fact that the school was impacted by national, state, and local politics: the national politics of race that informed the initial vision for and commitment to the school; the state politics of funding that made it so difficult for WOCS to remain financially secure; and the local politics of race, class, and public schooling that impacted how WOCS was received locally as a charter school in lean financial times and as an explicitly African American charter school in local and national times when an explicit focus on race often is deemed dangerous and anachronistic.

These entanglements between charter schools and the broader politics of race, class, place, and public schooling have the potential to create significant roadblocks to charter success. But, despite these, for this group of educators, parents, and activists, who came together in the spring of 1996, when their state faced a rollback of affirmative action and their city faced the realization that it was severely underserving African American students, the charter mechanism provided hope. WOCS founders and staff developed a race-specific remedy to racial inequality, and they spent 9 years building and implementing their vision. The charter mechanism also provided a terrain to work out many of the key questions of race and schooling of the day. As with the African American school choice efforts before it, for WOCS these questions were about the future of integration and multiracial organizing as a strategy of racial equality and the limits and possibilities of American institutions. It is to these debates, as they played out in the founding of WOCS, that I turn in the next chapter.

The West Oakland Community School, Charter Schooling, and Post-Civil Rights Politcs

If you have run a school or worked in one, you know that, no matter how grand your vision, most days, your work is no less important but much more mundane. Often you do not have time to consciously weigh in on the philosophical questions of the meaning of schooling or the definition of *community* as you struggle to pay the utilities bill for your rented space, teach a lesson on the Constitutional Convention, or practice for the upcoming Kwanzaa celebration. This was true with the West Oakland Community School as well. But, as I argue in this chapter, at a particularly politically charged historical moment, WOCS did provide a site to rethink some large political and sociological questions about the nature of schooling, race, and American participation.

Through WOCS, a group of predominantly African American educators worked to establish a new means through which public schools could participate in movements for social justice. Like their predecessors in other African American school choice initiatives, WOCS leaders worked to redefine *school quality*, as I discussed in Chapter 6. They also, like their predecessors, struggled with and built a strategy of *racial equality* that did not primarily focus on desegregation and that raised questions about the character of viable interracial cooperation and organizing, African American participation in mainstream American schools, and the limits and possibilities of public schools. I believe that charter schools are so contentious because they raise these fundamental questions about the nature of racial equality, American institutions, and public schooling. In this chapter, I examine some of these questions raised by WOCS founders as they made their way through the founding and implementation of the school.

PARTNERSHIP AND PARTICIPATION IN AMERICAN REFORM

Law professor Derrick Bell (1992) wrote a parable in which on the first day of the turn of the millennium, American leaders would be called upon to determine whether African Americans were truly Americans with an equal right to their freedom, self-determination, and livelihood. He wrote that White American leaders, backed by some powerful African American allies, would trade the freedom of African Americans for the prosperity, well-being, and security of White Americans. African Americans, on this day, would have no more standing than they did when many Africans entered the country in chains almost 400 years earlier. The turn of the millennium is indeed a time when the relationship of African Americans to America is under review, as some of the most significant tools of access to American institutions of the past 50 years—desegregation orders, civil rights laws, and affirmative action policies—are now under new attack.

The West Oakland Community School provided an opportunity for African American educators and activists to reassert the importance of a race-specific remedy to racial inequality. So, too, it furnished a site to negotiate another aspect of racial justice struggles: defining the most desirable and efficacious relationship between African Americans and American mainstream institutions and reforms and the most viable partnerships to build and sustain African American institutions. In building a school-based strategy of racial justice, WOCS founders grappled with the questions of the politics of affiliation and coalition-building in the charter school movement, the politics of funding, and the importance of multiracial participation in the school. These questions ultimately were about the politics of American participation and the possibilities and limitations of mainstream American institutions in serving African American citizens.

WOCS and the Charter Movement

As WOCS gained visibility over the years and charter schooling grew as a reform effort in Oakland, WOCS founders struggled with how closely to align with the charter school movement. While the founders felt that the charter movement had progressive potential, they also recognized that it was predominantly White and was impacted by some extremely conservative forces and tendencies. From the beginning, a number of WOCS members expressed simultaneous excitement about the opportunity that charter legislation gave them to found their own school and skepticism about the charter reform's ability to serve public education and African American students. The group's desire to affiliate with the charter movement and other charter schools was tested on a number of occasions.

Some of these occasions became touchstones in the group, as moments when WOCS members were made aware of the ways in which they and their school stood at the margins of the charter school movement. One of the most significant moments during the school's planning phase came in July 1998, at a regional charter school conference in Portland, Oregon, organized by the Northwest Regional Educational Laboratory. This conference featured days' worth of speakers, all of whom—according to WOCS participants—were White. Most of the charter school groups that attended were also White, with the exception of the WOCS group, an African American group from South Central Los Angeles, and a group from an Arizona Native American school. The four WOCS staff members who attended addressed this issue directly with the conference organizers and were met with a combination of defensiveness, lack of understanding, and apology.

Like the "race versus place" discussion, this experience, known later in the group just as "Portland," became a symbolic reference point for a number of reasons. First, the experience at the conference highlighted the extent to which most activists and visible leaders in the charter school movement were White and were not drawn to charter schools because they saw them as a vehicle for social change. Unlike the community control or the African American independent schools movements, which brought together school leaders from around the country who shared a political understanding of schooling and a common mission to serve students of color, the charter school movement was a much larger political tent. After Portland, Akiyu Hatano remarked that she and the others who attended from WOCS felt "like fish out of water." This occasion was just one instance among many charter school conferences, workshops, and meetings in which the WOCS group was among the only groups of color in attendance.

As the charter school movement proliferated, and as WOCS founders solidified their vision, they felt less and less drawn to identify with charter schools *as* charter schools and with the movement that supports these schools. In fact, WOCS leaders, especially as other charter schools in Oakland received heightened media attention on their financial and organizational difficulties, became increasingly willing to publicly disassociate from charter schooling as a so-called movement (Brumer, 1999; King, 2004).

WOCS founders also grappled with how to affiliate with the charter school movement on the issue of organized labor. They were aware that, like community control and voucher initiatives before it, charter schooling strains the traditional liberal–labor–civil rights coalition. In its place, it builds new, unlikely partnerships. Like vouchers, charter schools have drawn the support of both conservative White business leaders and progressive African American community activists (Bulman & Kirp, 1999; Carl, 1996; Henig, 1994). Particularly in the absence of a clarifying national social movement or a unifying political mission, these alliances are fluid and tenuous. Through their negotiation of these alliances, particularly with the teachers' union, WOCS founders over the years worked to define their allies and their relationship to mainstream education reform and reformers.

The WOCS group initially struggled with its relationship with the Oakland Education Association (OEA), the Oakland teachers' union, which claimed in a March 1998 meeting that WOCS could only avoid union opposition when its charter petition went before the state for approval if Wilkes promised *a priori* that the school's teachers would be unionized. Wilkes, whose career started at the United Federation of Teachers in New York (the New York teachers' union), made clear in this meeting, and in other public statements, that she supported the existence and the importance of teachers' unions. She felt, however, that she could not support their actions categorically, particularly when they jeopardized the education of students of color. Others in the group felt similarly uncomfortable either categorically denouncing or supporting both teachers' unions and charter schools. Many of the school's founders were labor union *and* charter school supporters, however reluctantly of both sometimes. Their dealings with and response to the union demonstrates another instance in which WOCS founders felt called upon to define and negotiate their allegiances. Their ultimate decision not to heed the OEA's demand aligned them with other charter schools in the district and the state. But their explicitly racial analysis of the political place of unions historically, along with their attempt to balance this critique with a progressive support of organized labor, demonstrates WOCS founders' attempt to carve out new allegiances and new political positions (Rofes & Stulberg, 2004).

The Politics of Charter Funding

The politics of funding and fundraising present another example of the way in which WOCS founders worked to define a strategy of racial justice, negotiating African American relationships to mainstream American institutions and reforms. Funding is clearly a substantial issue of viability for charter schools. Charter schools generally are allocated approximately the same per-pupil funding as their district counterparts. So, charter schools are subject to funding inequities tied to class and socioeconomic residential segregation. Urban charter schools, perhaps most in need of extra funds, tend to receive less money than their suburban counterparts. In its last year, the West Oakland Community School only received approximately $4,700 per average daily attendance, which was well below even the average per-pupil expenditure in the state.[1]

Research shows that charter schools in California—particularly in low-income and urban areas—generally cannot subsist on public funds (Scott & Holme, 2002; UCLA Charter School Study, 1998; Wells, Lopez, Scott, & Holme, 1999). This situation certainly is not unique to charter schooling. As we saw in New York, the public school community control project hinged on the support of the Ford Foundation and other private donors. As was the case in New York (and in the voucher movement, too), the financial reality of founding and running charter schools has created the opportunity for some very uncomfortable bedfellows.

For WOCS, the opportunity for an unlikely partnership came in the example of the School Futures Research Foundation. School Futures was a San Diego-based organization backed by philanthropist John Walton, of the Wal-Mart family, who had provided financial support to the voucher initiative on the November 1993 ballot in California, Proposition 174 (Bonsteel, 1997; Schorr, 2002). Walton also, in 1998, cofounded and cofunded a huge, nationwide private voucher program, the Children's Scholarship Fund, which, according to the organization's website, has served more than 86,000 low-income students to date (Children's Scholarship Fund, n.d; Hassel & Toch, 2006). The Walton family has since become the largest private funder of charter schools in the country (Hassel & Toch, 2006).

When the WOCS group first encountered School Futures, the organization supported just a small number of charter schools in California (Schorr, 1999d). School Futures provided start-up funds, and technical assistance and management if its partner schools wanted it. It also set up the governing boards at its school sites, which then had the power to hire the schools' principals. It used the traditional Core Knowledge curriculum in its schools. The foundation thus directed much of the operations and management of the schools it backed, leaving—despite its claims to the contrary—little room for local autonomy in school decision making.

Wilkes was given the name of the School Futures director of school operations, hearing that the organization was interested in supporting charter schools in the Bay Area. She received an enthusiastic response from him, and when members of the WOCS group met with him in September 1997, they learned that the organization planned to open a number of charter schools across the country. WOCS members left this meeting with the sense that School Futures was interested in funding charter schools particularly in communities of color so that it could soften public opinion on vouchers by demonstrating the inclusiveness of school choice.[2] "They're empire-building," Wilkes said, rejecting the possibility of a partnership. Citing political differences and concern for their ability to retain decision-making power through such a partnership, WOCS founders chose not to ally themselves with the Walton foundation. But School Futures eventually partnered with a large Bay Area community- and church-based organization, Oakland Community Organizations, which successfully submitted proposals for five new charter schools to the Oakland School Board in 1999 (Olszewski, 1999b; Schorr, 1999a; 1999b; 1999d; 1999e; 1999j; 2002).

Early on, WOCS founders felt some luxury to be able to turn down support from funders such as the Walton family. From the beginning, WOCS founders were aware of their professional status and the cultural and political capital they possessed, as evidenced by the occasional joking about the number of Ivy League degrees held by the school's founders. The group knew that it could rely on significant connections with foundations, corporate donors, and educational professionals. Founders also knew that they had the educational and class privilege to draw on connections in the nonprofit world and to use skills—such as grant-writing, budget-making, and organizational development—that they had as a result of their education and their professional experience. They also knew that their educational and class status gave them an "in" with charter school supporters and technical advisors in the state, who were eager to be able to tout their connection to successful charter groups of color. As Hatano said in an interview with me in November 1998:

> I think they more or less see us as potential stars. Because we have well-educated, articulate people who are on staff who speak the same kind of language as they do, who travel in the same circles as they do, they feel comfortable with us. If we were a group of parents from West Oakland saying "we really need a middle school," I think the reception there would be completely different, in all honesty.

The fact that WOCS founders had these skills and capital allowed them a degree of independence that other community-based charter school founders often do not have (Scott & Holme, 2002). This fact made the decision not to accept School Futures' backing easier and allowed some freedom to think innovatively about funding, despite the perennial funding challenges discussed in the previous chapter.

Unlike their private school counterparts in the Council of Independent Black Institutions (CIBI) and elsewhere, WOCS leaders did not have complete independence as their goal. Like public school community control leaders of the 1960s, charter school educators generally are beholden financially to both public and private interests. Independence is not feasible, given public school status and given that inadequate public funding frequently creates the need for supplemental private support. Charter school leaders thus often make *control* of key decisions, rather than explicit independence, a driving mission.

Because urban charter schools generally must rely on some private funds, their leaders confront choices about the kinds of partnerships they cultivate. Although they gain freedom from some public oversight, they often replace this with the demands of private foundations. WOCS founders learned, perhaps from predecessor movements, to draw on foundation and other support when necessary, without confrontation or public ideological wrangling. WOCS leaders were well positioned to have options here, given their professional connections. But these funding constraints placed on charter schools like WOCS raised many of the same challenges to full autonomy and control that both New York community control activists and African American independent school-builders faced. Like their predecessors, WOCS leaders were aware that the funding choices they made impacted the way in which they could define their institution. The partnerships they choose were political, as well as financial, decisions. WOCS leaders contended regularly with the reality that their potential partners in the charter school world held views that were often ideologically and politically incongruent with their own.

Non–African American Participation in WOCS

Aside from external partnerships, WOCS founders also negotiated their relationship to American mainstream institutions and reforms through their deliberations on the role of non–African Americans in the school and in African American education in general. During the founding phase, the WOCS group came to define its allies both by race and by a concern for the effects of enduring racism on African American children and their families. Wilkes defined the school group as a "community of affiliation" of those who "care deeply about African American children."

During the first few meetings of the planning group, its members talked a lot about why they chose to participate in building the school. Amid a broad discussion of social justice, this conversation centered on racial inequality in schooling, racial politics, and the interpersonal dynamics of race. A topic of discussion in these first few meetings was whether and how the planning of the school should involve non–African Americans, including me and others around the table in the first few meetings. Wilkes felt strongly that the planning should come from a multiracial group. During the second meeting, an African American man who taught at an African American independent school in Oakland was the only person to openly question the presence of non–African Americans. He said that, a few years ago, "if I had walked into the room and saw you two [nodding to me and the other White person in the room], I would have assumed that this project was going to be too watered down and I wouldn't want to be a part of it. Now," he said, mentioning White abolitionist John Brown, "I feel differently. Now I can sit at a table with you if you are willing to be down with this project, if you come knowing that we are talking about freeing African American people."

This issue of the role of non–African Americans in the building of this school arose, as well, in a number of conversations about whether all of the school's teachers and administrators should be African American. This issue of staffing is particularly important for charter schools, because their flexibility in hiring puts them in a unique position to actively address the dearth of teachers of color in urban schools.

In a November 1996 discussion of the school's staff, founder Anthony Reese said, "I'm less concerned that the staff of the school be all Black. But the staff needs to be down with this mission of fully arming Black kids to succeed in the world." Most of the others agreed with him. A small minority in the group, however, felt that it was important that the school—operating within its legal boundaries—should work to have an all-Black staff that also aligned with the political mission of the school. African American teachers, one member said, could "empower students in ways that non-Black teachers can't." Wilkes, however, said that it was important to her to have both African American role models *and* a multiracial group that could come together for a common mission of serving African American youth. In a 1999 interview with me, she reiterated this:

> The most important and most powerful thing that we're doing is that we are putting in front of these children African American people who have created other kinds of choices in their lives.

And we are putting in front of these children the image of
African American and White and Asian people working together
productively and peaceably on their behalf. There is no place else
in their lives where these children are going to see this at this age.

It also was important to her and others that, beyond a consideration
of racial background, the teachers be experienced and oriented toward
holding WOCS students to high academic standards. Subsequent group
conversations resulted in a decision that the staff and leadership of
the school should be *predominantly*, but not exclusively, African
American.

The staff and the leadership over the life of the school reflected
this. For the first 4 years of the school, Wilkes and Hatano served as
coleaders. Hatano, as the instructional leader, was the daily face of
the school to parents and students. Her appointment, as an Asian
American woman who was a central member of the initial founding
group, brought absolutely no opposition from the founding group or
others, and she served as a committed and popular advocate for and
confidante of parents and students throughout her years at the school.
After Wilkes and Hatano resigned, as discussed in the previous chapter,
an African American woman was hired to lead the school. When she
resigned midway through her first year, an African American teacher
at the school took her place. The core academic staff at the school
was almost exclusively African American, though there were some
non-African American volunteers and ancillary teachers and staff
members who, at various times, became integral members of the
WOCS community.

Perhaps ironically, the "race versus place" discussion in 1996, as
discussed in Chapter 6, became a turning point for some in the group
on the role of non–African Americans in the school. While this meeting
produced the unanimous decision to focus on African American
students rather than on West Oakland students, *per se*, it also made
clear for some founders why it was appropriate for a multiracial group
to build this school. As Wilkes said to me following the group decision,
the passage of Proposition 209 gave new urgency to the work of the
school and confirmed for her that this work should involve like-
minded non–African Americans. "There are not enough people like us
[politically] to go around anyway," she said.

For the non–African Americans in the group, of which there were
two at the time, the passage of Proposition 209 clarified their place
in the work of building an African American school. Hatano said in a
1998 interview with me that the "race versus place" discussion was
"the anchoring piece" for her:

> Being one of the . . . few non–African American members of the
> group, I felt like I needed to be clear—at least in my own mind—
> how it is that someone who is not African American finds herself
> in this group, very committed, and hopefully very central to the
> work.

I, as the other non–African American member of the founding group
at the time, felt similarly about the clarity that the November 1996
discussion provided. In my fieldnotes after the conversation, I wrote
that I felt that I had, for the first time in the group, "'come out' as
a white person with specific reasons *as* a white person why I would
want to be involved." I wrote that although self-reflection is always
important, feeling tentative about my involvement, given the current
racial politics of California, seemed self-indulgent. At a time of political
retreat on affirmative action, those active in the WOCS founding group
decided both that a focus on race was a necessary response *and* that
racial exclusivity in forming this response was a tactic they could not
afford.

The exceptions to this in the group were less explicit. During the
long planning process, the participation of members of the working group
intensified and waned, depending on what else was going on personally
and professionally in their lives. Wilkes's leadership remained steady,
as did my participation in the planning process. Hatano grew to take a
leadership role, particularly after she left her teaching position in San
Francisco to work with WOCS full-time. Derek Peake and Ted Uno,
cofounders of the Oakland-based nonprofit Quilombo, also grew to
take significant positions in the founding group for a short time during
the school's planning phase. At one point, particularly through 1998,
following the district's March approval of WOCS's charter application,
the group of five most actively involved founders was not primarily
African American, though the founding group as a whole remained
so. Also, a White man who had been a teacher in Berkeley joined the
working group for a short time, and sometimes clashed fairly vocally
with members of the group. During this period, Wilkes worried that the
African American members seemed less and less involved in the regular
decision making of the school. This pattern reversed itself as WOCS
moved from planning into actual program implementation, but some
of the initial founders did not retain their involvement. Although this
was never addressed explicitly in the group as a whole, it may have been
that for some, particularly those teachers involved in African American
independent schools, the WOCS group was not focused strongly enough
on race—on African American–centered curriculum and pedagogy or on
its commitment to building an exclusively Black staff.

Ultimately, WOCS leaders faced a very significant decision around the involvement of non–African Americans in the summer of 2005, when it confronted the choice to close or involve a new, unambiguously *not* African American–centered school group. Despite years of planning around what it meant to build a school that focused on African American students, a conclusive answer to the "race versus place" question, a vigilance about the politics of the partnerships it formed, and a decisive focus on hiring predominantly Black staff members, 9 years after the founding group came together, the question of what it meant to be an African American–centered school was still in flux. In forming the partnership with the Hyde School, as discussed in the previous chapter, WOCS leaders ultimately were quite flexible in their mission to serve African American students. For many, the decision to involve Hyde was filled with apprehension and conflict. But, out of organizational necessity, WOCS board members resolved that the school could better serve African American students by remaining open, even if the school had a very different educational and political vision under Hyde's leadership.

The Hyde team that assumed WOCS's charter for the 2005–06 school year was decidedly much Whiter than WOCS's initial founding group or the founding board. The founder of the Hyde boarding schools, Joseph Gauld, is White, as are many members of the national organization's leadership team and many of the WOCS board members who replaced the founding board in the summer of 2005. Although, during the 2005–06 school year, the day-to-day school leadership and staff at WOCS remained predominantly African American, as did the student body, it was clear that Hyde's mission and the demographics of its student bodies and governing teams were quite a shift for WOCS.

The flexibility that the WOCS board showed in ceding governance to Hyde demonstrates that what it means to focus on "race" is constantly shifting in the life of an institution like WOCS. So, too, is the question of who constitutes the relevant, appropriate partners in this institution-building. In the 10 years that the WOCS group existed, the answer to how it related and responded to American mainstream institutions, reforms, and reformers was never static or resolved.

DEBATING DESEGREGATION, AGAIN

Through building their school, WOCS founders and leaders articulated their vision of the relationship between racial justice and schooling, and they grappled with how to institutionalize this vision. Central to this was the question of the continued relevance and efficacy of school desegregation as a tool for racial equality. WOCS members confronted this question at a time in California and elsewhere when courts, legislatures, and other communities of color were doing likewise.

At this time of political flux, it makes sense that this prolific and controversial school reform, charter schooling and school choice in general, provided the latest site for the politics of desegregation (Stulberg, 2004; 2006). School choice movements at once both challenge desegregation policies and goals and revive them, politically and discursively. They have become sites to revisit many of the old desegregation questions on the limit of state involvement in schooling and the ability of desegregated schooling per se to provide equal educational opportunity for all schoolchildren. When, by contrast, few find it noteworthy enough to talk about the huge percentage of non-charter public schools that are de facto racially segregated, the degree of racial segregation in charter schools has arisen as a significant schooling issue. Charter schools and school choice more generally, therefore, have provided a vehicle for a recent national conversation to join the very local deliberations had by school-builders themselves, on the extent to which school desegregation is still a desired, effective, and politically and practically possible solution to racial and educational inequality.

The continued relevance of school desegregation and the role that schools of choice play in either advancing or setting back desegregation goals also became an important debate within the WOCS founding group. On some level, desegregation politics held little relevance for WOCS. The school's founders were not immediately responding to a failure of the city to implement its desegregation policy. The district is severely racially segregated. Yet, as noted in Chapter 6, the desegregation movement in Oakland was short-lived, and the city never had a significant desegregation policy (Kirp, 1982b). WOCS founders, though, were aware that they would be asked to justify a mission that seems to undermine school desegregation goals. The group did craft an answer to those who might accuse it of separatism, writing in its charter:

> Our goal is *not* to separate African Americans from other races and cultures. Quite the contrary, we recognize and celebrate the fact that our children must live and work in a diverse world. We also believe that they

must value and respect their own culture in order to value and respect the cultures of the many other groups that comprise California's increasingly diverse population. (West Oakland Community School, 1998a, pp. 5–6. Emphasis in original)

This paragraph was not simply a response to potential skeptics. It reflected a larger ideological grounding within the group.

WOCS founders built an alternative to desegregated schooling. But, contrary to the understanding of some school choice skeptics about the nature of school-based racial separatism,[3] WOCS founders were not romantically separatist by any means. Like their counterparts in the New York community control movement, WOCS founders and leaders held, rather, a nuanced, and sometimes ambivalent, approach to the goal of desegregation. This kind of approach has been historically quite common among both avowed integrationists and nationalists, as discussed in Chapter 2.

Given a narrow implementation of school integration—the kind provided by most current desegregation plans—WOCS founders generally rejected school desegregation as an effective tool of quality schooling or racial equality. Citing busing as her example, Hatano said in a 1998 interview with me: "The goal of integration in schools is something that's questionable in my mind, that simply putting kids of different races and backgrounds together could never serve as a real goal, a *meaningful* goal, to me." WOCS leaders also rejected as insufficient the existing models of desegregation alternatives, such as a "multiculturalism" that focuses only tokenistically and ceremonially on racial and cultural difference. As Peake said in a 1998 interview: "I'd hate it if we said 'we focus on multicultural education.' I . . . wouldn't be a part of WOCS at all. . . . I want a strong stance."

Given the limited existing models for either effective desegregation plans or genuine alternatives to desegregation, WOCS founders worked to define an approach that would best serve racial equality and quality schooling. Some grappled with a stance that would balance their belief that existing strategies were not serving African American students well with their desire (which varied from person to person, of course) for African American students to lead racially integrated lives.

While WOCS represented a fairly unusual educational strategy, even among current charter schools, it reflected a broader politics of race with respect to both schooling and interpersonal relationships. Some recent research shows that there has been a rise in support for political, economic, and cultural nationalist ideas among African Americans since the early 1980s (Levin, 1999; Muwakkil, 1997; Smith,

1996). Political scientist Robert C. Smith (1996) reports that a shift in attitudes of middle-class African Americans explains much of this phenomenon. But African Americans also are living increasingly integrated lives, reporting rising instances of interracial friendships, romantic relationships, and work collaborations, particularly among younger and more highly educated groups (Patterson, 1997). Some WOCS members lived this kind of seeming contradiction between ideology and daily reality. But I do not believe this constitutes a contradiction, as much as it demonstrates the complexity of racial identity. Of course, there was a lot of variation here. But many in the group had very close interracial friendships or relationships built around other shared similarities and interests, and many attended schools and then worked in organizations in which most of their colleagues were not African American. Some still, however—sometimes out of frustration, anger, exhaustion, or disappointment—expressed the difficulty of building such relationships.

In early discussions about the charter school, WOCS members tackled the tension between integrationism and nationalism in discussions of how they envisioned the school's graduates would choose to participate in American life. In the second meeting of the group, in the spring of 1996, in a discussion of the school's goals, members expressed that they would like WOCS graduates to go on to top colleges. This sparked a conversation about the goal of integration versus institution-building, about whether the group envisioned graduating young people who would enter existing institutions and excel in them without seeking to change them, enter institutions and change them from the inside, or build and participate in separate, alternative institutions. Group members agreed that they wanted to provide WOCS students with the tools they would need to make the choice to either participate in or opt out of mainstream American institutions.

The group reconciled this seeming contradiction in much the same way that their counterparts in the community control and Black Power movements had. Some WOCS leaders expressed that meaningful integration for African Americans could come only after a kind of "closing ranks": a knowledge and appreciation of African American history and culture and a focus on African American community-building. Hatano said in a 1998 interview:

> Someone who upholds integration as a goal is saying to me that one of the things that we can achieve through that is equality of experience and access for all kids. And it's interesting because *I* feel like the strategy that we're taking gets *closer* to achieving

that goal than just straight-out integration. . . . If we're going to talk about race, I think about empowering African American kids. At this age level, we have to create a safe place for them. And that safe place, I think especially at the middle school level, means. . . a place where kids with similar experiences are together and their experiences are validated. And, you know, it's from that position of strength that I think kids can really start to appreciate diversity.

Wilkes echoed this sentiment in an interview with a teacher candidate. She said:

> We want to focus on African Americans because we want students to know who they are. We want them to understand and love themselves. If they can't do that, then they can't understand and love others. We want to build their self-esteem so high that they can say: "I know who I am, now who are you?"

Hatano and Wilkes, among others in the group, believed that meaningful integration and interracial relationships could and should come to WOCS graduates through this kind of knowledge of self and community provided by a school that focused explicitly on African American history, identity, and community.[4]

CHARTER SCHOOLS AND THE PUBLIC SPHERE

The charter school movement and WOCS also provided a place for African American communities to confront the viability of public schooling in general, particularly as charter schooling is seen by many as kind of a hybrid form: still publicly supported and publicly accountable, but with substantially more autonomy than many public school options. Like the African American school choice initiatives before it, charter schooling raises significant critiques of public schooling—and of public institutions more generally. It also serves as a site to work out ambivalences toward public solutions to racial inequality and to weigh the limits and possibilities of public schools to serve racial equality.

CIBI and the Charter Option

I start this section with a non-WOCS example. The Council of Independent Black Institutions, as discussed in Chapter 4, always has been a federation of *private* schools, and CIBI members have greatly valued their freedom from public oversight and regulation. This independence was, in fact, a central piece of CIBI's founding mission. But, with the growth of the charter school movement, and of African-centered or Afrocentric charter schools, CIBI faced new competition for students and staff (Walker, 2001). While some CIBI schools began to investigate the charter school option, CIBI leaders considered whether charter schools could join the organization and whether existing CIBI schools could convert to charter status. With these deliberations, the organization confronted the question of what it meant, politically, to accept government support and oversight. The debate within CIBI turned on what it meant to be "independent" and whether CIBI could carry out its pan-African mission with substantial public support.

Some CIBI members saw charter schooling as an opportunity. The charter mechanism provided the possibility of a new, steady funding stream for the small, independent, largely tuition-driven schools in the CIBI network. Some CIBI schools sought to convert to charter school status. For instance, two long-standing CIBI members became charter schools: The New Concept Development Center in Chicago closed and reopened as the Betty Shabazz International Charter School and the Aisha Shule/W.E.B. Du Bois Preparatory Academy in Detroit converted to charter status (Walker, 2001).

Still others within CIBI saw charter schools as an absolute threat to CIBI's mission of independence. They saw charter schooling as an intrusion of government money, politics, and control into the project of African American nation-building and self-determination efforts. Former CIBI national executive officer Mwalimu J. Shujaa represents this position quite strongly. He has offered a stinging critique of charter schooling, arguing that charter schools are a new form of internal colonialism: rule and control by the U.S. government packaged as independence.

For example, in a speech to the CIBI Convention in November 2000, Shujaa urged:

> We can not [*sic*] forfeit the responsibility for doing that [nation] building work because somebody hands us a check. That's neo-colonialism. . . . In a sense, this is what we have done when we, in exchange for U.S. dollars, turn an institution that we have struggled to build into a charter school. (quoted in Walker, 2001, p. 95)

Noting the extent to which the debate on charter schools has been a challenge for CIBI, Shujaa theorized that the charter school option was a plot to ruin African American independent schooling, "undermining nationalist activity" (quoted in Hotep, 2001, p. 152), and dividing the IBI movement: "I honestly believe this charter school issue, if it wasn't intentionally put forward as a way of undermining independent African centered institutions, it's [sic] potential to do so is being exploited." He continued:

> I know that the analysts who work in government think tanks are paid well to figure out how to undermine progressive organizations. I don't think that CIBI has escaped the attention of those whose job it is to do this. And I think that they would certainly see the creation of charter schools as a way of doing that. (quoted in Hotep, 2001, p. 148)

Accepting government money for the project of gaining cultural, political, and financial independence from the same government seemed inconsistent and dangerous to Shujaa. It also, in his view and the view of others (see Walker, 2001), seemed to play right into the hands of those who opposed African American self-determination.

Shujaa and others also have talked about the fact that the charter school issue within CIBI has been a very contentious one. As Kofi Lomotey, a former CIBI national executive officer, summarized:

> We have a number of die-hards who believe that by definition a charter school cannot be an independent school. And we have another group of individuals who believe that we have to create charter schools within the public school system because that's the only way we're going to be able to sustain the organization. (quoted in Hotep, 2001, p. 87)

According to some CIBI activists, the charter school debate brought on a "period of crisis" and the threat of an "unraveling" of the organization (Shujaa, quoted in Hotep, 2001, pp. 146, 150). Ultimately, the organization decided to create an "associate membership" status for those schools within CIBI that had become charters before the organization took an official position on charter status (Lomotey, quoted in Hotep, 2001, p. 87). However, the organization's *Standards for Evaluating Afrikan-centered Educational Institutions*, updated in 2001, notes that charter schools do not meet CIBI's standard that its members receive funding "primarily from sources within and controlled by the Pan-Afrikan community" (CIBI, 2001, n.p.).

WOCS and Public Schooling

The West Oakland Community School was born just as CIBI debated whether it should join the charter movement. WOCS also began just as there was particular public attention to African American support of school privatization and vouchers. While debate on the role of African Americans in the voucher movement flourished, WOCS founders grappled with their own significant ambivalence about the public nature of their endeavor.

WOCS founders were glad for the space and freedom within the public sphere to build an alternative school. Unlike their predecessors in New York City in the 1960s, they were not seeking freedom from a predominantly White school board. Oakland's school leadership and city bureaucracy—like those in many cities across the country—was much more multiracial by the 1990s (Henig et al., 1999; Kirp, 1982b; Orfield, 1996e). Yet, like community control activists a generation earlier, WOCS leaders were skeptical about the amount of real freedom they would be "allowed." Many felt frustrated by the constraints that came with being a public school, particularly when weighed against the relatively meager financial benefits (particularly in California).

Some in the founding group also expressed skepticism about the truly radical potential of public schools, speaking of public schooling itself as antithetical to WOCS's mission. Wilkes said in an interview in 1999:

> There is a group of us who believe that education is about liberation. And so we're trying to create innovative schools. We're using charters as a strategy to create innovative schools that achieve that goal, when the truth is . . . public education has never been about liberation. Public education has been about preparing good soldiers. And so, at some point, the whole exercise becomes ridiculous. I mean . . . when I really sit myself down and say, "Okay, Marjorie, what do you want?" Well . . . I want children who are trained to think and fight for racial and economic justice. But . . . a charter school's not the right strategy to achieve that objective. . . . That's not what public education is after.

Public schools, many WOCS founders felt, generally maintained the kind of racial and economic inequality that they hoped to combat with their school.

Wilkes also expressed skepticism that WOCS founders could build the kind of school they dreamt of with public dollars and corresponding public oversight. She contended that charter schools were going to be increasingly regulated as the movement grew and became more entrenched. Echoing her counterparts in New York's community control movement, she said a number of times that charter schools were given a little freedom without the necessary support they needed to truly succeed in providing rigorous and relevant education for urban students of color. "Charter schools," she said in an interview with me in 1999, "are just public schools with enough rope to hang themselves."

But the relationship between WOCS and other public school options was complicated. For one thing, there was some difference of opinion within the group about the value of public schooling and public school reform. Not surprisingly, Greg Hodge, who had been a public school advocate through his nonprofit work at Urban Strategies and then his work as a member, then president, of the Oakland school board, expressed the opinion that charter schools were important to him as part of a broader project of public school change. He talked about charter schools as part of an ecology of schools in a neighborhood like West Oakland, and he envisioned that students could move in and out of charter and district schools during their school careers. Shawn Ginwright, by contrast, was skeptical of the potential of public schooling, as he questioned the limits of schooling, in general, to solve the individual and collective crises created by poverty and disenfranchisement. But, given "the limits to what the school can do given the crisis that our communities are in," even Ginwright saw a role for charter schools in public school reform. When asked about this in December 2003, he said of WOCS: "Certainly it provides an example of Black institution-building. . . . And then it simply provides a higher quality of education. And . . . it can push public schools to think differently about what it is they're doing with Black students."

WOCS founders also retained an affinity to other public schools in Oakland because they knew that they shared a significant political, financial, and educational fate with them. Politically, like their predecessors in the African American independent school movement, some WOCS founders remained attuned to the district schools out of their broad concern for African American education. They knew that most African American students in Oakland attended district schools, and the fact that WOCS could serve 50 students at a time did not erase their more general concern for African American educational equality. Financially, as well, WOCS founders knew that their school's viability was tied to the financial solvency of all California public schools— that they shared an interest with districts in working to increase state funding for public education (Forman, 2007). Educationally, also like their CIBI counterparts, WOCS founders expressed concern for public schooling in general because they recognized that most of their students would return to district schools for high school. Concern for post-WOCS high school options was one of the most frequent issues raised by parents of prospective WOCS students. Motivated by a concern for their students and the desire that the 3 years students spent at WOCS not be canceled out educationally by the 4 years they would then spend at the local public high school, WOCS leaders generally did not feel that they should simply retreat to their small school. In many ways, their institutional legacy depended on the quality of the education their graduates received once they left the charter middle school.

These political and institutional concerns were not all that linked WOCS to broader public schooling debates and concerns. WOCS also opened a small, newly energized space within public schooling, as it fostered a number of new partnerships and drew the involvement of people who might not have participated otherwise in public schools (Forman, 2007; Wells et al., 1999). Ultimately, as well, the school's founders placed substantial faith in the public system, despite their misgivings. A number of founding staff members quit stable jobs and placed themselves at considerable professional and personal financial risk to build the school within the public sphere, entrusting so much to a system that few in the group seemed to trust.

If the school's founding group could have started and sustained a tuition-free private school, many, though not all, might have been perfectly comfortable with this option. But, given the fact that WOCS founders chose a public option, the school provided a space to grapple with the limits and possibilities of public schooling. Through the school, WOCS founders reconciled a strong critique of public schooling with a recognition of the importance of schooling, particularly for African American students who were being underserved by Oakland's district schools.

NEW TERRAIN, SAME DEBATES

From 1996 to 2006, national and local politics of race and schooling came together in the West Oakland Community School. Its founders saw the charter school reform as a means to address the inadequate education that many of Oakland's African American students received. They also saw an opening through which to respond to the racial politics of the day. The failed "Ebonics" resolution in the district and, more significantly, the passage of the anti–affirmative action Proposition 209 in the state underscored the extent to which the public (particularly voters) generally no longer tolerated race-specific remedies to racial inequality in schooling. Unlike their predecessors in African American independent schools and their colleagues in the voucher movement, WOCS founders chose to counter this public sentiment with a public remedy. The existence and support of charter schooling in Oakland made a public alternative possible for WOCS founders, as they were able to build a semi-autonomous, self-governed small school within the public system. But, like IBI founders and like those community control activists who became disillusioned in New York City, many people involved with WOCS remained ambivalent about public schooling.

Like their counterparts in New York and in independent schools (voucher-supported or not) throughout the country, WOCS founders worked to define and build a strategy of racial justice through school choice. This group of predominantly African American educators and activists, endowed with relatively significant social and cultural capital, drew on a policy opening that allowed it to develop a state-sponsored African American–centered school. Within the story of this small school are embedded the most important questions of the race and school politics of our time. Within the story of this small school, as well, are the enduring questions and debates of African American politics of race and nation.

CHAPTER 9

School Choice and Hope

The existing debate on school choice is characterized by zealous oversimplification and lack of nuance on all sides. Some school choice reforms—particularly charter schools and vouchers—are now so contentious that there is almost no common ground in the vats of ink that have been spilled on them. As I have written about elsewhere (Rofes & Stulberg, 2004), the literature on school choice reforms often features scholars who talk past each other rather than to each other and who too-quickly and too-easily dismiss one another's work as overly dogmatic, methodologically problematic, or politically simplistic.

This narrow debate does not do justice to the complexity of choice reforms and the complexity of African American involvement in school choice efforts (Stulberg, 2004). Regardless of its educational contributions, school choice is a significant political development and set of reforms, in large part for the questions and insights about race and nation that it raises and the way in which it furnishes a site to debate central questions of racial equality and American participation. School choice reforms also are significant because they reveal a range of ways in which African American communities and leaders have retained involvement in schooling and hope for its potential, even in the face of frustration and despair with the educational status quo.

I have argued that the school choice mechanisms of the past 50 years have allowed many African American educators, parents, and leaders to remain hopeful about the possibility of schooling to impact social change and expand opportunity for African American young people. These mechanisms have provided a terrain to debate the meaning and means to racial equality, keeping active the long-standing conversation about whether and how the American welfare state and American institutions can and will serve a wide range of African American needs and interests.

How American institutions like schools can justly and equally serve African Americans is still—more than a half-century after the *Brown* decision—an open and urgent question. Sociologists and other social scientists of race and education, particularly those who dismiss as separatist and divisive any reform that hints of African American self-determination, would do well to learn from history. Scholars should acknowledge that the questions of race and nation that African American educators and their supporters have been asking for centuries lead to more complicated analyses and solutions than the ones that dominate our academic disciplines and our public debates.

AFRICAN AMERICAN SCHOOL CHOICE SINCE *BROWN*

The four school choice examples in this book—public school community control, African American independent schools, publicly funded school vouchers, and public charter schools—certainly are not identical in the way they approach issues of race and nation, integration and nationalism, and debates about American participation. They are each a product of the politics of their time, and this significantly informs their differences.

Ocean Hill–Brownsville's and East Harlem's community-controlled public schools were born during a heady time for the African American liberation movement, when Black Power emerged out of the civil rights movement and Black nationalism took new hold among African American activists, academics, and educators as a topic of discussion and a new approach to freedom struggles. Debates about the relative value of nationalism and integrationism filled coffee shops, dorm rooms, living rooms, meeting halls, classrooms, and the pages of the academic and popular press in the mid-1960s. The fight for community control of public schools in New York City became part of this broader conversation about how best to seek racial justice (Carmichael & Hamilton, 1967). The same can be said of schools that were part of the Council of Independent Black Institutions (CIBI) when the organization was founded in the early 1970s. Conversations within the African American independent school movement about how best to design educational institutions that served Black students reflected a larger conversation at the time among African American racial justice advocates and activists. These independent schools were an institutional site for the cultural nationalism and pan-Africanism of the late 1960s and early 1970s.

Charter schools and vouchers, in their latest and most politically viable iteration, developed in a political time when there was not the same kind of coordinated, national, social movement for racial justice. The national civil rights and Black Power movements had long waned by the time vouchers and charter schools became real policy options for African American communities. But, of course, racial justice activism has continued locally and nationally without a nationally unified movement. So, too, debates about integrationism and nationalism persist as part of broader debates about the meaning of racial justice and the extent to which it can be realized through American public institutions, regardless of whether they have a national and a mainstream forum. Voucher and charter school debates and reforms reflect these ongoing conversations and efforts. They also serve as responses to the local politics of race. We see, for instance, in the case of the West Oakland Community School (WOCS), that founders and school leaders began their school-building in large part as a response to African American underachievement in Oakland schools and as a response to the politics of affirmative action in the state of California.

Of course, the ways in which school-builders and reformers talk about the relevance of integrationism, the potential of America, public and private education, quality schooling, and racial equality are inflected with the language and politics of their time. Therefore, what it means to be integrationist or nationalist or something else altogether, for or against public schooling, supportive or opposed to participation in American mainstream institutions, varies in each of these cases.

So, too, each of the examples of school choice I examine here provides new and varied forms of hope. In the community control movement, many African Americans and other supporters of desegregation were losing hope that the city, after more than 10 years of broken promises, would act to integrate New York City schools. They turned to community control as a substitute to school desegregation. In the Council of Independent Black Institutions, independent school founders had lost hope in both public school community control and public school desegregation efforts, and they had little hope that the public school system could *ever* serve African American children well. They turned to independently run and financed schools that were fairly out of reach of public policy. The latest forms of vouchers and charter school reforms have come at a time of increasing school privatization, failing urban schools, a substantial and persistent racial and socioeconomic achievement gap, a lack of a national or unified movement for racial justice, and a retreat from civil rights–era remedies to racial inequality. For voucher and charter school supporters, these reforms have provided a new way for communities that were frustrated with the pace of district school change and flagging public attention to racial inequality in schooling to put new faith, effort, and hope into schooling.

Despite their differences, these four examples have some instructive commonalities. First, each example of African American school choice in this book demonstrates a strategy of effecting change from the relative margins, even the margins of African American activism. Though these initiatives were all fairly small and often did not represent the mainstream response to racial inequality in schooling in their time, each initiative impacted school and race reform in important (though not always positive) ways. Perhaps this is clearest in New York, where the community control movement's clash with the teachers' union brought the city's schools to a halt, eventually leading to state intervention in the form of legislation that divided the huge city into community districts. The community control movement affected race relations in the city as well, impacting community and citywide politics for years—even decades—to come.

Relatedly, each group of school choice activists in this book grappled with the kind of relationships they wanted to build with those from the relative center of politics and with the question of whether their more marginal movements required or could withstand support from the center. Each considered building precarious alliances, and in each example (with the exception of most IBIs), we see school solutions that were, to varying degrees, founded on and sustained by unstable coalitions. The New York groups, for example, relied—albeit skeptically—on the funding of the Ford Foundation and the political support of the Republican mayor, while WOCS leaders found themselves linked with colleagues in other charter schools with whom they often felt they had little in common. WOCS founders, like many African American voucher advocates in Milwaukee and elsewhere, also grappled with whether to seek out and accept funding from foundations and philanthropists with whom they shared little politically.

The four choice examples here share other similarities. In each case, participants defined the fundamental purpose of schooling quite broadly, heaping a heavy charge on their schools. All shared the belief that schools were institutions especially worthy of focus and relevant to the struggle for racial justice and equality. In this general view of schooling, they reflected the thinking of their counterparts for generations and their immediate predecessors in the civil rights movement (Tyack & Hansot, 1982). Yet participants and supporters of these school choice efforts envisioned a role for schools in movements for racial justice in a number of ways that were specific and common to these choice strategies.

Activists in all four school choice initiatives believed that their schools should serve racial justice by promoting community-building, personal and collective transformation, self-esteem- and racial identity–building, and leadership training. In all four cases, the school founders and reform activists I have introduced here intended for their schools to act as community institutions, contributing to the economic, social, and political life and growth of the communities they served. Participants in each of these efforts also envisioned African American futures and legacies through their schools, and they held their schools responsible for building these futures. Thus, each believed that their schools should act to cultivate African American leaders who had a strong and abiding sense of themselves as individuals and as part of political collectives. Schools that were part of the CIBI network, for example, stressed a heavily politicized Black identity grounded in the cultural nationalism and pan-Africanism of the time. Founders of these independent schools, like their counterparts in the public school community control movement and the West Oakland charter school, believed that building African American identity, community, and legacy should be a central purpose of African American schooling.

School choice activists in each example envisioned schools as life-or-death institutions, capable of bringing either cultural strength or cultural devastation to African American individuals and communities. This focus on schooling as potentially redemptive and healing was a prominent organizing force and rhetorical strategy in each of the four school reform efforts in this book. When Preston R. Wilcox (1970), a scholar and activist in New York who helped define and build the community control movement, wrote in 1970 that "[e]ducation must become a process that educates for liberation and survival—nothing less" (p. 11), he spoke for many of his descendents in the African American independent school movement, the voucher movement, and WOCS.

This understanding of schooling is a distinctive feature of the school choice efforts I examine here, but it certainly is not new or unfamiliar to American conceptions of schooling. As David Tyack and Elisabeth Hansot (1982) argue, common school reformers were institution-builders of the 19th century who were engaged in the "bureaucratization of redemption" (p. 34) as they built a system of American public schooling. They were motivated by a similar, if more explicitly religious, belief in the power of schools to redeem individuals and to build the burgeoning American nation on a common understanding of morality and purpose (see also Tyack, Kirst, & Hansot, 1980). Diane Ravitch (1974) argues that efforts like New York's community control movement demonstrated "a direct assault on the idea of the common school, that is, a school which is supported by all, controlled by all, and which propagates no particular religious, ideological, or political views" (p. 397). Yet these African American school choice reforms shared a basic fervor for schooling and deep belief in its redemptive power with their 19th-century (perhaps unlikely) predecessors.

Despite their faith in schooling as a mechanism for social change, leaders in each of these efforts also grappled with their faith in *public* schooling as the viable arena for such change. Each group was motivated by frustration and anger with existing public schools and public school bureaucracies. Choice activists wrestled with the extent to which they were willing to give up on the public schools, even as they challenged the very legitimacy of these schools. Leaders and educators in the New York and Oakland schools both demonstrated some desire to resuscitate the public sphere, as they worked to carve out semi-autonomous spaces that could be free and accessible to all students yet could benefit from some of the freedoms the private schools enjoyed. Despite their lack of faith in the public bureaucracy, they chose to place the fate of their efforts in this system. Independent school-builders in the 1970s and voucher advocates through the decades showed more of a willingness to opt out of public schooling, motivated by the belief that public schools were unlikely ever to adequately serve African American needs and interests. Yet even these private school activists struggled to maintain relationships with their public counterparts and to impact African American education more broadly. In the case of vouchers, advocates relied on public policy and public dollars to support their reform.

Whatever their orientation toward public schooling, school choice advocates in each case obscured the lines between public and private. They did so primarily through governance and funding relationships and concerns. In this, they joined, rather than departed from, much of American public schooling. As New York community control supporters pointed out, suburban schools relied on local control and a certain kind of self-determination in the way they were governed. All four school choice efforts in my work stressed independence in governance, despite the fact that the public alternatives were still subject to local and state oversight. On funding, the New York demonstration districts and WOCS, although public, could not have survived without private—primarily foundation—support. Similarly, a number of independent schools of the 1970s received public money to fund their programs, and vouchers were publicly funded, even as they were used to pay for private schooling.

Finally, school choice advocates in each of these examples grappled with the meaning and strategy of *racial equality* and worked to institutionalize their vision of racial justice through their school reform efforts. In each case, they strove for equality outside of explicitly desegregated schooling. After the access fights of the 1950s and early 1960s, New York community control provided an early alternative to Northern school desegregation. Independent schools in the 1970s offered a way to opt out of public school politics and their desegregation battles, as did vouchers. Charter schools like WOCS offered a solution, via school choice, that both emphasized the irrelevance of desegregation as an immediate goal *and* made desegregation relevant again by gaining the skeptical attention of desegregationists and furnishing a new site for the desegregation debate.

Each instance of African American school choice represented a response to desegregation politics (see Levin, 1999). There is some difference here within each of these cases, as we have seen that supporters of each initiative expressed varying degrees of apprehension about rejecting the goal of desegregation. There are also differences between the cases, given the progression of history. Born at a time when Northern cities were just beginning to contend with the mandate of *Brown*, the New York movement for community control was more entangled in the local politics of desegregation than were subsequent school choice reforms. By contrast, WOCS was certainly, in part, a response to the protracted failure of school desegregation. Yet the historical lack of desegregation mandate or marked enthusiasm in Oakland combined with the national turn away from desegregation as a remedy to unequal schooling meant that desegregation politics were not the most salient, or most inhibiting, to WOCS founders and supporters.

Despite these differences, activists in each effort shared a frustration with the way in which school desegregation was applied and a belief that school integration was not the most efficacious strategy of equal schooling at the time. More precisely, in each case, school activists focused primarily on African American educational self-determination and the importance of some autonomy in defining and meeting African American communities' varied needs through schools and other central institutions. Each, therefore, demonstrates a turn away from White-controlled institutions and multiracial public bureaucracies and a broadening of the definition of *racial equality* to include the redistribution of control, resources, and decision-making power.

School choice activists in each case derived their visions of racial justice from and in relationship to the social movements of the day. For instance, the focus on educational self-determination in both the public school community control and CIBI examples reflects Black nationalist thinking of the time, set against that of the civil rights movement. Similarly, the explicit focus on race by the West Oakland group grew, in the absence of a strong national movement, as a direct response to the California anti–affirmative action movement's denial of race as a still-important social and political category. Each group also understood its school efforts to be a contribution to a broader social movement, believing African American educational self-determination to be an important strategy of African American racial justice.

THE LIMITS OF SCHOOL CHOICE

School choice has been and remains part of a broader debate about the meaning of and means to educational equality for underserved students. The question of whether and how school choice mechanisms can serve as a way to equalize schooling for African American students and others who typically are not well served by American public schools is an open question and a very contentious one, given the political and politicized nature of the research and debate on school choice.

The historical and sociological importance of school choice reforms does not negate the important question of whether these reforms are educationally and politically successful. Academic outcomes matter, too, to the achievement of racial equality. As Christopher Jencks and Meredith Phillips reported in 1998, schooling matters now in ways that it did not even a generation ago, such that school achievement is now a significant determinant of adult attainment and earnings. A focus on reducing the enduring racial and socioeconomic achievement gap is, therefore, imperative to a concern for racial equality and justice. Hope unrealized in academically unsuccessful reforms is of limited utility to racial justice efforts. Unfortunately, thus far, we have reason to be quite modest about the impact that school choice reforms have had on African American educational equality.

Historical Assessment

History tells us that leaders of the African American school choice initiatives that I have examined here have been driven by the broader school and race politics of their time and considered that they had a contribution to make to these politics. History also tells us that these choice efforts have had an impact beyond their doors, particularly when they played a major role in city school politics or national race politics. Yet many of these school choice examples remained fairly marginal in their day.

Marginality cannot be read automatically as failure. Participants in some of these initiatives—such as WOCS and the schools that were part of CIBI—had a desire to remain independent and low-key and to go about the business of running successful alternative institutions. But, at the same time, even these small institutions hoped to make a broader impact on their geographic and racial communities.

A number of factors contributed to the fact that these choice reforms often remained small, outside of the center of broader school reform efforts in their cities, and were sometimes short-lived. First, resource challenges limited the impact of many of these schools. These challenges prevented them from expanding to serve significantly more students and made it difficult for some of these initiatives— like WOCS—to fulfill their missions and serve the students with the greatest needs. For example, in New York City in the late 1960s, the autonomy given to the community boards was never clearly defined and was not sufficiently publicly funded. In the case of vouchers, laws have specified that the dollar value of the voucher given to parents is fairly small, even when compared with the amount spent by the state on the same student in a public school. In the case of charter schools, state laws often do not provide full support to charter schools in the form of aid for school facilities, transportation, and special education services.

Relatedly, some of these choice schools faced the kind of organizational challenges that many new, underresourced institutions experience: challenges of leadership and mission maintenance, for example. These challenges sometimes, as in the case of WOCS, prevented these choice initiatives from flourishing and becoming more central players in their local districts. Also, leaders of these initiatives often had little time, inadequate resources, and few official channels, to partner with district schools or school systems. This limited their broader impact.

Finally, many of these reforms faced external scrutiny and pressure, and reformers needed to take time away from the business of teaching and learning to address this pressure. This limited the extent and success of the educational program they developed. The community control movement is the primary example of this: Political battles over the existence of the community district detracted from the success of the educational project in Harlem and Brooklyn. Even community control supporters conceded that—for a number of reasons—they did not sufficiently define how their vision should be realized in the classroom (Gittell, 1971; Wilson, 1970).

When we assess the extent to which these choice reforms and others like them can serve African American educational equality, we must contend with the fact that they often remained small, were sometimes quite short-lived, and sometimes—despite broad missions—could only serve quite small groups of young people. We can learn from history here, as we go about the messy business of assessing current choice reforms and their ability to mitigate educational inequality.

The Limits of Charters and Vouchers

Individual schools supported by choice mechanisms *can* offer empowering, educationally superb, life-changing options for some students and communities. They can provide opportunities for communities of color and urban communities—which have often been severely underserved by the public schools—to define and meet their needs through their schools (Rofes & Stulberg, 2004). There are also, as I have noted earlier, many forms of daily and systemwide school choice that I do not assess here. But, as they now exist, the current forms of school choice that are at the center of American attention and debate—vouchers and charter schools, in particular—are *not* poised to be systemic solutions to the continuing problem of educational inequality for African American students and communities. This is true, I believe, for a number of reasons.

For many scholars, the primary reason that charter schools and vouchers could never be systemic solutions to educational inequality is that these reforms ostensibly exacerbate—or at least do nothing to alleviate—racial segregation in schooling (see citations in Chapter 6). I am less concerned about this than many others are. This is not because I do not care about racial integration or do not believe that school integration and the racial integration of social life are worthy and important goals. Clearly, they are, and there are many documented benefits of integrated schooling for children of color and White children see "Brief of 553 Social Scientists as Amici Curiae in Support of Respondents," amicus brief nos. 05-908 & 05-915, *Parents Involved in Community Schools v. Seattle School District No. 1*). But, as it has been implemented in the past few decades and in the context of a diminished political will to create and maintain strong school integration programs, I do not believe that school desegregation is the only remedy to unequal schooling for African Americans. I also remain critical of school choice literature that is too narrowly focused on supporting desegregated schooling above all else (see Rofes & Stulberg, 2004). Furthermore, I believe that racially homogenous charter schools in communities of color are not necessarily an affront to racial integration. These schools, when they are successful, may, in fact, prepare their graduates to have the option to live more integrated personal and professional lives.

This question of the relationship between segregated schooling and integrated adult lives deserves significant research attention in the future (Wells & Crain, 1994; see also "Brief of 553 Social Scientists as Amici Curiae in Support of Respondents").

I do, however, have other concerns about the systemic potential of charter schools and vouchers. For one, charter schools—like the schools of the public school community control movement before them—generally face the same funding and other resource inequalities between urban and suburban, White and African American, poor and wealthy districts as their district counterparts do (Fuller, Gawlik, Gonzales, Perk, & Gibbings, 2003; Wells et al., 1999). As education scholars Jean Anyon (1997), Pedro Noguera (2003), and Jeffrey Henig and his colleagues (1999) have argued, urban school politics are intricately tied to urban politics in general, which are heavily inflected with the politics of race and class that produce unequal and inadequate schooling for low-income students and students of color. Second, charter schools—like their predecessors in the African American independent school movement—still serve very few students. This, I believe, is unlikely to change, particularly if we (as we should) pay careful attention to quality when chartering and renewing school applications. Finally, I believe that charter schools like the West Oakland Community School will lose vital support, as African American alternative schools have in the past, when they appear too separatist, too militant, or too political. This limits charter school innovation.

Vouchers, even more than charters, have significant limitations as a systemic option. First, for political reasons, I doubt that vouchers ever will be worth enough money to fund the kind of educational options that are available to upper-middle-class and wealthy families. The approximately $2,250, $6,300, or $7,500 that publicly funded vouchers are maximally worth in Cleveland, Milwaukee, and the District of Columbia, respectively, does not buy elite private schooling in these cities (for these figures, see Haynes, 2005; Wisconsin Department of Public Instruction, n.d.; *Zelman*, 2002). Rather, this limited funding restricts the choices available to its recipients, providing a semblance of full choice while leaving in place the choice gap between wealthy and low-income families (Bulman, 2006). Vouchers, then, act as a reform on the cheap, generally costing the state much less than it would cost to educate a child in the relevant public districts (Forman, 2005). For example, according to National Center for Education Statistics data, compiled by the pro-voucher Center for Education Reform in April 2006, the District of Columbia spends $15,489 per pupil on its public school students, while the vouchers it provides are worth about half of this amount (Center for Education Reform, 2006). Vouchers do not, therefore, significantly redistribute educational resources to low-income families, and the political possibilities are slim that they will ever be significantly redistributive.

Relatedly, a voucher is a tuition check to private schools; it is not an acceptance letter. Schools still exercise choice over whom they admit. So, vouchers do not greatly improve access. We have seen that the schools that do accept vouchers generally are limited to schools in central cities, often religious schools. This only expands options for students in a limited way. For example, as noted in the *Zelman* decision, while 56 private schools chose to accept vouchers as part of the Cleveland program, 82% of these schools were religious and none of the participating schools was a suburban public school. Similarly, a *Washington Post* story in September 2005 reported that the number of high schools that participated in the District of Columbia's voucher program was limited by the fact that the voucher did not cover the cost of tuition at many private high schools in and around D.C. (Haynes, 2005).

Another shortcoming of both charter schools and vouchers as systemic reform possibilities is the extent to which they actually impact school districts and spur districtwide change. According to both charter and voucher proponents, these choice mechanisms are supposed to inject competition into public systems and, thus, spur innovation—or, at least, improvement—in district schools. Although this subject needs much more research attention (e.g., Campbell, DeArmond, Guin, & Warnock, 2006), there is some evidence from the earlier years of these reforms that this is not happening to the extent imagined by proponents, particularly in larger and urban districts (Rofes, 1998).

Finally, and quite importantly, it is not clear that charter schools or vouchers can be systemic solutions to the underachievement of African American students. Research on the impact of vouchers and charter schools on student achievement often gets caught in the bitter debate about school choice. Within the contentious politics of choice, there is no agreement about whether charters and vouchers work to boost student achievement. More work needs to be done in the area of student achievement and choice mechanisms, and the work should remain as much above the political fray as possible. We have yet to reach conclusive answers to the question of whether voucher programs and charter schools serve the academic interests of African American students. And these results vary significantly by local context. But we do have evidence that these reforms certainly are not cure-alls.

There are a number of stellar charter schools that serve predominantly African American student bodies. These are truly the best of the best of American schooling. They top the schools in their states, combining rigorous academics with caring, small-school environments that allow students to thrive academically and socially. There is also careful quantitative evidence to suggest that, when compared with students in their neighboring district schools, charter school students generally achieve at higher levels on reading and math state tests. This is true, as well, for African American students in charter schools (e.g., Hoxby, 2004). These kinds of local comparisons provide meaningful, quality data that indicate that charter schools may be quite effective in boosting student achievement (for a useful discussion of the issues surrounding the assessment of charter schools and student achievement, see Betts & Hill, 2006).

But there also is some evidence that charter school students are underperforming on standardized tests. This examination of charter effectiveness is quite blunt, in that it compares students in different local contexts in very different types of schools, using performance on the nationally administered National Assessment of Educational Progress (NAEP) test (see Christensen & Angel, 2005, for an important discussion of the limitations of drawing conclusive comparisons between district and charter schools from NAEP data). But it provides a broad way to compare district and charter school performance. The highly publicized and hotly debated teachers' union study of 2003 NAEP data suggested that, in general, charter school students on fourth- and eighth-grade math tests and fourth-grade reading tests tended to score about a half-grade level of schooling behind their district school counterparts (Nelson et al., 2004). A study of the same 2003 data by the federal Education Department, which supports charter schools under President George W. Bush, confirmed that charter school fourth graders underperformed relative to their district school counterparts (see Schemo, 2006b). But, interestingly, despite these very broad differences, there was no statistically significant disparity between African American student NAEP achievement in charter and noncharter public schools, nor was there a larger gap between the scores of White and African American students at charters and noncharter public schools (Nelson et al., 2004). Data released in October 2005, on the 2005 NAEP tests, seem to indicate that the gap between fourth graders in district and charter schools had closed, but that charter school fourth graders on the math test and eighth graders on both the reading and math tests still underperformed relative to their district peers (National Alliance for Public Charter Schools, 2006; Schemo, 2006b).

Like the research on charter school effectiveness, the work on the impact of vouchers on student performance is incredibly contested, perhaps even more so. Given the methodological complexity of isolating the singular impact of vouchers on educational achievement, compounded by the controversial nature of vouchers themselves, it is difficult to assess the punch line of this research (for a range of findings on various voucher programs, see, e.g., American Federation of Teachers, 2005; Greene, Peterson, & Du, 1999; Greene & Forster, 2002; Hoxby, 2001; Metcalf, Muller, Boone, Tait, Stage, & Stacey, 1998; Rouse, 1998; 2000; Witte, 1998). Studies generally fail to document much academic success in either publicly or privately funded voucher programs. Voucher opponents, of course, assert the ineffectiveness of vouchers (American Federation of Teachers, 2005), and even pro-voucher researchers acknowledge that vouchers have had limited impact on academic achievement to date (Howell, Wolf, Campbell, & Peterson, 2002).

In highly publicized findings in 2000, a group of researchers provided evidence that African American students receive the only significant boost from voucher program participation. This research team conducted studies of privately funded voucher programs in New York City; Dayton, Ohio; and Washington, D.C. It found that only African American students, after 2 years in the program, demonstrated a test-score gain (Howell, Wolf, Peterson, & Campbell, 2001; Howell et al., 2002). This conclusion was widely reported in the national media (Mathews, 2000; Safire, 2000; Wyatt, 2000). It drew significant criticism from scholars who questioned the findings, political motivation, rhetorical strategies, and methodological choices of the researchers (Carnoy, 2001; Molnar & Achilles, 2000; Rothstein, 2000; Zernike, 2000). One such criticism even came from a research group that helped collect data for the study (Mathematica, 2000).

Unlike their choice counterparts in preceding decades, charter schools and vouchers often are hailed as a potential systemic solution to unequal schooling, even despite their mixed achievement reviews and the organizational and political challenges they face. These choice mechanisms often stand in for an educational policy for all public schools, as they are offered up as a substitute for a school reform plan when city leaders do not know what to do about the failing schools for which they are responsible. In this way, they take much-needed public policy attention away from public school systems and systemic reform efforts (Gittell, 1998; Henig, 1994). Cities like Oakland, that are documented failures in providing adequate education for their African American students, need systemic solutions. Charter schools and vouchers can be important tools of self-governance, educational excellence, political and educational organizing, and community development (Rofes & Stulberg, 2004). They also can promote vigorous and useful public discussion on and attention to the limits and possibilities of public schooling. But, so far, they are not the equivalent of systemwide reform in schooling or in racial inequality more broadly.

THE POTENTIAL OF SCHOOL CHOICE

African American participation in school choice reforms over the past 50 years can be seen as a hopeful act, a retention of faith in schooling; and, until there is broad equality in educational opportunity and results, African Americans will continue to turn to school choice options for hope. But, as we have seen, this hope will not be easily realized. I believe that some school choice reforms can provide part of the solution to educational inequality. But an analysis of history and of current choice reforms teaches us that the existence of these choice reforms cannot be an excuse for the state to abdicate its responsibility to educate all of its citizens. For hope to be realized in these reforms, we need a strong state.

I believe that school choice mechanisms have the best chance of effecting significant change if we can carve out a more active role for the state in educational reform. This is counter to the rationale of some choice supporters who believe that small government serves citizens best. I believe that charter schools must have more government support and oversight in some areas if they are to best serve African American students; and vouchers are simply too much of an opt-out from public regulation and public protection, particularly in the form that would be politically palatable to most of the American public, to adequately serve educational equality.

There is some evidence, from the American Federation of Teachers study of NAEP data, that charter schools that are more tightly regulated and are held highly accountable to state oversight do better, academically, than their counterparts in states that provide more autonomy and less oversight to their charters (Nelson et al., 2004). This question of the relationship between charter school autonomy and student achievement deserves much more research attention.

For a political progressive, the recommendation for a stronger state requires a hefty dose of optimism. But I believe that the best model for school reform lies with an active and involved federal government, with funding and protection geared toward equity and resource redistribution, but with space for local freedom, innovation, and control. That an expanded state and federal government should support an enlivened and emboldened local polity is a concept that New York community control participant and advocate Marilyn Gittell and her coauthor Laura McKenna call "progressive federalism" (Gittell & McKenna, 1998, p. 4; see also Gittell, 1998). Along with Gittell and McKenna, a number of African American scholars and others concerned with racial and economic justice recognize the importance of the balance between the devolution and centralization of power. Many believe that African American freedom and equality are best served by active government participation, not its opposite (Noguera, 2003; Patterson, 1997; Unger & West, 1998).

With an actively involved and progressively minded state, one that focuses on redistributing resources to lower-income students and their schools, charter schools—but not vouchers—could be a part of systemic school reform (Rofes & Stulberg, 2004). Charters can be one of many kinds of school options—"one tool among many" (Henig, 1994, p. 205)—that are available to parents, who have the right to choose schooling for their children. Charter schools of this kind will serve students best when there is substantial, deliberate, nongratuitous oversight and quality control that is combined with the provision of local autonomy and educational self-determination: "a stronger, more astute, and more confident bureaucracy, not its opposite" (Henig, 1994, p. 211). To be sure, this is a challenging combination of centralization and decentralization (Wells, 1993). How to achieve this requires much more research attention and much more innovation on the part of school leaders and public policymakers.

"AMERICA WILL BE . . ."

After the *Brown* decision in 1954, African American educators and civil rights leaders had a lot of hope that the public schools could open up to serve—and serve equally—African American children. In fact, attorney Thurgood Marshall, who had argued the desegregation cases before the Supreme Court for the NAACP, predicted that school segregation would be eliminated completely within 5 years (Kluger, 1975). This hope, after a decade of inaction on desegregation in cities and towns across the country, had eroded. African American activists and their supporters began to demand alternatives, in the form of school choice efforts like community control of public schools, the building of private schools, and the support of private schooling through voucher programs. Since the 1950s, school choice has been a site to grapple with despair, anger, and hope in America and its institutions.

There is no neat resolution to this. The American welfare state continues to fail African Americans time and time again. We witnessed this in a profound and tragic way in August 2005, when Hurricane Katrina ravaged New Orleans and the Gulf Coast. To the average consumer of 24-hour cable news, it seemed as if most White people escaped the hurricane relatively unscathed, while those wading through the waters looking for loved ones and personal belongings, those stuck in filthy rescue centers, and those who simply did not survive, were almost entirely African American. As scholar and prolific commentator on American race politics Michael Eric Dyson (2006) eloquently wrote of the sight after Katrina: "The suffering on screen created cognitive dissonance. . . . This surely couldn't be the United States of America—and how cruelly that term seemed to mock those poor citizens who felt disunited and disconnected and just plain dissed by their government" (p. 2). Katrina was a very visual moment of despair. It signified a failure of the American welfare state to protect and save African Americans and a loss of faith, by many African Americans, in the will of the state to do so.

In this context, we need more than school choice to redeem American education and to achieve racial equality in schooling, just as, as is currently being attempted, we need more than charter schools to resurrect public schooling in post-Katrina New Orleans. As a country, we still have a long way to go to create schooling that would live up to Langston Hughes's vision of what America and its institutions should be. We have a long way to go before we reach a time when African American children have unimpeded access to rigorous and relevant schooling and African American communities have the autonomy and power to define and meet their own needs through their schools. We have a long way to go until *all* Americans believe that this struggle for racial equality—in schooling and otherwise—is *their* struggle.

In December 2003, reflecting on both the difficulties and joys of her involvement in the West Oakland Community School, founder Marjorie Wilkes mentioned the Black National Anthem, "Lift Every Voice and Sing," which begins hopefully with a call to action and faith in a "new day." She said that she had been thinking, in particular, about these lines of the Anthem:

Stony the road we trod,
Bitter the chastening rod,
Felt in the days when hope unborn had died

Hope has died, she reflected, in communities like West Oakland. The power of schools like WOCS, she said, was that, at their best, they could change this. She envisioned that WOCS could train young leaders who could "catalyze hope" in their communities.

In the African American school choice examples in this book, we see parents, educators, and activists living in tension with the promises and the perils of America. They have the courage to dream a future through American public schools, to hope that schools will actually serve the needs of African American families and communities. This is a very American dream: a dream that, in the face of centuries of evidence to the contrary, hope will not go unborn. Schools will be the birthplace of hope.

Notes

Chapter 2

1. Madhubuti (1973) explains his choice to use the designation *Afrikan*, with a "k," which he views as a more indigenous and authentic spelling than *Africa(n)*, with a "c": "Most vernacular or tradtional languages on the continent spell Afrika with a K; therefore the use of K is germain [*sic*] to us" (p. 13).

Chapter 3

1. The story of I.S. 201 in the context of New York desegregation and community control politics has been told by a number of participants and historians. See, for instance, Berube and Gittell, 1969; Eisenberg, 1971; Fantini et al., 1970; Jones, 1966; Minter, 1967; Ports, 1970; and Wasserman, 1970.

2. Ford provided material resources to the community control movement, in the form of seed money and continued financial and technical support. The foundation made clear from the beginning of its involvement that it felt its financial role should be to support the start-up phase of the demonstration projects. It did award additional funds, mostly through its grants to Marilyn Gittell's Institute for Community Studies. But it continued to insist that the Board of Education needed to provide the bulk of financial support. In a November 13, 1968, press release, Ford claimed that, despite its financial backing, the support it provided for the Ocean Hill project made up less than 3% of the district's $7.3 million budget (p. 5). The districts also raised additional public and private funds from a number of local and national foundations and universities, such as the Carnegie Corporation and the New York Foundation (Fantini & Magat, 1968; Gittell, 1971).

Chapter 4

1. Before the passage of the Civil Rights Act of 1964, during the 1962–63 academic year, 99% of African American students in the South attended schools that were virtually all-Black. By 1974–75, this number had dropped

to 14%, while, during the same year, in the Northeast and Midwest, 32% and 45%, respectively, of Black students attended such segregated schools (Orfield, 1981, p. 25).

2. For Latino students, the schools were significantly more segregated. For African Americans, there was a large national drop in the percentage of Black students attending schools that were comprised predominantly of students of color, from 76.6% of Black students in 1968, to 63.3% in 1986. But the largest drop occurred between 1968 and 1972, and numbers have remained fairly steady since then. The same trend is true of Black students attending schools that are "intensely" segregated, with student bodies that are 90–100% students of color. This number fell from 64.3% of Black students in 1968 to 38.7% in 1972 to 32.5% in 1986 (Orfield et al., 1989).

3. These principles, also the foundation of the Kwanzaa holiday that Karenga developed, are *Umoja* (unity), *Kujichagulia* (self-determination), *Ujima* (collective work and responsibility), *Ujamaa* (cooperative economics), *Nia* (purpose), *Kuumba* (creativity), and *Imani* (faith).

4. African American enrollment in private schools rose in the 1970s and declined a little in the early 1980s. Williams (1986) attributes the decline in the 1980s to a decrease in African American enrollment in parochial schools. Slaughter and Johnson (1988) report that by the end of the 1970s, approximately 7.3% of African American elementary school students enrolled in private (including parochial) schools. They note that the percentage of private school student bodies comprised of African American students rose from 3.7% in 1967 to 5.5% a decade later (p. 2). This number reflects, as well, the opening up of previously unavailable private schools, such as elite independent and boarding schools (Schneider & Shouse, 1992; Williams, 1986). African American enrollment in these institutions was helped by the development of programs in the 1960s, like the well-known A Better Chance (ABC) program, designed to enroll students of color in the country's most prestigious independent schools (Griffen & Johnson, 1988; Speede-Franklin, 1988; Zweigenhaft & Domhoff, 1991).

Chapter 5

1. As Henig (1994) notes in his discussion of the race politics of school choice, many Southern states employed two related choice strategies to evade desegregation. First, they instituted "freedom of choice" plans, designed to give a choice of desegregated public schooling in name only by making it bureaucratically and logistically difficult, generally unthinkable, and sometimes outright dangerous for African American students to choose to attend White public schools. Second, they employed versions of these private school tuition grant programs, many of which were considered part of the "freedom of choice" option (see also Phillips, 1961; "U.S. Court Rules," 1969).

2. Milwaukee had an early history with vouchers, as it was one of the districts that—prompted by African American parents and school leaders—

debated and ultimately rejected involvement in Jencks's OEO program in the early 1970s (Holt, 2000).

Chapter 6

1. For a few important exceptions, for broader research on race and choice, see Forman (2005) for an extensive historical look at school choice, and Saporito and Lareau (1999) for an interesting study of how school choices are made with respect to race by White and African American parents.

2. West Oakland's residents remain largely African American. According to the 2000 census count, approximately 35% of Oakland residents were African American, compared to almost 65% of West Oakland residents (City of Oakland, n.d.; Urban Strategies Council, n.d). During the 2005–06 school year, the school-going population at the middle school across the street from WOCS, Lowell Middle School, was 79% African American, and 71% of Lowell's students participated in the free or reduced-price lunch program (California Department of Education, 2007).

Chapter 7

1. The demographics of WOCS and its neighboring school, Lowell, were quite similar by race and class, and, for the most part, Lowell is the district school that most of the students at WOCS would have attended had they remained in the district. But there were some differences. While the vast majority of WOCS students lived in West Oakland and otherwise would have attended Lowell, some WOCS students came from outside of the city to attend the charter school. So, these data compare schools without identical student populations. Comparing WOCS scores with scores of students in the neighboring school and the district as a whole might not capture some of the differences in student population. To isolate and measure school effects and success, therefore, we would need to control for these differences.

2. Use of an initial rather than a name to identify a WOCS staff member indicates that I did not have permission to use this staff member's real name.

3. There is some effort under way now to change the tenor of this relationship between Oakland Unified and similar districts and their charter schools. According to Rofes (2005), the recognition that charter–school district relations in California (as elsewhere) seemed to be "heading for an explosive confrontation" (p. 25), prompted Alameda County's superintendent of schools, Sheila Jordan, to organize a task force of district, charter, and other education leaders to improve district-charter relationships and "support the equitable coexistence of school districts and charter schools" (p. 27). Oakland Unified's charter school coordinator was a member of this task force.

4. Wilkes stepped down from her co-director role at the end of the 2001–02 school year, but she remained on staff, as development director, until June 2003. Hatano moved from co-director for curriculum and instruction to executive

director for the 2002–03 school year, took a short-term transitional position as a development advisor, and then resigned as a staff member at the school. Both Wilkes and Hatano remained formally connected to WOCS as board members through the summer of 2005 and remained informally very involved, in almost a daily way, as advisors to WOCS staff members and parents.

Chapter 8

1. A WOCS budget drafted in late 2003 estimated that the school would receive $4,716 per pupil during the 2004–05 school year, allotted by average daily attendance (ADA). The 2004–05 state average per ADA expenditure (or cost) was $7,127, while Oakland Unified's expense per ADA was $9,019 (California Department of Education, 2006).

2. Bulman and Kirp (1999) identify this tactic as a broader trend in the current politics of choice, writing that "voucher advocates support charters as a foot in the door of the public school monopoly" (p. 61).

3. See, for instance, Wells and Crain's (1997) discussion of African American "separatists" in their study of the voluntary metropolitan desegregation program in St. Louis and their classification of White and Black political ideologies in the city (p. 16).

4. Fuller and his colleagues (1996) identify a tension between "ethnic localisms" and "assimilation" among school choice activists of color. They write: "In Milwaukee, the vibrant inner-city voucher program was begun by ethnic activists on the Left who sought higher-quality schools (implicitly linked to the goal of assimilation) *and* schools that would focus directly on African-American or Latino topics within the curriculum (a particularistic, community-centered goal). Historically, the modern state has seen ethnic localisms as provincial or backward, threatening to nation-building. But many parents in pluralistic America seem to want both assimilation and particularistic forms of socialization" (p. 14).

References

25 years later, Foster remains education hero. (1998, November 6). *Oakland Tribune*, p. news-1.

A. Philip Randolph Institute. (1968, September 19). An appeal to the community from Black trade unionists. *New York Times*, p. 39.

Abubadika, M. I. (1972). *The education of Sonny Carson*. New York: W. W. Norton.

African-American Teachers Association. (1967, September). *African-American Teachers Association demands self-control, self-determination, and self-defense for schools in the Black community*. Robert F. Wagner Labor Archives of the Tamiment Institute Library. New York University. UFT collection.

Akoto, A. (1994). Notes on an Afrikan-centered pedagogy. In M. J. Shujaa (Ed.), *Too much schooling, too little education: A paradox of Black life in White societies*. Trenton, NJ: Africa World Press.

Allen, R. L. (1990). *Black awakening in capitalist America*. Trenton, NJ: Africa World Press, Inc.

American Federation of Teachers, AFL-CIO. (2005). *School vouchers: The research track record: student achievement*. Washington, DC: American Federation of Teachers, AFL-CIO. Retrieved October 27, 2006, from http://www.aft.org/pubs-reports/teachers/VoucherTrackRecord2005.pdf.

Anderson, J. (1997). *Bayard Rustin: Troubles I've seen. A biography*. Berkeley: University of California Press.

Anderson, J. D. (1988). *The education of Blacks in the South, 1860–1935*. Chapel Hill: The University of North Carolina Press.

Anti-Semitism?: A statement by the teachers of Ocean Hill–Brownsville to the people of New York. (1968, November 11). *New York Times*, p. 55.

Anyon, J. (1997). *Ghetto schooling: A political economy of urban educational reform*. New York: Teachers College Press.

Apple, M. W., & Pedroni, T. C. (2005, September). Conservative alliance building and African American support of vouchers: The end of *Brown's* promise or a new beginning? *Teachers College Record, 107*(9), 2068–2105.

Applebome, P. (1996, December 20). School district elevates status of Black English. *New York Times*, p. A8.

Archer, J. (1998b, June 24). Black parents at heart of tug of war. *Education Week, 17*(41), 1.

Areen, J., & Jencks, C. (1972). Educational vouchers: A proposal for diversity and choice. In R. C. Rist (Ed.), *Restructuring American education: Innovations and alternatives.* New Brunswick, NJ: Transaction Books

Asante, M. K. (1994, Autumn). Afrocentricity, race, and reason. *Race & Reason, 1*(1), 20–22.

Associated Press. (1993, November 3). Voters in California reject proposal on school vouchers. *New York Times,* p. A24.

Associated Press. (1999a, February 17). San Francisco settles lawsuit on desegregation of schools. *New York Times,* p. A17.

Associated Press. (1999b, August 17). Florida begins voucher plan for education. *New York Times,* p. A15.

Associated Press. (2006, February 5). Hyde School becomes a model for public charter schools. Retrieved February 8, 2006 from http://www.boston.com/news/local/maine/articles/2006/02/05/hyde_school_becomes_a_model_for_public_charter_schools

Ayers, B. (2001). *Fugitive days: A memoir.* Boston: Beacon Press.

Bailey, C. (1998, September 21). Brown urges "make our own change." *Oakland Tribune,* p. 2.

Baker, R. E. (1957, March 3). Virginia "buys" a year of segregation. *Washington Post and Times Herald,* p. E3.

Bell, D. (1989). The case for a separate Black school system. In W. D. Smith & E. W. Chunn (Eds.), *Black education: A quest for equity and excellence.* New Brunswick, NJ: Transaction Publishers.

Bell, D. (1992). *Faces at the bottom of the well: The permanence of racism.* New York: Basic Books.

Bellamy, C. (1973, August 30). Voucher system gets mixed reactions. *Bay State Banner,* p. 1.

Belluck, P. (1998, June 15). School ruling shakes Milwaukee. *New York Times,* p. A12.

Benson, J. (2006, April 16). Newark, the next generation. *New York Times,* section 14NJ, p. 6.

Berube, M. R. (1969a, April 11). Black Power and the learning process. *Commonweal,* 98–101.

Berube, M. R. (1969b). Maurice Berube replies. In M. R. Berube & M. Gittell (Eds.), *Confrontation at Ocean Hill–Brownsville: The New York school strikes of 1968.* New York: Frederick A. Praeger.

Berube, M. R., & Gittell, M. (Eds.). (1969). *Confrontation at Ocean Hill–Brownsville: The New York school strikes of 1968.* New York: Frederick A. Praeger.

A better option than busing? (1978, September 19). *Chicago Tribune,* p. B2.

Betts, J., & Hill, P. T. (2006, May). *Key issues in studying charter schools and achievement: A review and suggestions for national guidelines.* NCSRP White Paper Series, No. 2. Seattle: National Charter School Research Project, Center on Reinventing Public Education.

Black teachers hold 3–Day meeting here (1972, 22 April). *Amsterdam News.*

Bonsteel, A. (1997). The Proposition 174 story. In A. Bonsteel & C. A. Bonilla. *A choice for our children: Curing the crisis in America's schools.* San Francisco: ICS Press.

Bordett, D. (1970, February 26). Parents look at tuition voucher plan. *Bay State Banner,* p. 6.

Bositis, D. A. (2001, August 15). School vouchers along the color line. *New York Times,* p. A23.

Bowers, M. A. (1984). *The Independent Black Educational Institution: An exploration and identification of selected factors that relate to their survival.* Ed.D. dissertation. Atlanta University.

Bracey, J. H., Jr., Meier, A., & Rudwick, E. (Eds.). (1970). *Black nationalism in America.* Indianapolis: The Bobbs-Merrill Company, Inc.

Brief of 553 social scientists as amici curiae in support of respondents. Amicus brief nos. 05-908 & 05-915. *Parents Involved in Community Schools v. Seattle School District No. 1.* Retreved November 16, 2007 from http://www.civilrightsproject.ucla.edu/research/deseg/amicus_parents_v_seatle.pdf.

Brooke, J. (1997, December 27). Minorities flock to cause of vouchers for schools. *New York Times,* p. A1.

Brookins, C. C. (1984). *A descriptive analysis of ten independent Black educational models.* M.A. thesis. Michigan State University.

Brown, E. (1992). *A taste of power: A Black woman's story.* New York: Anchor Books.

Brown, J. (1998, May 12). Mayoral candidates discuss ways to market Oakland. *Oakland Tribune,* p. local–3.

Brown, P. L. (2001, August 24). Oakland school's military bearing rankles some. *New York Times,* p. A11.

Brownsville, Ocean-Hill Independent Local School Board of District 17. (1966, October 18). *Memorandum and petition.* Mayors Advisory Panel Collection, box 14566, folder 2, "IS 201," Ford Foundation Archives.

Brumer, L. (1999, September). Charter school blues. *East Bay Monthly, 29*(12), 19–21.

Bulman, R. C.(2006, August). *The progressive potential of school vouchers.* Paper presented at the American Sociological Association Annual Meeting. Montreal, Canada.

Bulman, R. C., & Kirp, D. L. (1999). The shifting politics of school choice. In S. D. Sugarman & F. R. Kemerer (Eds.), *School choice and social controversy: Politics, policy, and law.* Washington, DC: Brookings Institution Press.

Burawoy, M. (1991a). The extended case method. In M. Burawoy et. al., *Ethnography unbound: Power and resistance in the modern metropolis.* Berkeley: University of California Press.

Burawoy, M. (1991b). Introduction. In M. Burawoy et. al., *Ethnography unbound: Power and resistance in the modern metropolis.* Berkeley: University of California Press.

Byndloss, D. C. (2001, November). Revisiting paradigms in Black education: Community control and African-centered schools. *Education and Urban Society, 34*(1), 84–100.

California Department of Education. (n.d.). *Charter school database.* Retrieved October 18, 2006, from http://www.cde.ca.gov.

California Department of Education. (2001). *Comparing scores.* Retrieved August 10, 2004, from http://star.cde.ca.gov/star2001/help/ScoreComparisons. html.

California Department of Education. (2006, March 27). *2004–05 current expense per Average Daily Attendance (ADA).* Retrieved June 5, 2007, from http://www.cde.ca.gov/ds/fd/ec/documents/currentexpense0405.xls.

California Department of Education. (2007, April 10). *School demographic characteristics: 2006 Base Academic Performance Index (API) report.* Retrieved June 11, 2007, from http://api.cde.ca.gov/AcntRpt2007/2006BaseSchDC.aspx?allcds=01-61259-6057053&c=R.

Campbell, C., DeArmond, M., Guin, K., & Warnock, D. (2006, September). *No longer the only game in town: Helping traditional public schools compete.* Seattle: Center on Reinventing Public Education. Retrieved March 26, 2007, from http://www.crpe.org/dscr/pubs/pdf/DSCR_DistrictResponse_sept1.pdf.

Campbell, L. (1970). The devil can never educate us. In N. Wright, Jr. (Ed.), *What Black educators are saying.* New York: Hawthorn Books.

Carl, J. (1996, Winter). Unusual allies: Elite and grass-roots origins of parental choice in Milwaukee. *Teachers College Record, 98*(2), 266–285.

Carmichael, S., & Hamilton, C. V. (1967). *Black power: The politics of liberation* (1992 ed.). New York: Vintage Books.

Carnoy, M. (2001, January 1–15). Do school vouchers improve student performance? *The American Prospect, 12*(1). Retrieved October 30, 2006 from http://www.prospect.org/print/V12/1/carnoy-m.html.

Cave, D., & Benson, J. (2006a, April 17). Voucher issue a touchy topic in Newark race. *New York Times,* p. B1.

Cave, D., & Benson, J. (2006b, May 4). In Newark, Booker runs against his own fame. *New York Times,* p. A1.

Center for Education Reform. (1999, May). Newsletter. Washington, DC: Center for Education Reform.

Center for Education Reform. (2006). *Education in America: State-by-state scorecard.* Retrieved October 30, 2006, from http://www.edreform.com_/upload/CER_state_edstates_snapshot_apr06.pdf.

Center for Education Reform. (2007). *National charter school data: 2007–2008 new school estimates.* Retrieved September 27, 2007, from http://www.edreform.com/_upload/CER_charter_numbers.pdf.

Chapman, W. (1964, December 15). Federal court hearing begins on tuition plan. *Washington Post, Times Herald,* p. C1.

Chávez, L. (1998). *The color bind: California's battle to end affirmative action.* Berkeley: University of California Press.

Children's Scholarship Fund. (n.d.) *About csf.* Retrieved June 7, 2007, from http://www.scholarshipfund.org/about/facts.asp.

Christensen, J., & Angel, L. (2005, December 7). What NAEP can't tell us about charter school effectiveness. *Education Week, 25*(14), 35.

Chubb, J. E., & Moe, T. M. (1988, December). Politics, markets, and the organization of schools. *American Political Science Review, 82*(4), 1065–1087.

Chubb, J. E., & Moe, T. M. (1990). *Politics, markets, and America's schools.* Washington, DC: The Brookings Institution.

Citizens League. (1988, November 17). *Chartered schools = choices for educators + quality for all students.* Minneapolis: Citizens League.

City of Oakland. (n.d.) *Race and ethnicity. Oakland, 2000.* Retrieved August 4, 2005, from http://www.oaklandnet.com/government/hcd/policy/docs/Census/CensusChart4.pdf.

Clark, K. B. (1968). Thoughts on Black Power. *Dissent,* 98.

Clark, K. B. (1969). The social scientists, the Brown decision, and contemporary confusion. In L. Friedman (Ed.), *Argument: The oral argument before the Supreme Court in Brown v. Board of Education of Topeka, 1952–55.* New York: Chelsea House Publishers.

Cleaver, E. (1968). *Soul on ice* (1992 ed.). New York: Dell Publishing.

Clemetson, L. (2003, August 8). Younger Blacks tell Democrats to take notice. *New York Times,* p. A1.

Cohen, M. (1981, December 14). Harvard reformers resurrect school-option plan. *Los Angeles Times,* p. F14.

Cole, V. S. (1998). *African Village: A case study of an African centered public elementary school.* Ph.D. dissertation. University of Pennsylvania.

Coleman, J. S. (1981). The role of incentives in school desegregation. In A. Yarmolinsky, L. Liebman, & C. S. Schelling (Eds.), *Race and schooling in the city.* Cambridge: Harvard University Press.

Coleman, J. S. (1994). Quality and equality in American education: Public and Catholic schools. In J. Kretovics & E. J. Nussel (Eds.), *Transforming urban education.* Boston: Allyn and Bacon.

Coleman, J. S., Campbell, E. Q., Hobson, C. J., McPartland, J., Mood, A. M., Weinfeld, F. D., & York, R. L. (1966). *Equality of educational opportunity.* Washington, DC: U.S. Government Printing Office.

Coleman, J. S., Hoffer, T., & Kilgore, S. (1982). *High school achievement: Public, Catholic, and private schools compared.* New York: Basic Books.

Collins, P. H. (1991a). *Black feminist thought: Knowledge, consciousness, and the politics of empowerment.* New York: Routledge.

Collins, P. H. (1991b). Learning from the outsider within: The sociological significance of Black feminist thought. In M. M. Fonow, & J. A. Cook (Eds.), *Beyond methodology: Feminist scholarship as lived research.* Bloomington: Indiana University Press.

Comer, J. P. (1981, April 19). Coleman's bad report. *New York Times,* p. E15.

Cone, J. H. (1991). *Martin & Malcolm & America: A dream or a nightmare.* Maryknoll, NY: Orbis Books.

Council of Independent Black Institutions (IBI). (2001, March 12 ed.). *Standards for evaluating Afrikan-centered educational institutions.* Retrieved June 5, 2007 from http://www.cibi.org/pdfs/standards.pdf.

Cremin, L. A. (1980). *American education: The national experience, 1783–1876.* New York: Harper & Row.

Cremin, L. A. (1988). *American education: The metropolitan experience, 1876–1980.* New York: Harper & Row.

Cruse, H. (1967). *The crisis of the Negro intellectual: A historical analysis of the failure of Black leadership* (1984 ed.). New York: Quill.

Cunningham, B. (1968, November). The Shankers in suburbia. *SCOPE Bulletin,* 3–4.

Dao, J. (1997, September 29). How to make a poor school change. *New York Times,* p. B1.

DeFao, J. (2001, January 21). At midterm, is Jerry Brown making grade in Oakland? *San Francisco Chronicle,* p. A17.

DeFao, J. (2002, March 6). Oakland Mayor Brown wins second term. *San Francisco Chronicle,* p. A17.

DelVecchio, R. (1998a, January 20). In Oakland, Jerry Brown finds all politics is local. *San Francisco Chronicle,* p. A1.

DelVecchio, R. (1998b, June 3). Jerry Brown returns triumphant: Oakland's next mayor wins by huge margin. *San Francisco Chronicle,* p. A1.

Dewar, H. (1968, December 19). NAACP challenges state aid for private school pupils. *Washington Post, Times Herald,* p. D1.

Dillard, E. (1998, March 22). Where are Oakland's Black leaders? *Oakland Tribune,* p. news–5.

Dillon, S. (2005, July 13). For parents seeking a choice, charter schools prove more popular than vouchers. *New York Times,* p. B8.

Dillon, S. (2006, January 6). Florida Supreme Court blocks school vouchers. *New York Times,* p. A16.

Diringer, E., & Olszewski. L. (1996, December 21). Critics may not understand Oakland's Ebonics plan. *San Francisco Chronicle,* p. A17.

Dougherty, J. (2004). *More than one struggle: The evolution of Black school reform in Milwaukee.* Chapel Hill: The University of North Carolina Press.

Doughty, J. J. (1973). *A historical analysis of Black education— Focusing on the contemporary Independent Black School Movement.* Ph.D. dissertation. Ohio State University, 1973.

Douglas, W. B. (1964, November 5). Suit assails Prince Edward private school grants. *Washington Post, Times Herald,* p. B20.

Du Bois, W. E. B. (1935, July). Does the Negro need separate schools? *Journal of Negro Education, 4*(3), 328–335.

Du Bois, W. E. B. (1903). *The souls of Black folk* (1989 ed.). New York: Penguin Books.

Dwyer, R. (1997, December 31). Vouchers appeal to minorities. *Columbus Dispatch,* p. 11A.

Dyson, M. E. (2006). *Come hell or high water: Hurricane Katrina and the color of disaster.* New York: Basic Civitas Books.

Eaton, S. E. (2001). *The other Boston busing story: What's won and lost across the boundary line.* New Haven: Yale University Press.

Eisenberg, C. W. (1971). *The parents movement at I.S. 201: From integration to Black Power, 1958–1966: A case study of developing ideology.* Ph.D. dissertation. Columbia University.

Elmore, R. F., & Fuller, B. (1996). Empirical research on educational choice: What are the implications for policymakers? In B. Fuller & R. F. Elmore with G. Orfield (Eds.), *Who chooses? Who loses?: Culture, institutions, and the unequal effects of school choice.* New York: Teachers College Press.

Evans, P. B., Rueschemeyer, D., & Skocpol, T. (1985). On the road toward a more adequate understanding of the state. In P. B. Evans, D. Rueschemeyer, & T. Skocpol (Eds.), *Bringing the state back in.* Cambridge: Cambridge University Press.

Fantini, M. D. (1972). Participation, decentralization, community control and quality education. In R. C. Rist (Ed.), *Restructuring American education: Innovations and alternatives.* New Brunswick, NJ: Transaction Books.

Fantini, M. D., & Magat, R. (1968). Decentralizing urban school systems. In A. Toffler (Ed.), *The schoolhouse in the city.* New York: Frederick A. Praeger.

Fantini, M., Gittell, M., & Magat, R. (1970). *Community control and the urban school.* New York: Praeger Publishers.

Farkas, S., & Johnson, J., with Immerwahr, S., & McHugh, J. (1998). *Time to move on: African-American and White parents set an agenda for public schools.* New York: Public Agenda.

Farmer, J. (1971). Develop "group pride" and then "cultural pluralism." In A. Meier, E. Rudwick & F. L. Broderick (Eds.), *Black protest thought in the twentieth century* (2nd ed.). The American Heritage Series. Indianapolis: Merrill Educational Publishing.

Fein, L. J. (1970). Community schools and social theory: The limits of universalism. In H. M. Levin (Ed.), *Community control of schools.* Washington, DC: The Brookings Institution.

Feinberg, L. W. (1972, April 25). Calif. school system to test educational vouchers. *Washington Post, Times Herald,* p. A6.

Feinberg, L. (1978, June 20). Desegregation expert backs tuition credit. *Washington Post,* p. A3.

Feldstein, H. S. (1969, February 5). Letter to Lawrence Robbins. PA 670–0426, Ford Foundation Archives.

Feron, J. (1973, October 21). Voucher bid dies in New Rochelle. *New York Times,* p. 46.

Ferretti, F. (1969). Who's to blame in the school strike. In M. R. Berube, & M. Gittell (Eds.), *Confrontation at Ocean Hill-Brownsville: The New York school strikes of 1968.* New York: Frederick A. Praeger.

Flake, F. (1998a, Fall). More on school choice by the Rev. Floyd Flake. *School Voices,* 6(1), 20.

Flake, F. H. (1998b, Fall). We cannot afford to wait any longer: An interview with the Rev. Floyd H. Flake. *School Voices*, 6(1), 18–20.

Ford Foundation. (1969, May). *And then, there were the children . . . : An assessment of efforts to test decentralization in New York City's public school system*. Report #002149, Ford Foundation Archives.

Fordham, S. (1988, February). Racelessness as a factor in Black students' school success: Pragmatic strategy or pyrrhic victory? *Harvard Educational Review*, 58(1), 54–84.

Fordham, S., & Ogbu, J. U. (1986). Black students' school success: Coping with the "burden of 'acting White.'" *Urban Review*, 18(3), 176–206.

Forman, J. (1985). *The making of Black revolutionaries*. Seattle: Open Hand Publishing.

Forman, J., Jr. (2005). The secret history of school choice: How progressives got there first. *The Georgetown Law Journal*, 93, 1287–1319.

Forman, J., Jr. (2007, May). Do charter schools threaten public education?: Emerging evidence from fifteen years of a quasi-market for schooling. *University of Illinois Law Review*, 2007. Retrieved June 11, 2007, from http://lsr.nellco.org/cgi/viewcontent.cgi?article=1008&context=georgeto wn/fwps.

Forté-Parnell, C. E. (1998). *Meeting the challenge of permanence: A case study of three k–8 Independent Black Institutions (IBIs) in the state of California*. Ed.D. dissertation. University of La Verne.

Foster, G. (1992, Spring). New York City's wealth of historically Black independent schools. *Journal of Negro Education*, 61(2), 186–200.

Frankenberg, E., & Lee, C. (2002, August). *Race in American public schools: Rapidly resegregating school districts*. Cambridge: The Civil Rights Project at Harvard University.

Frankenberg, E., & Lee, C. (2003, July). *Charter schools and race: A lost opportunity for integrated education*. Cambridge: The Civil Rights Project at Harvard University.

Friedman, M. (1955). The role of government in education. In R. A. Solo (Ed.), *Economics and the public interest*. New Brunswick, NJ: Rutgers University Press.

Friedman, M. (1962). *Capitalism and freedom*. Chicago: University of Chicago Press.

Friedman, M. (1973, September 23). The voucher idea. *New York Times Magazine*, p. 22.

Friedman, M. (1975, October 6). Whose intolerance? *Newsweek*, p. 73.

Fuller, B. (Ed.). (2000). *Inside charter schools: The paradox of radical decentralization*. Cambridge: Harvard University Press.

Fuller, B., Elmore, R. F., & Orfield, G. (1996). Policy-making in the dark: Illuminating the school choice debate. In B. Fuller & R. F. Elmore with G. Orfield (Eds.), *Who chooses? Who loses?: Culture, institutions, and the unequal effects of school choice*. New York: Teachers College Press.

Fuller, B., Gawlik, M., Gonzales, E. K., Park, S., with Gibbings, G. (2003, April). *Charter schools and inequality: National disparities in funding, teacher quality, and student support.* PACE Working Paper Series 03–2. Berkeley: Policy Analysis for California Education.

Fuller, H. L. (2000). The continuing struggle of African Americans for the power to make real educational choices. Retrieved August 14, 2006, from www.schoolchoiceinfo.org/data/research/construg.pdf.

Funnye, C. (1967, November 16). Bundy & Black Power: A retreat to reality. *The Village Voice.*

Gammon, R. (2005, April 27). The caustic reformer: Randolph Ward has proposed the boldest school reforms in America. But can Oakland's most hated man sell his vision? *East Bay Express.* Retrieved June 2, 2005, from http://www.eastbayexpress.com/Issues/2005-04-27/news/feature_print.html.

Garinger, L. (1971, February 4). Nixon to Catholic educators: "You must not retreat." *Christian Science Monitor,* p. 7.

Gates, R. L. (1962). *The making of massive resistance: Virginia's politics of public school desegregation, 1954–1956.* Chapel Hill: The University of North Carolina Press.

Gehring, J. (2005, March 2). Dips in enrollment posing challenges for urban districts. *Education Week, 24*(25), 1.

George, G. R., & Farrell, W. C., Jr. (1990). School choice and African American students: A legislative view. *Journal of Negro Education, 59*(4), 521–525.

Gewertz, C. (2000, March 15). Oakland voters give Brown broader say over schools. *Education Week, 19*(27), 10.

Giddings, P. (1984). *When and where I enter: The impact of Black women on race and sex in America.* New York: Quill/William Morrow.

Ginwright, S. A. (2004). *Black in school: Afrocentric reform, urban youth, and the promise of hip-hop culture.* New York: Teachers College Press.

Gittell, M. (1969, May). New York City school decentralization. *Community, 1,* 1–2.

Gittell, M. (1970, February). The community school in the nation. *Community Issues, 2*(1).

Gittell, M. (1971). *Demonstration for social change: An experiment in local control.* New York: Institute for Community Studies, Queens College of the City University of New York.

Gittell, M. (1998). Conclusion: Creating a school reform agenda for the twenty-first century. In M. J. Gittell (Ed.), *Strategies for school equity: Creating productive schools in a just society.* New Haven: Yale University Press.

Gittell, M., & McKenna, L. (1998). Introduction: The ends and the means in education policy. In M. J. Gittell (Ed.), *Strategies for school equity: Creating productive schools in a just society.* New Haven: Yale University Press.

Goldberg, G. S. (1966–1967, Winter). I.S. 201: An educational landmark. *IRCD Bulletin, 2*(5)–3(1), 1–8.

Goldbloom, M. J. (1968, November 15). *A critique of the New York Civil Liberties Union report on the Ocean Hill–Brownsville school controversy.* New York: Ad Hoc Committee to Defend the Right to Teach.

Gordon, J. A. (2001). *Why they couldn't wait: A critique of the Black-Jewish conflict over community control in Ocean Hill–Brownsville (1967–1971)*. New York: Routledge Falmer.

Graubard, A. (1972, August). The Free School Movement. *Harvard Educational Review, 42*(3), 351–373.

Gray Report text. (1955, November 13). *Washington Post and Times Herald*, pp. A14–15.

Greene, J. P., Peterson, P. E., & Du, J. (1999, February). Effectiveness of school choice: The Milwaukee experiment. *Education and Urban Society, 31*(2), 190–213.

Greene, J. P., & Forster, G. (2002, October). Rising to the challenge: The effect of school choice on public schools in Milwaukee and San Antonio. *Civic Bulletin* (27). Retrieved January 10, 2006, from http://www.manhattan-institute.org/html/cb_27.htm.

Greenhouse, L. (2003, June 24). Justices back affirmative action by 5 to 4, but wider vote bans a racial point system. *New York Times*, p. A1.

Greenhouse, L. (2006, December 5). Court reviews race as factor in school plans. *New York Times*, p. A1.

Greenhouse, L. (2007, June 29). Justices, voting 5–4, limit the use of race in integration plans. *New York Times*, p. A1.

Griffen, J. B., & Johnson, S. (1988). Making a difference for a new generation: The ABC story. In D. T. Slaughter & D. J. Johnson (Eds.), *Visible now: Blacks in private schools*. New York: Greenwood Press.

Grove, S. (2004, May 16). At charter schools, the issue is diversity. Quality? At many. The lack, critics say, is in the racial mix. *Boston Globe*, p. city weekly–1.

Gurin, P., Hatchett, S., & Jackson, J. S. (1989). *Hope and independence: Blacks' response to electoral and party politics*. New York: Russell Sage Foundation.

Guthrie, J. (1999, February 18). Admission policy to hit Blacks, Latinos hardest. *San Francisco Examiner*.

Hamilton, C. V. (1968, Fall). Education in the Black community: An examination of the realities. *Freedomways, 8*, 319–324.

Harlem Parents Committee. (1965). *The education of minority group children in the New York City public schools, 1965*. Daniel Perlstein's personal files.

Harrington, M. (1969). The freedom to teach: Beyond the panaceas. In M. R. Berube, & M. Gittell (Eds.), *Confrontation at Ocean Hill–Brownsville: The New York school strikes of 1968*. New York: Frederick A. Praeger.

Hart, G. K., & Burr, S. (1996, September). The story of California's charter school legislation. *Phi Delta Kappan, 78*(1), 37–40.

Haskins, K. W. (1973, November). A Black perspective on community control. *Inequality in Education, 15*, 23–34.

Hassel, B. C., & Toch, T. (2006, November). *Big box: How the heirs of the Wal-Mart fortune have fueled the charter school movement*. Washington, DC: Education Sector. Retrieved November 16, 2006, from http://www.educationsector.org/usr_doc/CTDWalton.pdf.

Haynes, V. D. (2005, September 20). Voucher program at full capacity; D.C. high schools have too few slots. *Washington Post*, p. B01.

Hechinger, F. M. (1975, November 16). Where have all the innovations gone? *New York Times*, p. 30.

Hendrie, C. (1998a, June 10). Buffalo seeks a smooth transition after release from court oversight. *Education Week*, *17*(39), 10.

Hendrie, C. (1998b, March 25). N.C. lawsuit revives historic integration case. *Education Week*, *17*(28), 3.

Hendrie, C. (1998c, June 10). New magnet schools policies sidestep an old issue: Race. *Education Week 17*(39), 10–12.

Hendrie, C. (1998d, April 29). Plan for Little Rock would shift away from busing. *Education Week*, *17*(33), 3.

Hendrie, C. (1998e, June 17). Pressure for community schools grows as court oversight wanes. *Education Week*, *17*(40), 23.

Henig, J. R. (1994). *Rethinking school choice: Limits of the market metaphor*. Princeton: Princeton University Press.

Henig, J. R., Hula, R. C., Orr, M., & Pedescleaux, D. S. (1999). *The color of school reform: Race, politics, and the challenge of urban education*. Princeton: Princeton University Press.

Henry, T. (2001, May 7). Alliance promotes vouchers. *USA Today*. Retrieved October 24, 2002, from wysiwyg://39/http://www.usatoday.com/life/2001-05-07-vouchers.htm.

Herrnstein, C. M., & Murray, C. (1994). *The bell curve: intelligence and class structure in American life*. New York: The Free Press.

Holmes, S. A. (1999, May 30). Black groups in Florida split over school voucher plan. *New York Times*, p. 17.

Holt, M. (2000). *Not yet "free at last." The unfinished business of the civil rights movement: Our battle for school choice*. Oakland: Institute for Contemporary Studies.

Hoover, M.E.R. (1992, Spring). The Nairobi Day School: An African American independent school, 1966–1984. *Journal of Negro Education, 61*(2), 201–210.

Hopkins, R. (1997). *Educating Black males: Critical lessons in schooling, community, and power*. Albany: State University of New York Press.

Hotep, U. (2001). *Dedicated to excellence: An Afrocentric oral history of the Council of Independent Black Institutions, 1970–2000*. Ph.D. dissertation. Duquesne University.

Howell, W. G., Wolf, P. J., Peterson, P. E., & Campbell, D. E. (2001, February 7). In defense of our voucher research. *Education Week*, *20*(21), 52.

Howell, W. G., Wolf, P. J., Campbell, D. E., & Peterson, P. E. (2002). School vouchers and academic performance: Results from three randomized field trials. *Journal of Policy Analysis and Management, 21*(2), 191–217.

Hoxby, C. M. (2001). *How school choice affects the achievement of public school students*. Paper prepared for the Koret Task Force Meeting. Hoover Institution, Stanford, CA. Retrieved October 27, 2006, from http://www.economics.harvard.edu/faculty/hoxby/papers/choice_sep01.pdf.

Hoxby, C. M. (2004, December). *Achievement in charter schools and regular public schools in the United States: Understanding the differences.* Retrieved October 14, 2005, from http://www.innovations.harvard.edu/showdoc.html?id=4848.

Hughes, E. C. (1984). *The sociological eye: Selected papers.* New Brunswick, NJ: Transaction Publications.

Hughes, L. (1995). Let America be America again. In A. Rampersad & D. Rosessel (Eds.), *The collected poems of Langston Hughes.* New York: Alfred A. Knopf.

Hyde Leadership Public Charter School. (n.d.). *Hyde Schools to open charter school in NYC in September '06.* Retrieved October 19, 2006, from http://www.hydedc.org/PR_NYschool.htm.

Hyde Schools. (n.d.). *About Hyde.* Retrieved October 19, 2006, from http://www.hyde.edu/podium/default.aspx?+=50437.

Institute for Independent Education. (1991). *On the road to success: Students at independent neighborhood schools.* Washington, DC: Institute for Independent Education.

Isaacs, C. et al. (1970). Charles Isaacs and others. In M. I. Urofsky (Ed.), *Why teachers strike: Teachers' rights and community control.* Garden City, NY: Anchor Books.

Isaacs, C. S. (1969). A JHS 271 teacher tells it like he sees It. In M. R. Berube & M. Gittell (Eds.), *Confrontation at Ocean Hill–Brownsville: The New York school strikes of 1968.* New York: Frederick A. Praeger.

Jackson, J. (2004, May 18). Bush's education reforms mock the promise of Brown. *Chicago Sun-Times,* p. 35.

Jacobs, R. (1997). *The way the wind blew: A history of the Weather Underground.* London: Verso.

Jacoby, S. (1968, March 3). New "private" schools drain public system. *Washington Post, Times Herald,* p. B3.

Jacoby, T. (1998). *Someone else's house: America's unfinished struggle for integration.* New York: The Free Press.

Jencks, C. (1966, Winter). Is the public school obsolete? *The Public Interest, 2,* 18–27.

Jencks, C. (1968, November 3). Private schools for Black children. *New York Times Magazine,* p. 30.

Jencks, C. (1970, July 4). Giving parents money to pay for schooling: Education vouchers. *The New Republic, 163,* 19–21.

Jencks, C., & Phillips, M. (Eds.) (1998). *The Black-White test score gap.* Washington, DC: Brookings Institution Press.

Jencks, C., Smith, M., Acland, H., Bane, M. J., Cohen, D., Gintis, H., Heyns, B., & Michelson, S. (1972). *Inequality: A reassessment of the effect of family and schooling in America.* New York: Basic Books.

Joffe, C. (1986). *The regulation of sexuality: Experiences of family planning workers.* Philadelphia: Temple University Press.

Johnson, C. (2004a, January 19). Oakland schools' loss is Elk Grove's gain. *San Francisco Chronicle,* p. B1.

Johnson, C. (2004b, May 17). Ax-grinding in Oakland over schools takeover. *San Francisco Chronicle*, p. B1.

Johnson, J. W., & Johnson, J. R. (2000). Lift every voice and sing. In J. Bond & S. K. Wilson (Eds.), *Lift every voice and sing: A celebration of the Negro national anthem.* New York: Random House.

Johnston, R. C. (1999, December 8). Oakland to vote on giving mayor school say. *Education Week, 19*(15), 3.

Jones, D. S. (1966). The issues at I.S. 201: A view from the parent's committee. *Integrated Education,* 23.

Jordan, V. (1972, April 29). To be equal. *Sun Reporter,* p. 8.

Karenga, M. (1982). *Introduction to Black studies.* Los Angeles: University of Sankore Press.

Katznelson, I., & Weir, M. (1985). *Schooling for all: Class, race, and the decline of the democratic ideal.* New York: Basic Books.

Kemble, E. (n.d.). *New York's experiments in school decentralization: A look at three projects.* New York: United Federation of Teachers.

Kertscher, Tom. (2005, July 10). Bond comes out swinging at Bush: He denounces president in speech. *Milwaukee Journal Sentinel Online.* Retrieved July 13, 2005 from http://www.jsonline.com/news/metro/jul05/340205.asp

King, M. L., Jr. (1967). *Where do we go from here? Chaos or community?* Boston: Beacon Press.

King, M. L., Jr. (1986). The ethical demands for integration. In James M. Washington (Ed.), *A Testament of hope: The essential writings and speeches of Martin Luther King, Jr.* New York: HarperCollins Publishers.

King, M. S. (2004). Voices of progressive charter school educators. In E. Rofes & L. M. Stulberg (Eds.), *The emancipatory promise of charter schools: Toward a progressive politics of school choice.* Albany: State University of New York Press.

Kirp, D. L. (1982a, January 5). Public money and private education. *Christian Science Monitor,* p. 23.

Kirp, D. L. (1982b). *Just schools: The idea of racial equality in American education.* Berkeley: University of California Press.

Kluger, R. (1975). *Simple justice: The history of* Brown v. Board of Education *and Black America's struggle for equality.* New York: Vintage Books.

Kozol, J. (1991). *Savage inequalities: Children in America's schools.* New York, HarperPerennial.

LaCayo, R. (1997, October 27). They'll vouch for that. *Time, 150*(17), 72–74.

Ladner, J. A. (1973). Tomorrow's tomorrow: The Black woman. In J. Ladner (Ed.), *The death of White sociology.* New York: Random House.

Lawton, M. (1990, October 10). 2 schools aimed for Black males set in Milwaukee. *Education Week, 10*(6), 1.

Lee, C. D. (1992, Spring). Profile of an independent Black institution: African-centered education at work. *Journal of Negro Education, 61*(2), 160–177.

Lee, C. D. (1994). African-centered pedagogy: Complexities and possibilities. In M. J. Shujaa (Ed.), *Too much schooling, too little education: A paradox of black life in white societies.* Trenton, NJ: Africa World Press.

Leedom, J. (1970, February 18). Voucher plan proposed to bring competition into schools. *Christian Science Monitor,* p. 6.

Lerman, S. (1999, July 1). Black leaders ponder how to reclaim power. *Oakland Tribune,* pp. local–1–2.

Levin, B. (1999). Race and school choice. In S. D. Sugarman & F. R. Kemerer (Eds.), *School choice and social controversy: Politics, policy, and law.* Washington, DC: Brookings Institution Press.

Lewis, A. E. (2003). *Race in the schoolyard: Negotiating the color line in classrooms and communities.* New Brunswick, NJ: Rutgers University Press.

Lewis, N. A (1998, November 10). School vouchers survive as justices sidestep a debate. *New York Times,* p. A1.

Locke, M. (1999, March 26). Jerry Brown is strong Oakland mayor. Associated Press.

Lomotey, K., & Brookins, C. C. (1988). Independent Black institutions: A cultural perspective. In D. T. Slaughter & D. J. Johnson (Eds.), *Visible now: Blacks in private schools.* New York: Greenwood Press.

Lomotey, K. (1992, Fall). Independent Black institutions: African-centered education models. *Journal of Negro Education, 61*(4), 455–462.

Lublin, J. S. (1973, June 4). California purchase: "Buying" your school with a voucher looks like good deal so far. *Wall Street Journal,* p. 1.

Madhubuti, H. R. (1973). *From plan to planet. Life studies: The need for Afrikan minds and institutions.* Chicago: Third World Press.

Madhubuti, H. R. (1994). Cultural work: Planting new trees with new seeds. In M. J. Shujaa (Ed.), *Too much schooling, too little education: A paradox of Black life in White societies.* Trenton, NJ: Africa World Press.

Magat, R. (1967, April 17). *The Ford Foundation's new currency: Advancing social change on the quiet and on the cheap.* Report #010718, Ford Foundation Archives.

Magnusson, P. (2003, October 13). The split over school vouchers. Businessweek Online. Retrieved February 6, 2006, from http://www.businessweek.com.

Mahiri, J. (1998, 14 October). Interview with author.

Marable, M. (1990, August). A new Black politics. *The Progressive, 54*(8), 18–23.

Marable, M. (1991). *Race, reform, and rebellion: The second Reconstruction in Black America, 1945–1992* (2nd ed.). Jackson: University Press of Mississippi.

Marable, M. (1992). *The crisis of color and democracy: Essays on race, class and power.* Monroe, ME: Common Courage Press.

Marshall, C. (1968, Spring). *Report to governing board Ocean Hill school district from personnel committee.* PA 670–0426, Ford Foundation Archives.

Mathematica Policy Research, Inc. (2000, September 15). *Voucher claims of success are premature in New York City: Second-year results show no overall differences in test scores between those who were offered vouchers and those who were not.* Press release. Retrieved October 12, 2005, from http://www.mathematica-mpr.com/press%20releases/past%20releases/voucherrelfinal.asp.

Mathews, J. (2000, September 19). Some researchers question voucher study. *Washington Post*, p. B4.

Matusow, A. J. (1972). From civil rights to black power: The case of SNCC, 1960–1966. In B. J. Bernstein & A. J. Matusow (Eds.), *20th Century America: Recent Interpretations* (2nd ed.). New York: Harcourt Brace Javanovich.

May, M. (2002, December 8). Oakland schools broke, face bailout. *San Francisco Chronicle*, p. A1.

May, M. (2003, June 3). State's take-charge guy walks and talks in Oakland. *San Francisco Chronicle*, p. A1.

Maynard, R. C. (1967, November 12). Ultimate solution recommended for schools. *Washington Post, Times Herald*, p. B4.

McCartney, J. T. (1992). *Black Power ideologies: An essay in African-American political thought*. Philadelphia: Temple University Press.

McCoy, R. A. (1970). Why have an Ocean Hill–Brownsville? In N. Wright Jr. (Ed.), *What Black educators are saying*. New York: Hawthorn Books.

McGroarty, D. (1996). *Break these chains: The battle for school choice*. Rocklin, CA: Forum.

McWhorter, J. H. (1997, Spring). Wasting energy on an illusion. *The Black Scholar, 27*(1), 9–14.

Metcalf, K. K., Muller, P., Boone, W., Tait, P., Stage, F., & Stacey, N. (1998, November 18). *Evaluation of the Cleveland Scholarship Program: Second year report (1997–1998)*. Bloomington, IN: The Indiana Center for Evaluation, Indiana University. Retreived October 27, 2006, from http:// ceep.indiana.edu/projects/PDF/199811b_clev_2_report.pdf.

Minter, T. K (1967, 2 June). *Intermediate School 201, Manhattan: Center of controversy. A case study*. Cambridge: Harvard University Graduate School of Education.

Moe, T. M. (1999, May 9). A look at school vouchers: The public revolution private money might bring. *Washington Post*, p. B3.

Molnar, A., & Achilles, C. (2000, October 25). Voucher and class-size research. *Education Week, 20*(8), 64.

Morgan, D. (1980, September 12). Reagan, opponents differ sharply on educational policy. *Washington Post*, p. A8.

Morrison, D. (1972, 12 May). NYC Black teachers hold convention. *The Militant*, p. 14.

Mothner, I. (1969, May 13). The war for city schools. *Look*, 42–49.

Murphy, D. E. (2003, June 8). Dream ends for Oakland school chief as state takes over. *New York Times*, p. 30.

Murphy, D., Nelson, F. H., & Rosenberg, B. (1997). *The Cleveland voucher program: Who chooses? Who gets chosen? Who pays?* Washington, DC: The American Federation of Teachers.

Muse, B. (1961). *Virginia's massive resistance*. Bloomington: Indiana University Press.

Muwakkil, S. (1997, November 2). Letting go of the dream: African-Americans turn their backs on integration. *In These Times, 21*, 13–15.

Nakamura, D. (2004, May 16). Disparity threatens case's legacy: Panelists celebrate decision, push for continued changes. *Washington Post*, p. C8.

Nathan, J. (1996a). *Charter schools: Creating hope and opportunity for American education.* San Francisco: Jossey-Bass Publishers.

Nathan, J. (1996b, September). Possibilities, problems, and progress: Early lessons from the charter movement. *Phi Delta Kappan, 78*(1), 18–23.

Nathan, J. (1998, March). Heat and light in the charter school movement. *Phi Delta Kappan, 79*(7), 499–505.

National Alliance for Public Charter Schools. (2006, May 22). *What NAEP is really telling us about charter performance.* Retrieved October 27, 2006, from http://www.publiccharters.org/content/publication/detail/1101.

Negro Teachers' Association. (1967, May 28). *Resolutions: Negro Teachers' Association's conference.* Robert F. Wagner Labor Archives of the Tamiment Institute Library. New York University. UFT Collection. Shanker subject files. Box 1, folder 9.

Nelson, F. H., Rosenberg, B, & Van Meter, N. (2004, August). *Charter school achievement on the 2003 National Assessment of Educational Progress.* Washington, DC: American Federation of Teachers.

Newby, R. G., & Tyack, D. B. (1971, Summer). Victims without "crimes": Some historical perspectives on Black education. *Journal of Negro Education, 40*(3), 192–206.

Newton, H. P. (1991). The founding of the Black Panther Party. In C. Carson, D. J. Garrow, G. Gill, V. Harding, & D. C. Hine (Eds.), *The Eyes on the Prize civil rights reader: Documents, speeches, and firsthand accounts from the Black freedom struggle, 1954–1990.* New York: Penguin Books.

New York-Harlem CORE. (1967). *A proposal for an independent board of education for Harlem.* Daniel Perlstein's personal files.

Nixon asks broader pupil aid. (1968, October 21). *Washington Post, Times Herald,* p. A12.

Noguera, P. A. (1996). Confronting the urban in urban school reform. *The Urban Review, 28*(1), 1–19.

Noguera, P. A. (2003). *City schools and the American dream: Reclaiming the promise of public education.* New York: Teachers College Press.

Oakland Citizens Committee for Urban Renewal. (1998). *Neighborhood profiles: West Oakland.* Oakland: Oakland Citizens Committee for Urban Renewal.

Oakland Coalition of Congregations, in partnership with the Oakland Unified School District, the Oakland Education Cabinet and the Oakland Tribune. (1997, November 9). 1997 Annual report to the community on Oakland public schools. *Oakland Tribune* supplement.

The Oakland Ebonics Resolution. (1998). In T. Perry & L. Delpit (Eds.), *The real Ebonics debate: Power, language, and the education of African-American children.* Boston: Beacon Press.

Oakland Unified School District. (2000, May 16). *New Small Autonomous Schools district policy.* Retrieved July 12, 2005, from http://webportal.ousd.k12.ca.us/news/revised_nse_%20policy.htm.

Oakland Unified School District. (2005, April 14). *Multi-year fiscal recovery plan.* Retrieved June 1, 2005, from http://bex.ousd.k12.ca.us/frp.asp.

Obama, B. (2006). *The audacity of hope: Thoughts on reclaiming the American dream.* New York: Crown Publishers.

Ocean Hill–Brownsville School District. (n.d.). *We demand total control of our schools.* Flier for March 28 march at J.H.S. 271. Department of Special Collections, Milbank Memorial Library, Teachers College, Columbia University. New York City Board of Education Papers. Rose Shapiro Collection. Box 8, folder 12.

Ocean Hill–Brownsville Teaching Staff. (1968, 16 October). *We the teachers of Ocean/Hill–Brownsville deny that police controlled schools are "normal."* Robert F. Wagner Labor Archives of the Tamiment Institute Library. New York University. UFT Collection. Shanker subject files. "Decentralization" box 3, folder 95.

Olszewski, L. (1999a, February 11). Charter school fever hits Oakland: Failing public system leads parents to seek alternatives. *San Francisco Chronicle,* p. A19.

Olszewski, L. (1999b, February 12). Oakland Board dilutes plan to shift power to schools: Charter–school backers say panel is resisting change. *San Francisco Chronicle,* p. A21.

Open letter to Albert Shanker from very angry parents and children in New York City. (Christmas, 1968). *SCOPE Bulletin,* 8.

Opening Pandora's box: An interview with Oakland School Board member Toni Cook. (1998). In T. Perry & L. Delpit (Eds.), *The real Ebonics debate: Power, language, and the education of African-American children.* Boston: Beacon Press.

Orfield, G. (1978). *Must we bus?: Segregated schooling and national policy.* Washington, DC: The Brookings Institution.

Orfield, G. (1981). Why it worked in Dixie: Southern school desegregation and its implications for the North. In A. Yarmolinsky, L. Liebman, & C. S. Schelling (Eds.), *Race and Schooling in the City.* Cambridge: Harvard University Press.

Orfield, G. (1995, Summer). Public opinion and school desegregation. *Teachers College Record, 96*(4), 654–670.

Orfield, G. (1996a). The growth of segregation: African Americans. Latinos, and unequal education. In G. Orfield, S. E. Eaton, and the Harvard Project on School Desegregation. *Dismantling desegregation: The quiet reversal of* Brown v. Board of Education. New York: The New Press.

Orfield, G. (1996b). *Plessy* parallels: Back to traditional assumptions. In G. Orfield, S. E. Eaton, and the Harvard Project on School Desegregation. *Dismantling desegregation: The quiet reversal of* Brown v. Board of Education. New York: The New Press.

Orfield, G. (1996c). Toward an integrated future: New directions for courts, educators, civil rights groups, policymakers, and scholars. In G. Orfield, S. E. Eaton and the Harvard Project on School Desegregation. *Dismantling desegregation: The quiet reversal of* Brown v. Board of Education. New York: The New Press.

Orfield, G. (1996d). Turning back to segregation. In G. Orfield, S. E. Eaton, and the Harvard Project on School Desegregation. *Dismantling desegregation: The quiet reversal of* Brown v. Board of Education. New York: The New Press.

Orfield, G. (1996e). Unexpected costs and uncertain gains of dismantling desegregation. In G. Orfield, S. E. Eaton, and the Harvard Project on School Desegregation. *Dismantling desegregation: The quiet reversal of* Brown v. Board of Education. New York: The New Press.

Orfield, G. (1998, January 2). Charter schools won't save education. *New York Times*, p. A15.

Orfield, G. (1999, December 10). Affirmative action works—but judges and policy makers need to hear that verdict. *Chronicle of Higher Education*, B7–8.

Orfield, G., Eaton, S. E., & the Harvard Project on School Desegregation. (1996). *Dismantling desegregation: The quiet reversal of* Brown v. Board of Education. New York: The New Press.

Orfield, G., Monfort, F., & Aaron, M. (1989). *Status of school desegregation, 1968–1986.* Alexandria, VA: National School Board Association Council of Urban Boards of Education.

Orfield, G., & Yun, J. T. (1999, June). *Resegregation in American schools.* Cambridge: The Civil Rights Project at Harvard University.

Owens, M. L. (2002, February 26). Why Blacks support vouchers. *New York Times*, p. A25.

Paddock, R. C. (2006, November 26). Affirmative action era over, foe says. *Los Angeles Times*, p. B1.

Page, C. (1996, December 25). Linguistic apartheid?: The uses and abuses of "Black" English. *Chicago Tribune*, p. 27.

Parents ponder tuition voucher plan. (1970, March 19). *Bay State Banner*, p. 1.

Parker, W. (2001, February). The color of choice: Race and charter schools. *Tulane Law Review*, 75(3), 563–630.

Parsons, T. (1970, December). The community school movement. *Community Issues, 2.*

Patterson, O. (1997). *The ordeal of integration: Progress and resentment in America's "racial" crisis.* Washington, DC: Civitas/Counterpoint.

Payton, B. (1998, November 1). African Americans need to reclaim power. *Oakland Tribune*, p. local–9.

Pedroni, T. C. (2005, June). Market movements and the dispossessed: Race, identity, and subaltern agency among Black women voucher advocates. *The Urban Review,* 37(2), 83–106.

Perkinson, H. J. (1995). *The imperfect panacea: American faith in education* (4th ed.). New York: McGraw-Hill.

Perlstein, D. (1993, Spring). The case against community: Bayard Rustin and the 1968 New York school crisis. *Educational Foundations,* 7(2), 45–67.

Perlstein, D. (1994). *The 1968 New York City school crisis: Teacher politics, racial politics and the decline of liberalism.* Ph.D. dissertation. Stanford University.

Perlstein, D. H. (2004). *Justice, justice: School politics and the eclipse of liberalism.* New York: Peter Lang.

Perry, T., & Delpit, L. (Eds.). (1998). *The real Ebonics debate: Power, language, and the education of African-American children.* Boston: Beacon Press.

Peterson, P. E. (1976). *School politics Chicago style.* Chicago: University of Chicago Press.

Phillips, C. (1961, July 25). School closings argued in court. *New York Times,* p. 24.

Pinkney, A. (1976). *Red, Black, and green: Black nationalism in the United States.* Cambridge: Cambridge University Press.

Placier, M. (1998, April). Uses of history in present-day qualitative studies of schools: The case of the junior high school. *Qualitative Studies in Education, 11*(2), 303–322.

Podair, J. E. (1994, Spring). "White" values, "Black" values: The Ocean Hill–Brownsville controversy and New York city culture, 1965–1975. *Radical History Review, 59,* 36–59.

Podair, J. E. (2002). *The strike that changed New York: Blacks, Whites, and the Ocean Hill–Brownsville crisis.* New Haven: Yale University Press.

Ports, S. (1970). Racism, rejection, and retardation. In A. T. Rubinstein (Ed.), *Schools against children: The case for community control.* New York: Monthly Review Press.

Powledge, F. (1991). *Free at last?: The civil rights movement and the people who made it.* Boston: Little, Brown and Co.

Proposal for academic excellence: Community and teachers assume responsibility for the education of the ghetto child. (1967, April 26). PA 670–0431, Ford Foundation Archives.

Raspberry, W. (1987, June 29). Schools: The "voucher-plus" system. *Washington Post,* p. A13.

Raspberry, W. (1998a, March 9). Not enough lifeboats. *Washington Post,* p. A19.

Raspberry, W. (1998b, June 26). School options. *Washington Post,* p. A27.

Raspberry, W. (1999, September 3). Failing schools? No, failing parents. *Washington Post,* p. A27.

Raspberry, W. (2001a, June 15). Selling out our schools. *Washington Post,* p. A33.

Raspberry, W. (2001b, August 6). Solidly for vouchers. *Washington Post,* p. A15.

Raspberry, W. (2003a, September 15). Give poor students a choice. *Washington Post,* p. A23.

Raspberry, W. (2003b, September 29). Echoes of an earlier school fight. *Washington Post,* p. A19.

Ratteray, J. D. (1986, June 27). *Access to quality: Private schools in Chicago's inner city.* Heartland Policy Study n. 9. Chicago: Heartland Institute. ED: 272613.

Ratteray, J. D. (1994). The search for access and content in the education of African-Americans. In M. J. Shujaa (Ed.), *Too much schooling, too little education: A paradox of Black life in White societies.* Trenton, NJ: Africa World Press.

Ratteray, J. D., & Shujaa, M. (1987). *Dare to choose: Parental choice at independent neighborhood schools.* Washington, DC: Institute for Independent Education.

Rauh, G. (2006, September 17). Charter school movement finds a boomtown in Oakland. *Alameda Times Star*. Retrieved September 20, 2006, from http://www.insidebayarea.com/timesstar/ci_4352467.

Ravitch, D. (2000). *The great school wars. A history of the New York City public schools* (2000 ed.). Baltimore: The Johns Hopkins University Press. (Original work published in 1974)

Ravitch, D. (1981). The evolution of school desegregation policy, 1964–1979. In A. Yarmolinsky, L. Liebman, & C. S. Schelling (Eds.), *Race and schooling in the city*. Cambridge: Harvard University Press.

Ravitch, D. (1983). *The troubled crusade: American education, 1945–1980*. New York: Basic Books.

Reid, K. S. (2001a, May 30). Black Alliance weighs in with pro-voucher campaign. *Education Week, 20*(38), 8.

Reid, K. S. (2001b, October 3). Charlotte schools desegregated, court rules. *Education Week, 21*(5), 3.

Reinhold, R. (1975, June 4). School vouchers: Quick defeats raise question on test validity. *New York Times*, p. 18.

Reynolds, M. G. (1998, October 18). Castlemont parents seek solutions. *Oakland Tribune*, pp. local–1–2.

Rofes, E. (1998, April). *How are school districts responding to charter laws and charter schools?* Berkeley: Policy Analysis for California Education.

Rofes, E. (2005, June). *How can we reduce conflict between charter schools and school districts?* Hayward, CA: Alameda County Office of Education.

Rofes, E., & Stulberg, L. M. (2004). Conclusion: Toward a progressive politics of school choice. In E. Rofes & L. M. Stulberg (Eds.), *The emancipatory promise of charter schools: Toward a progressive politics of school choice*. Albany: State University of New York Press.

Rogers, D. (1968). *110 Livingston Street: Politics and bureaucracy in the New York City schools*. New York: Random House.

Rossell, C. H. (1990). *The carrot or the stick for school desegregation policy: Magnet schools or forced busing*. Philadelphia: Temple University Press.

Rothstein, R. (2000, December 13). Judging vouchers' merits proves a difficult task. *New York Times*, p. B11.

Rouse, C. E. (1998, May). Private school vouchers and student achievement: An evaluation of the Milwaukee Parental Choice Program. *The Quarterly Journal of Economics, 113*(2), 553–602.

Rouse, C. E. (2000, January 31). *School reform in the 21st century: A look at the effect of class size and school vouchers on the academic achievement of minority students*. Working Paper #440. Princeton University Industrial Relations Section. Retrieved January 20, 2006, from http://www.irs.princeton.edu/pubs/working_papers.html.

RPP International. (2000, January). *The state of charter schools 2000: Fourth-year report*. Washington, DC: Office of Educational Research and Improvement, U.S. Department of Education.

Ruenzel, D. (1998, September 16). War of attrition. *Education Week, 18*(2), 32–37.

Rustin, B. (1969, January 21). *Some Items for Discussion: Memorandum to participants of February 5–6 Conference on School Decentralization.* Robert F. Wagner Labor Archives of the Tamiment Institute Library. New York University. UFT Collection. Shanker subject files. "Decentralization" box 3, folder 72.

Rustin, B. (1976). *Strategies for freedom: The changing patterns of Black protest.* New York: Columbia University Press.

Safire, W. (2000, August 31). Vouchers help Blacks. *New York Times,* p. A25.

Salisbury, D., & Lartigue, C., Jr. (2004). *Educational freedom in urban America: Brown v. Board after half a century.* Washington, DC: Cato Institute.

Sanchez, R. (1996, December 20). Oakland school system recognizes "Black English" as second language. *Washington Post,* p. A8.

Saporito, S., & Lareau, A. (1999). School selection as a process: The multiple dimensions of race in framing educational choice. *Social Problems, 46*(3), 418–439.

Schemo, D. J. (2006a, April 6). Federal program on vouchers draws strong minority support. *New York Times,* p. A1.

Schemo, D. J. (2006b, August 23). Study of test scores finds charter schools lagging. *New York Times,* p. 14.

Schneider, B. L. (1988). Private schools and Black families: An overview of family choice initiatives. In D. T. Slaughter & D. J. Johnson (Eds.), *Visible now: Blacks in private schools.* New York: Greenwood Press.

Schneider, B., & Shouse, R. (1992, Spring). Children of color in independent schools: An analysis of the eighth-grade cohort from the National Education Longitudinal Study of 1988. *Journal of Negro Education, 61*(2), 223–234.

Schuman, H., Steeh, C., & Bobo, L. (1985). *Racial attitudes in America: Trends and interpretations.* Cambridge: Harvard University Press.

The schools we get. . . are the schools we pay for. (1997, March 6). *New York Times,* p. A18.

Schorr, J. (1999a, January 22). Parents turn to charter schools. *Oakland Tribune,* p. news–1.

Schorr, J. (1999b, January 28). Parents turn out for new schools plan. *Oakland Tribune,* pp. local–1–2.

Schorr, J. (1999c, February 9). Charter schools herald change for Oakland students. *Oakland Tribune,* p. news–1.

Schorr, J. (1999d, February 9). A chart to Oakland's charters. *Oakland Tribune,* p. news–1.

Schorr, J. (1999e, February 11). Packed petition shows support for charter schools. *Oakland Tribune,* p. news–1.

Schorr, J. (1999f, February 28). Fix-it plan for Oakland schools scrutinized. *Oakland Tribune,* pp. local–1–2.

Schorr, J. (1999g, March 19). Quan says spending was wrong but legal. *Oakland Tribune,* p. news–1.

Schorr, J. (1999h, March 21). Possible deal for Quan to bow out. *Oakland Tribune,* p. news–1.

Schorr, J. (1999i, April 8). Six charter schools set for approval. *Oakland Tribune*, pp. local–1–2.

Schorr, J. (1999j, April 9). Oakland Board expands charter school sites by six. *Oakland Tribune*, p. news–11.

Schorr, J. (1999k, April 14). Departure might end takeover bid. *Oakland Tribune*, p. news–1.

Schorr, J. (1999l, April 14). Quan quits. *Oakland Tribune*, p. news–1.

Schorr, J. (2002). *Hard lessons: The promise of an inner city charter school*. New York: Ballantine Books.

Scott, J., & Holme, J. J. (2002). Public schools, private resources: The role of social networks in California charter school reform. In A. S. Wells (Ed.), *Where charter school policy fails: The problems of accountability and equity*. New York: Teachers College Press.

Shanker, A. (1970). Albert Shanker. In M. I. Urofsky (Ed.), *Why teachers strike: Teachers' rights and community control*. Garden City, NY: Anchor Books.

Shanker, A. (1988, March 31). National Press Club Speech. Washington, DC: American Federation of Teachers.

Sharp, J. M. (1976). *Evaluation and authority in Independent Black Educational Institutions*. Ed.D. dissertation. Teachers College, Columbia University.

Shokraii, N. (1996, November–December). Free at last: Black America signs up for school choice. *Policy Review, 80,* 20–26.

Shujaa, M. J. (1994). Education and schooling: You can have one without the other. In M. J. Shujaa (Ed.), *Too much schooling, too little education: A paradox of Black life in White societies*. Trenton, NJ: Africa World Press.

Shujaa, M. J., & Afrik, H. T. (1996). School desegregation, the politics of culture, and the Council of Independent Black Institutions. In M. J. Shujaa (Ed.), *Beyond desegregation: The politics of quality in African American schooling*. Thousand Oaks, CA: Corwin Press.

Simmel, G. (1950). The stranger. In K. H. Wolff (Ed. and Trans.), *The sociology of Georg Simmel*. London: The Free Press of Glencoe.

Sitton, C. (1961, April 17). Prince Edward County adamant on refusing school integration. *New York Times*, p. 33.

Skocpol, T. (1984). Emerging agendas and recurrent strategies in historical sociology. In T. Skocpol (Ed.), *Vision and method in historical sociology*. Cambridge: Cambridge University Press.

Skocpol, T. (1985). Bringing the state back in: Strategies of analysis in current research. In P. B. Evans, D. Rueschemeyer, & T. Skocpol (Eds.), *Bringing the state back in*. Cambridge: Cambridge University Press.

Slaughter, D. T., & Johnson, D. J. (1988). Introduction and Overview. In D. T. Slaughter & D. J. Johnson (Eds.), *Visible now: Blacks in private schools*. New York: Greenwood Press.

Sleeper, J. (1990). *The closest of strangers: Liberalism and the politics of race in New York*. New York: W. W. Norton & Company.

Sleeper, J. (1997). *Liberal racism*. New York: Penguin Books.

Smith, D. E. (1987). *The everyday world as problematic: A feminist sociology.* Boston: Northeastern University Press.

Smith, R. C. (1996). *We have no leaders: African Americans in the post–civil rights era.* Albany: State University of New York Press.

Sowell, T. (1974, Spring). Black excellence—the case of Dunbar High School. *The Public Interest, 35,* 1–21.

Sowell, T. (1976, Spring). Patterns of Black excellence. *The Public Interest, 43,* 26–58.

Speede-Franklin, W. A. (1988). Ethnic diversity: Patterns and implications of minorities in independent schools. In D. T. Slaughter & D. J. Johnson (Eds.), *Visible now: Blacks in private schools.* New York: Greenwood Press.

Staples, B. (1998, January 4). Schoolyard brawl: The new politics of education casts Blacks in a starring role. *New York Times,* p. EL35.

Staples, B. (2002, August 5). School vouchers: A small tool for a very big problem. *New York Times,* p. A14.

Stephens, S. (2002, June 30). An unlikely team brings about vouchers success. *Plain Dealer,* p. A1.

Stevens, W. K. (1971, July 2). Education voucher plan is making slow progress. *New York Times,* p. 14.

Stinnett, P. (1999, June 4). Brown tackles schools, crime and "ossification" at forum. *Oakland Tribune,* pp. local-1–2.

St. John, K. (2003, May 30). Oakland schools plan goes to Davis. *San Francisco Chronicle,* p. A23.

Stulberg, L. M. (2004). What history offers progressive choice scholarship. In E. Rofes & L. M. Stulberg (Eds.), *The emancipatory promise of charter schools: Toward a progressive politics of school choice.* Albany: State University of New York Press.

Stulberg, L. M. (2006). School choice discourse and the legacy of *Brown. Journal of School Choice, 1*(1), 23–45.

Sturrock, C. (2005, January 13). District's plans anger teachers. *San Francisco Chronicle,* p. B5.

Suddes, T. (1995, March 29). It's not in the budget: Black lawmakers say GOP proposal excludes interest. *Plain Dealer,* p. 5B.

Sweezy, P. M. (1970). Afterword: The implications of community control. In A. T. Rubinstein (Ed.), *Schools against children: The case for community control.* New York: Monthly Review Press.

Swidler, A. (1979). *Organization without authority: Dilemmas of social control in free schools.* Cambridge: Harvard University Press.

Task Force on the Education of African American Students. (1996, December 18). *Resolution of the board of education.* Oakland United School District.

Tate, R. (1998, November 12). The G.O.P.'s chance to reach out. *New York Times,* p. A29.

Tepperman, J. D. (2002, April 28). Complicating the race. *New York Times Magazine.* Retrieved May 2, 2002, from http://www.nytimes.com/2002/04/28/magazine/28BOOKER.html.

Thorne, B. (1983). Political activist as participant observer: Conflicts of commitment in a study of the draft resistance movement of the 1960s. In R. M. Emerson (Ed.), *Contemporary field research: A collection of readings*. Prospect Heights, IL: Waveland Press.

Thorne, B. (1993). *Gender play: Girls and boys in school*. New Brunswick: Rutgers University Press.

Toppo, G. (2005, June 23). Father of vouchers foresees "breakthrough." *USA Today*, p. 9D.

Townsend, A. (2006, July 4). More than 2,500 in Ohio apply for school vouchers. *Plain Dealer*, p. B4.

Tuition aid again hit by NAACP. (1968, August 1). *Washington Post, Times Herald*, p. B2.

Tyack, D., & Cuban, L. (1995). *Tinkering toward utopia: A century of public school reform*. Cambridge: Harvard University Press.

Tyack, D., & Hansot, E. (1982). *Managers of virtue: Public school leadership in America, 1820–1980*. New York: Basic Books.

Tyack, D. B., Kirst, M. W., & Hansot, E. (1980, Spring). Educational reform: Retrospect and prospect. *Teachers College Record, 81*(3), 253–269.

Tyack, D., Lowe, R., & Hansot, E. (1984). *Public schools in hard times: The great depression and recent years*. Cambridge: Harvard University Press.

UCLA Charter School Study. (1998). *Beyond the rhetoric of charter school reform: A study of ten California school districts*. Los Angeles: UCLA Charter School Study.

Unger, R. M., & West, C. (1998). *The future of American progressivism: An initiative for political and economic reform*. Boston: Beacon Press.

United Federation of Teachers. (1967). *The United Federation of Teachers looks at school decentralization: A critical analysis of the Bundy Report with UFT proposals*. New York: United Federation Teachers, AFL-CIO.

Urban Coalition. (Christmas, 1968). If it works for Scarsdale, it can work for Ocean Hill. *SCOPE Bulletin*, 7.

Urban Strategies Council. (1995). *A chance for every child 2: Prospects for Oakland's infants, children and youth in the 1990s and beyond*. Oakland: Urban Strategies Council.

Urban Strategies Council with the Youth Development Initiative Working Group. (1996). *Call to action: An Oakland blueprint for youth development*. Oakland: Urban Strategies Council.

Urban Strategies Council. (n.d.). West Oakland 2000 census data. Personal files.

U. S. court rules out state aid to Mississippi private schools. (1969, January 31). *New York Times*, p. 20.

Van Deburg, W. L. (1992). *New day in Babylon: The Black Power movement and American culture, 1965–1975*. Chicago: The University of Chicago Press.

Van Deburg, W. L. (Ed.). (1997). *Modern Black nationalism: From Marcus Garvey to Louis Farrakhan*. New York: New York University Press.

Vann, A. (1970). "Community involvement" in schools. In N. Wright, Jr. (Ed.), *What Black educators are saying*. New York: Hawthorn Books.

Vanourek, G. (2005, May). *State of the charter movement 2005: Trends, issues, & indicators*. Washington, DC: Charter School Leadership Council.

Virginians plan Negro schooling. (1959, December 16). *New York Times*, p. 23.

Voucher system—A challenge to education. (1971, March 27). *Sun Reporter*, p. 6.

Walker, I. (2001). *African-centered education: An Afrocentric analysis of its purposes, principles, and practices in an Independent Black Institution*. Ph.D. dissertation. Temple University.

Walker, V. S. (1996a). Can institutions care?: Evidence from the segregated schooling of African American children. In M. J. Shujaa (Ed.), *Beyond desegregation: The politics of quality in African American schooling*. Thousand Oaks, CA: Corwin Press.

Walker, V. S. (1996b). *Their highest potential: An African American school community in the segregated South*. Chapel Hill: The University of North Carolina Press.

Walsh, M. (1998a, June 17). Court allows vouchers in Milwaukee. *Education Week, 17*(40).

Walsh, M. (1998b, November 25). Court blocks race-based school policy. *Education Week, 18*(13), 1.

Ward, F. C. (1967, 26 June). Grant request: Division of education and research. PA 670–0426, Ford Foundation Archives.

Wasserman, M. (1970). *The school fix, NYC, USA*. New York: Outerbridge & Dienstfrey.

We cannot afford to wait any longer: An interview with the Rev. Floyd H. Flake. (1998, Fall). *School Voices, 6*(1), 18–20.

Wells, A.S. (1990, August 22). Experiment pioneered the school choice concept. *New York Times*, p. A1.

Wells, A. S. (1993). *Time to choose: America at the crossroads of school choice policy*. New York: Hill and Wang.

Wells, A. S. (2000a, November 2). In search of uncommon schools: Charter school reform in historical perspective (part 1)—revisiting the ideology of the common school. Retrieved March 28, 2003, from http//: www.tcrecord. org/PrintContent.asp?ContentID=10630.

Wells, A. S. (2000b, November 2). In search of uncommon schools: Charter school reform in historical perspective (part 3)— charter schools as uncommon schools. Retrieved on March 28, 2003, from http//:www. tcrecord.org/PrintContent.asp?ContentID=10632

Wells, A. S. (2002). Why public policy fails to live up to the potential of charter school reform: An introduction. In A. S. Wells (Ed.), *Where charter school policy fails: The problems of accountability and equity*. New York: Teachers College Press.

Wells, A.S., & Crain, R. L. (1994, Winter). Perpetuation theory and the long-term effects of school desegregation. *Review of Educational Research, 64*(4), 531–555.

Wells, A. S., & Crain, R. L. (1997). *Stepping over the color line: African-American students in White suburban schools*. New Haven: Yale University Press.

Wells, A. S., Lopez, A., Scott, J., & Holme, J. J. (1999, Summer). Charter schools as postmodern paradox: Rethinking social stratification in an age of deregulated school choice. *Harvard Educational Review, 69,* 172–204.

West, C. (1996). Black strivings in a twilight civilization. In H. L. Gates, Jr. & C. West, *The future of the race.* New York: Alfred A. Knopf.

West, C. (1997). *Restoring hope: Conversations on the future of black America.* Boston: Beacon Press.

West-Burns, N. (1997). *African-centered education: Reflections and perspectives from one institution.* Ph.D. dissertation. Syracuse University.

West Oakland Community School. (1997, June 13). *Funding proposal: Joint community development program.* Personal files.

West Oakland Community School. (1998a, January). *Charter application.* Personal files.

West Oakland Community School. (1998b, March 17). *Addendum to charter school petition.* Personal files.

West Oakland Community School. (1998c, May). *Grant application: Submitted to the California Department of Education.* Personal files.

West Oakland Community School. (1999a, January). *Funding proposal: Submitted to the Walter S. Johnson Foundation.* Personal files.

West Oakland Community School. (1999b, February). *Draft: Charter school program design.* Personal files.

West Oakland Community School. (1999c, December). *Newsletter, 1*(1). Personal files.

West Oakland Community School. (2001, December 3). *Memorandum: December 5th Board of Directors meeting.* Personal files.

West Oakland Community School. (2003a). *Charter renewal application.* Personal files.

West Oakland Community School. (2003b). *Student-family handbook: 2003-2004 school year.* Personal files.

Wilcox, P. R. (1968, Fall). Africanization: The new input to Black education. *Freedomways, 8,* 395–398.

Wilcox, P. R. (1969). The meaning of community control. *Foresight Bulletins.* Robert F. Wagner Labor Archives of the Tamiment Institute Library. New York University. UFT Collection. Shanker subject files. "Decentralization" box 6, folder 157.

Wilcox, P. R. (1970). Education for Black humanism: A way of approaching it. In N. Wright, Jr. (Ed.), *What Black educators are saying.* New York: Hawthorn Books.

Wilgoren, J. (2000, October 9). Young Blacks turn to school vouchers as civil rights issue. *New York Times,* p. A1.

Wilkerson, I. (1990, December 19). For 345, poverty is key to door of private school. *New York Times,* p. B6.

Williams, M. F. (1986). Private school enrollment and tuition trends. Reprint from *The Condition of Education.* Washington, DC: U.S. Department of Education Center for Education Statistics.

Williams, P. (1998, Fall). School choice: A vehicle for achieving educational excellence in the African-American community. *School Voices, 6*(1), 6.

Willie, C. V. (1989). The intended and unintended benefits of school desegregation. In W. D. Smith & E. W. Chunn (Eds.), *Black education: A quest for equity and excellence.* New Brunswick, NJ: Transaction Publishers.

Willis, P. (1977). *Learning to labour: How working class kids get working class jobs.* New York: Columbia University Press.

Willis, P. (1980). Notes on method. In the Center for Contemporary Cultural Studies. *Culture, Media, Language: Working Papers in Cultural Studies, 1972–79.* London: Hutchinson.

Wilson, C. E. (1969, August). *The beginnings of a miracle: Interim report for the I.S. 201 complex demonstration district 33.* PA 670–0431, Ford Foundation Archives.

Wilson, C. E. (1970). 201—First steps toward community control. In A. T. Rubinstein (Ed.), *Schools against children: The case for community control.* New York: Monthly Review Press.

Wilson, Y. (1995, May 10). Many Whites say they feel cheated. *San Francisco Chronicle,* p. A8.

Wisconsin Department of Public Instruction. (n.d.). *Milwaukee Parental Choice Program (MPCP): MPCP facts and figures for 2005–2006, as of January 2006.* Retrieved October 30, 2006, from http://dpi.wi.gov/sms/choice.html.

Witte, J. F. (1998, Winter). The Milwaukee voucher experiment. *Educational Evaluation and Policy Analysis, 20*(4), 229–251.

Wolfe, A. (2003). The irony of school choice: Liberals, conservatives, and the new politics of race. In A. Wolfe (Ed.), *School choice: The moral debate.* Princeton: Princeton University Press.

Woodson, C. G. (1933). *The Mis-education of the Negro* (1990 ed.). Trenton, NJ: Africa World Press.

Worth a try. (1970, July 29). *Christian Science Monitor,* p. 12.

The wrong prescription. (1970, June 8). *New York Times,* p. 36.

Wyatt, E. (2000, August 29). Study finds higher test scores among Blacks with vouchers. *New York Times,* p. A14.

X, M., & Haley, A. (1964). *The autobiography of Malcolm X.* New York: Ballantine Books.

Zelman v. Simmons-Harris, No. 00-1751, slip. op. (June 27, 2002).

Zernike, K. (2000, September 15). New doubt is cast on study that backs voucher efforts. *New York Times,* p. A26.

Zinn, H. (1994). *You can't be neutral on a moving train: A personal history of our times.* Boston: Beacon Press.

Zweigenhaft, R. L., & Domhoff, G. W. (1991). *Blacks in the White establishment?: A study of race and class in America.* New Haven: Yale University Press.

Index

About the Author

Lisa M. Stulberg is Assistant Professor of Educational Sociology at New York University's Steinhardt School of Culture, Education, and Human Development. Her research examines the politics of schooling, with a particular focus on African American education in the post-*Brown* era and on school choice politics and policies. Her work includes a coedited volume (with Eric Rofes) entitled *The Emancipatory Promise of Charter Schools: Toward a Progressive Politics of School Choice.* She received a Ph.D. in Sociology from the University of California, Berkeley. While in graduate school, she was part of the founding group of the West Oakland Community School, a public charter middle school in Oakland, California.